Deleuze and Becoming

Bloomsbury Studies in Continental Philosophy

Presents cutting edge scholarship in the field of modern European thought. The wholly original arguments, perspectives and research findings in titles in this series make it an important and stimulating resource for students and academics from across the discipline.

Breathing with Luce Irigaray, edited by Lenart Skof and Emily A. Holmes
Deleuze and Art, Anne Sauvagnargues
Deleuze and the Diagram: Aesthetic Threads in Visual Organization, Jakub Zdebik
Derrida, Badiou and the Formal Imperative, Christopher Norris
Desire in Ashes: Deconstruction, Psychoanalysis, Philosophy, edited by Simon Morgan Wortham and Chiara Alfano
Early Phenomenology, edited by Brian Harding and Michael R. Kelly
Egalitarian Moments, Devin Zane Shaw
Ernst Bloch and His Contemporaries, Ivan Boldyrev
Why there is no Post-Structuralism in France, Johannes Angermuller
Gadamer's Poetics: A Critique of Modern Aesthetics, John Arthos
Heidegger, History and the Holocaust, Mahon O'Brien
Heidegger and the Emergence of the Question of Being, Jesús Adrián Escudero
Husserl's Ethics and Practical Intentionality, Susi Ferrarello
Immanent Transcendence: Reconfiguring Materialism in Continental Philosophy, Patrice Haynes
Merleau-Ponty's Existential Phenomenology and the Realization of Philosophy, Bryan A. Smyth
Mortal Thought: Hölderlin and Philosophy, James Luchte
Nietzsche and Political Thought, edited by Keith Ansell-Pearson
Nietzsche as a Scholar of Antiquity, Helmut Heit
Philosophy, Sophistry, Antiphilosophy: Badiou's Dispute with Lyotard, Matthew R. McLennan
The Poetic Imagination in Heidegger and Schelling, Christopher Yates
Post-Rationalism: Psychoanalysis, Epistemology, and Marxism in Post-War France, Tom Eyers
Revisiting Normativity with Deleuze, edited by Rosi Braidotti and Patricia Pisters
Towards the Critique of Violence: Walter Benjamin and Giorgio Agamben, Brendan Moran and Carlo Salzani

Deleuze and Becoming

Samantha Bankston

BLOOMSBURY ACADEMIC
LONDON • NEW YORK • OXFORD • NEW DELHI • SYDNEY

BLOOMSBURY ACADEMIC
Bloomsbury Publishing Plc
50 Bedford Square, London, WC1B 3DP, UK
1385 Broadway, New York, NY 10018, USA

BLOOMSBURY, BLOOMSBURY ACADEMIC and the Diana logo
are trademarks of Bloomsbury Publishing Plc

First published 2017
Paperback edition first published 2019

ISBN: HB: 978-1-4742-3356-9
PB: 978-1-3501-4386-9
ePDF: 978-1-4742-3355-2
eBook: 978-1-4742-3358-3

Series: Bloomsbury Studies in Continental Philosophy

Typeset by Deanta Global Publishing Services, Chennai, India

To find out more about our authors and books visit
www.bloomsbury.com and sign up for our newsletters.

To Silverton

Contents

Acknowledgements

I would like to thank Daniel W. Smith for his generosity of spirit, brilliance and guidance in my studies of Deleuze, and academia, more broadly. At Purdue University I had the privilege of studying with Geraldine Friedman, Arkady Plotnitsky and William McBride, all of whom enriched my philosophical journey in countless ways. Prior to joining the Philosophy Department at Purdue University, a handful of individuals helped shape my academic life; I would like to extend my gratitude to Martin Matustik, Edward S. Casey, Yirmiyahu Yovel and Jay Bernstein. I would like to thank my first philosophy professor and good friend, Robert Parsons Baker, whose chance encounter served as a pivotal moment in the course of my studies, to which I eternally return. I would like to thank Purdue University and the Philosophy and Literature Ph.D. program, in particular, for funding my doctoral studies. I was able to complete my research, thanks to welcoming institutions that temporarily housed me as a visiting scholar: The Saxo Institute at the University of Copenhagen and Smith College. Finally, thank you to my family and friends for your continued support and love. Communism will win.

All translations are those of the author, except where noted.

Introduction

What is becoming? *Who* or what becomes? *How much* does becoming condition the state of affairs? *How* can we theorize becoming on its own terms? *Where* might processes of becoming dwell? *When* is the time of becoming? In many ways, this line of investigation is the driving force behind Gilles Deleuze's philosophical project. While the concept of becoming is essential to his philosophy, Deleuze never wrote an explicit theory systematizing the concept. The present book systematizes a theory of becoming from Deleuze's collected works. However, an immediate difficulty arises in the terminological variance used by Deleuze to describe the processes of becoming. There are vast differences between the formulation of the concept of becoming in, say, *Nietzsche and Philosophy, The Logic of Sense*, and *A Thousand Plateaus*. Not only is the concept of becoming subjected to shifts in terminology across Deleuze's corpus, but also the specific problematics established in each text draws out different features of the concept, leading to further mystification. The key to untangling the knot of becoming is time. By tracking the temporal processes that subtend expressions of becoming throughout Deleuze's writings (with and without Félix Guattari), the logic of becoming emerges out of the fog.

When surveying the concept of becoming in Deleuze, two divergent temporal logics surface again and again; one unfolds in the realm of ideas, the other in matters of expression. The former is Deleuze's version of Friedrich Nietzsche's eternal return, while the latter is his re-appropriation of Henri Bergson's duration. These two divergent temporal processes correspond to two modes of becoming that constellate in disjunctive synthesis: the becoming of events and the becoming of sensation, respectively. Thus, becoming is both statically and dynamically generative, and to adequately grasp and apply Deleuze's concept of becoming requires an understanding of its underlying temporal logic(s). Neglecting the temporal complex of becoming leads to an ontological distortion and betrayal of Deleuze's metaphysics. In making visible the temporal and (counter)causal mechanisms of becoming(s) as they interrelate with effectuated being, Deleuze's tripartite ontology shines forth, dispelling claims that he is a philosopher of the One.

Deleuze's pre-eminent treatise, *Difference and Repetition*, could very well have been titled *Becoming and Time*, presenting a poststructuralist alternative to Martin Heidegger's work of fundamental ontology, *Being and Time*. The problematic established in this book is indebted to the interrogation of Being launched by Heidegger. We begin with the realization that the concept of becoming has, like Being, been overused and oversimplified throughout the history of philosophy. Poststructuralist metaphysics attempts to correct the overlooked presuppositions of the concept of becoming by appealing to the notion of difference in-itself. Deleuze is one such philosopher, and he takes seriously the task of developing a system of becoming that is not founded on the four shackles of representational thought: identity, analogy, opposition and resemblance.[1] The illusions of the four tendencies of representational thought can be traced to a fundamental temporal error: the attempt to conceive of change as a structural derivative of the immutable. Henri Bergson and Friedrich Nietzsche converge on the criticism of mechanistic causality and its employment of 'reason' to freeze pure flux in order to construct an image of becoming. Deleuze connects these criticisms and asks how a counter-causal process appropriate to the concept of becoming might be created. Deleuze sets out to sketch a concept of becoming that is not distorted by the temporal frameworks of representational thought.

The madman's untimely pronouncement of the death of God in *The Gay Science* immediately changes the landscape of metaphysics.[2] Removing the transcendental placeholder of God unhinges all other transcendental signifiers, such as Being, Truth, Reason, and – as Michel Foucault poignantly observed – Man.[3] The death of God in Nietzsche signals the end of metaphysics as we know it, for metaphysical systems had thus far operated according to a transcendental ordering of concepts. In a conventional metaphysical system, the concept of becoming is invariably subordinated to the concept of Being. As conceived by Deleuze, Being externally regulates individuated forms through a hierarchical, fixed homogeneous structure which employs chronological time. However, abruptly following the death of God, the concept of Being loses its transcendental footing. And rather than accept the declaration of the end of metaphysics, Deleuze revolutionizes what it means to create a metaphysical system. The result is a non-hierarchical, univocal ontology that replaces transcendental signifiers with immanent processes. Deleuze's philosophy is, arguably, a metaphysical systematization of Nietzsche's philosophy. In one of his first published monographs, *Nietzsche and Philosophy*, Deleuze states that the text is, above all, an analysis of Nietzsche's theory of becoming.[4] His engagement with the processes of becoming would come to dominate the course of his philosophical trajectory. This book extracts the concept of becoming from Deleuze's collective works and creates a comprehensive theory of becoming, exposing the temporal processes that are contained within the concept.

The reason this book looks to Deleuze for an understanding of becoming should now be clear: Deleuze is the philosopher of becoming *par excellence*. He provides a constructive ontology that articulates becoming on its own terms. Post-Kantian critiques of the separation of the transcendental subject from temporality are remedied in Deleuze's concept of becoming. Additionally, the metaphysical trappings of subjectivity that arise from the death of God are defeated by an immanent conception of becoming and time. To the extent that Deleuze's philosophy is deemed a transcendental empiricism, it remains transcendental in the sense that his philosophy describes the conditions of experience without requiring his ontological processes to be transcendent to something else. The way these conditions are accomplished, however, is through immanent processes and disjunctive temporal syntheses.

In the preface to *Difference and Repetition,* Deleuze describes his philosophical method according to what he calls the double nature of becoming.[5] The dual nature of becoming is adopted from Bergson's theory of memory, which splits the present into two simultaneous streams of the in-itself pure past and the not-yet of the future. In other words, as we see in *A Thousand Plateaus,* 'Becoming is always double, that which one becomes becomes no less than the one that becomes.'[6] There are no fixed and immobile islands in an immanent system of becoming. The restlessness of becoming discloses the nature of things to be pure relationality, where terms are in the perpetual process of vanishing. In this case, Deleuze looks to Gottfried Wilhelm Leibniz's theory of infinitesimal differential calculus to demonstrate how terms may vanish without rendering their relation indeterminable. Fixed terms undergo an infinite dissimulation on the line of becoming, and all ontological processes are caught in the middle, in-between what they were and what they are not yet. This duality of becoming informs Deleuze's philosophical process. His notorious characterization of philosophy as the creation of concepts includes the ways in which he apprehends the history of philosophy. After Nietzsche, Deleuze states that it is becoming less and less possible to write a text on the history of philosophy in the 'old style'. Glaring examples of this reworking of the history of philosophy include his monographs on such philosophers as Bergson, Nietzsche, Leibniz, Spinoza and so on. The product of a true artist-philosopher, all of Deleuze's works exemplify the double nature of becoming he theorizes. On this score, he proclaims,

> It seems to us that the history of philosophy should play a role roughly analogous to that of *collage* in painting. The history of philosophy is the reproduction of philosophy itself. In the history of philosophy, a commentary should act as a veritable double and bear the maximal modification appropriate to a double. (One imagines a *philosophically* bearded Hegel, a *philosophically* clean-shaven Marx, in the same way as a moustached Mona Lisa.) It should be possible to recount a real book of past philosophy as if it were an imaginary and feigned book.[7]

Deleuze is a true philosophical collagist in this sense – his works, a philosophical pastiche. Each of his texts is produced through the extraction of certain concepts from different philosophers and arranged in new neighbourhoods of thought. Re-appropriation provides Deleuze the space to mobilize concepts and push their limits through innovative arrangement and expression. As concepts are released from their previous texts, they are reanimated across times in simultaneous planes superimposed upon one another. This is how the history of philosophy operates for Deleuze; it is not eternal and it is not temporal – it is untimely. The history of philosophy is both too late and too early, and he seeks to repeat the history of philosophy in his texts at the same moment that the texts in the history of philosophy repeat his thought. Concepts are not immutable, as Plato would claim, but they endlessly become other. When that which becomes becomes at the same moment as the one becomes, we are presented with a labyrinthine philosophical garden of forking paths.[8] New futures ceaselessly diverge and are all interconnected in the absence of a dominant centre. Becoming is immanent to itself, and as we will see, this requires a new set of temporal concepts.

The re-articulation of what a concept can do in light of becoming makes Deleuze's philosophy especially challenging. A particular concept may be re-appropriated from another philosopher and redeployed in varying ways throughout different texts that he has written, or often within the same text. For example, he extracts the concept of the eternal return from Nietzsche, and depending on which text we analyse, this concept has taken on several masks, such as the synthesis of the future; the line of Aion; the perverse moment; the ritornello. Each of these concepts is a radical reordering of the eternal return and its intensive components (features), and so each expresses different tendencies of the concept, causing the concept to become.

Accordingly, it can be difficult for a reader of Deleuze to detect the different masks of a single concept. As we discover, each mask, once removed, reveals another mask *ad infinitum*; such is the case with the concept of becoming. There are no originary Ideas, and when analysing a particular concept in the history of philosophy, we find that the concept already in the middle is always in the middle, *au milieu*. Thus many critiques of Deleuze attempt to denounce his philosophy on the merit of consistency. The same critique that is often levelled against Nietzsche – that his works contain internal contradictions and, therefore, ought to be dismissed – is founded on a notion of consistency that is inexorable from a logic that inscribes identity in the concept. To criticize Deleuze's philosophy on the basis that his concepts do not operate universally across texts is to miss the point entirely. This is the very image of thought that Deleuze wishes to put into question. The moment philosophy stops questioning its dearest presuppositions, it risks falling into institutionalized dogma. The pillars of 'reason', namely propositional logic, the principle of identity, the universality of truth and representation, must be put to the test and extricated from their ideological positions in the history of philosophy. If not, we begin to view historical constructs as *a priori* essences.

Philosophy has long been the source of heterodox thinking, and Deleuze's philosophy breathes life into ossified structures, forcing us to re-evaluate that which we have taken as given. One must redefine the notion of consistency to interrogate the becoming of concepts according to its own logic. Rather than circumscribe chaos by freezing it on a plane of reference, thereby ascribing general variables and constants to the concept, a philosophy of immanent becoming defines consistency in accordance with the contingency of chaos. Here, Deleuze (and Félix Guattari) separate philosophy from science and explain that 'science and philosophy take opposed paths, because philosophical concepts have events for consistency whereas scientific functions have states of affairs or mixtures for reference'.[9] The successive, linear apprehension of the concept is the attempt of science to resituate becoming in the discrete, extensive functions of Being, or what Deleuze calls the actual, where virtual processes are individuated. It is an imposition of science to level complaints of inconsistency in a philosophical system whose concepts do not function as constant variables.[10] On the contrary, concepts have internalized difference in their movements and they vary intensively in a continuum. Seeing that concepts operate according to a logic separate from scientific propositions, dismissing a philosophical system on the basis of inconstant expressions of a concept is no longer valid. We must evaluate a philosophical system based instead on a new definition of consistency that corresponds to the chaotic logic of becoming, or a term Deleuze adopts from Bergson, the virtual. And this is precisely what Deleuze and Guattari do in their treatise which examines the life of the philosophical concept: *What Is Philosophy?*

> Chaos is not an inert or stationary state, nor is it a chance mixture. Chaos makes
> chaotic and undoes every consistency in the infinite. The problem of philosophy
> is to acquire a consistency without losing the infinite into which thought
> plunges (in this respect chaos has as much a mental as a physical existence).
> *To give consistency without losing anything of the infinite* is very different from
> the problem of science, which seeks to provide chaos with reference points, on
> condition of renouncing infinite movements and speeds and of carrying out a
> limitation of speed first of all. Light, or the relative horizon, is primary in science.
> Philosophy, on the other hand, proceeds by presupposing or by instituting the
> plane of immanence: it is the plane's variable *curves* that retain the infinite
> movements that turn back on themselves in incessant exchange, but which also
> continually free other movements which are retained.[11]

In this passage, Deleuze and Guattari show the problem with using a scientific
system of reference points to reduce the infinite variation of chaos. They offer
another critical look at the fixing mechanism of representational thought
to describe the chaotic flux of the real. Deleuze repudiates the distortive
cinematographic model of the intellect and the illusory construction of binaries
in mechanistic causation, echoing the critiques offered by Bergson and Nietzsche,
respectively. What Bergson described as a logical equivocation between intensive
quality and extensive quantity is reconciled in Deleuze's notion of intensive
quantity. Heterogeneous, continuous processes of duration were subjected to
discrete, static extensity, invoked by representational time, a schematic error that
denatured time in the name of homogeneous quantification. To Deleuze's mind,
this is not simply a case of subordinating the qualitative to the quantitative.

There is a third option that retains the relation of quantities in modes of
becoming: the differential relation of intensive quantities. A theory of intensive
quantity installs a precise mathematical model into the notion of force in
Nietzsche's philosophy. *Nietzsche and Philosophy* argues that the concept of
force involves relations of quantity as well as quality. Deleuze states that any
time Nietzsche criticizes the tendency of science to reduce qualitative difference
to extensive quantities of equal measure that he is calling for a differentially
quantitative understanding of force. Qualitative difference always includes a
quantitative difference, and this notion of intensive quantitative difference is
central to Deleuze's theory of becoming: 'Difference in quantity is the essence
of force and of the relation of force to force.'[12] Any qualitative difference that is
expressed by the theory of forces calls forth a quantitative difference in relations.
Conceiving of difference through processes of intensive quantity opens up a
theory of becoming that is premised on *relations* and not fixed terms. This is

the point at which Deleuze enlists Leibniz into his elaboration of becoming; he restructures the Leibnizian calculus through processes of immanence and thus provides a foundation for a quantitative theory of Nietzschean force that will be integrated into Deleuze's ontology.

Creating a new concept of becoming, along with other new concepts that are required for an immanent ontology, Deleuze develops a metaphysical system in keeping with Nietzsche's affirmation of chaos. For the first time in the history of philosophy, the concept of becoming does not fall back into the trappings of identity. This, of course, is Deleuze's dissatisfaction with one of history's greatest philosophers of becoming: Hegel. Hegel's theory of becoming was unable to escape the logic of representation, according to Deleuze, on the grounds that the dialectic is inoperable without maintaining the primacy of identity through negation.[13] If we are to investigate the processes of absolute becoming, difference cannot be derived from identity. The old conceptual tools used in the construction of representational thinking must be discarded in favour of new tools. Likewise, the theory of time that is based on a re-presentation of perceived presents cannot serve as the mobilizing force beneath becoming. Mechanistic causality provides an insufficient account of processes in becoming. To look beyond the illusory effects of representation, we need to articulate the mode of individuation evoked in immanent processes. It is not enough to describe two parallel realms, each replete with independent causalities and temporalities. How are individuated bodies connected to incorporeal virtual processes? How does becoming produce states of being? By constructing a philosophical pastiche of re-appropriated concepts Deleuze's innovative ontology answers these questions.

While Deleuze's collective works aim to develop an immanent ontological system of becoming, explicating the concept of becoming from his philosophy is no easy task. The reason for this is attributable to Deleuze's dramatization of his concept of becoming within his writings. That is to say, concepts *become*, and this is evident in his collective works; they are perpetually engaged in a dance of self-differing. Concepts are said to be infinite and absolute in their survey, yet finite and relative in their movements, according to Deleuze and Guattari.[14] They are complex combinations of singular components (intensive features) whose condensation is absolute.[15] Their relativity arises in external relations with other concepts, the arrangement of components, the medium of expression and the problematic with which they are elaborated. That concepts are inexorably linked to the sensible is crucial to a non-hierarchical ontology, but the consequence is a varying expression throughout philosophical works. Deleuze creates his philosophy fully cognizant of the implications of form and content folded into one another. The concept of becoming varies in Deleuze's writings depending on the posed problematic of the text or the concept's proximity to other concepts. Mapping the concept of becoming requires tracking its consistency – in other words, the condensation of its intensive features, or 'singularities'. This is the task of the study upon which we are embarking. Working as conceptual detectives, we will apprehend the various formulations of becoming in Deleuze's works in order to outline the concept's temporal processes.[16] We will learn the conceptual language of becoming's masks and extract the concept from the text.

Upon examination, two temporal processes resurface again and again in Deleuze's writings on becoming. It immediately becomes clear that the concept of becoming is double. Deleuze uses the language of generality and particularity to express becoming, denoting two different sets of onto-temporal processes. The first clue of the dual nature of becoming is the tendency in Deleuze's writings to refer to it either in the plural (becomings, or 'a' becoming),[17] or in terms of a single, absolute process (becoming).[18] These two expressions of becoming should not be equated with one another. They correspond to the double nature of the concept, as outlined above: the absolute, unconditioned features of becoming differ in kind from the relative, fragmentary features of becomings. We see the two concepts of becoming operating throughout Deleuze's writings, but it is not until the publication of *What Is Philosophy?* that they are expressly named: sensory becoming and conceptual becoming ('conceptual becoming' will be changed to 'absolute becoming' in this study).[19] The plurality of becomings will henceforth be referred to in the study as sensory becoming, while the single, unconditioned concept of becoming will be referred to as absolute becoming. Sensory becoming pertains to expression in matter, while absolute becoming pertains to events in ideation. Together, they combine to form a multiplicity of becoming that is related through disjunctive syntheses.[20] Determining which of these two concepts of becoming is being utilized in a particular text helps us construct the temporal processes and logic that correspond to each. It turns out that sensory becomings involve a re-appropriation of Bergson's duration, and absolute becoming involves a re-appropriation of Nietzsche's eternal return. In a reconstruction of the conceptual history of the concept of becoming in Deleuze, we will begin to sketch its relevant temporal processes. Both of the temporal logics intertwine in a comprehensive theory of becoming that bridge the virtual and the actual, defeating criticisms that Deleuze's philosophy consists of two incompatible ontologies;[21] it is the third term, the becoming of sensation, which keeps his concept of becoming from lapsing into dualism. Whenever the phrase 'the concept of becoming' is used in this book, the combination of the components of sensory becoming and conceptual (absolute) becoming in one continuous multiplicity is intended.

The methodological approach undertaken by this study reflects Deleuze's call for a double movement in philosophical commentary. This means that creating a theory of becoming from Deleuze's philosophy unabashedly does so through a particular lens. The scope of this project is restricted and does not seek to restate a history of the concept of becoming in philosophy, nor does it pretend to provide an exhaustive account of every re-appropriated philosopher who influences Deleuze's ontology. Deleuze's masterful knowledge of the history of philosophy results in a vital kaleidoscope effect, whereby one concept can be read as an opening onto any single philosopher he engages, and is still a seamless collage of different philosophers. For example, Daniel W. Smith reads many of Deleuze's concepts as an immanent reconstruction of Leibniz's philosophy,[22] while Keith Ansell-Pearson sees the same concepts as an expression of a long-standing dialogue with Bergson.[23] Both of these notable Deleuze scholars recognize the combinatory process in Deleuze's philosophy, wherein he draws from multiple thinkers in areas of philosophy, art, science and other disciplines. However, they interpret Deleuze's philosophy from separate axes, and this process vitalizes his concepts.

One of the unique aspects of Deleuze's philosophical method is its utilization of conceptual components to force philosophers throughout history into confrontation. The result is an interchange of components which releases different concepts from their respective histories, and they converge in the formation of new concepts. Thus, the technique of philosophical collage validates the simultaneous interpretations of Deleuze through any number of re-appropriated philosophers. It is equally valid to read his philosophical project as an immanent Leibnizism as it is to read it as a metaphysical Nietzscheanism. Other scholars argue that Deleuze interprets a particular philosopher, such as Nietzsche, through the conceptual framework of another philosophy, such as Bergson.[24] Must these different interpretations of Deleuze exclude one another? Not at all. While certain commentaries are more convincing and forceful than others, the practice of diverse commentators – reading the same concept through separate philosophers – reinforces Deleuze's project.

Deleuze's philosophy is at once a re-appropriated concatenation of different pieces of philosophers as well as a proliferation of divergent philosopher-lines inscribed by pure difference. Deleuze's philosophy evokes a both/and approach, as opposed to an either/or approach. Concepts are dynamic, and while one thinker may argue that the concept of the virtual is a simulation of Leibniz, another thinker may argue that the concept of the virtual is a simulation of Bergson. What is common to both analyses is a dramatization of concepts. Since concepts become according to the problems posed to them, different analyses will emphasize certain intensive features more than others. Thus, the kaleidoscopic effect of Deleuze's philosophy reflects the splintering of concepts in each unique viewing. In order to map a concept and explore its expressive and ideational tendencies, it is important to dramatize it according to different conceptual valences. Coming to understand the temporal processes initiated by different conceptual arrangements provides the tools to paint Deleuze's concept of becoming. As we will see, the varying temporal tendencies of concepts are disjunctively synthesized in a faithful rendering of the redoubling of becoming. Thus the return to the task of explicating the concept of becoming in Deleuze via two main axes: Bergson and Nietzsche.

Key temporal concepts of Bergson and Nietzsche – duration, the eternal return and the moment – are essential to Deleuze's concept of becoming. The two conceptual galaxies presented by Bergson and Nietzsche are developed in combination with other influential thinkers; those specifically addressed in this study include Proust, Riemann, Leibniz, Carroll, Klossowski, Worringer, Spinoza, Hume and Borges. In addition to forming a conceptual constellation with the figures listed, certain artistic works will be invoked to concretize the concept of becoming. In particular, works by Odilon Redon, Jackson Pollock and Rainer Maria Rilke will lend sensory expression to the ontological and temporal processes condensed by Deleuze. There are alternative conceptual constellations that could undoubtedly be formed through the axiomatic analysis of other thinkers;[25] however, this study reads the aforementioned thinkers as providing the pertinent intensive features condensed in Deleuze's concept of becoming. As far as the consideration of Deleuze's works, they are not treated as a teleological progression in chronological history. They are considered along separate lines that indicate a particular text's articulation of a different set of problems. The restless becoming of each concept and each text is enforced by a non-chronological reading.

Deleuze understands concepts operating on the plane of immanence which curves and causes them to fold onto each other as they exchange singularities and release tendencies that may have been stifled in a previous arrangement. Accordingly, the present book is structured as a ritornello. Our methodological process is twofold: 1. we intend to map the different folds of the concepts which inform Deleuze's concept of becoming and 2. we dramatize these concepts by folding them throughout the chapters. In 'The Method of Dramatization' Deleuze describes his treatment of concepts as staged combinations, rather than abstract definitions.[26] It is misguided to ask *what* a concept is, says Deleuze, and more appropriate questions begin instead with '*who? how much? how? where? when?*'[27] Posing problems in such a way places emphasis on what a concept can do and how it is expressed in spatiotemporal dynamisms. In a dramatized method, concepts are incorporated in materiality, which is necessary to reveal their conceptual limits and temporal logics. The method of dramatization performs the tripartite ontology that Deleuze theorizes: absolute becoming, sensory becoming and effectuated being.

Concepts are not static essences but dynamic processes. Drama occurs when a concept is examined in its resonance with other concepts and according to the specific (im)material plane upon which it is unfolded. The current text dramatizes concepts in this fashion, as they are repeated and folded in order to map their intense features which are then synthesized in the concept of becoming. Each chapter poses a different problem that exposes varying tendencies of the concept of becoming and its relationship to time. Mapping the consistency of the concept of becoming – its condensed intensive features – sheds light on the myriad masks which disguise and differentiate the concept. We will disambiguate the different terminological expressions that Deleuze uses to indicate the concept of becoming, including learning the temporal logics that denote whether sensory becoming or absolute becoming is at work. Ultimately, the method of conceptual mapping and dramatization allows us to extract a theory of becoming from Deleuze's collective works and demonstrate the intricate temporal processes entailed in actualization of the virtual and the virtualization of the actual. Bergson's claim that posing a problem brings about its immediate solution structures Deleuze's philosophical project.[28] His philosophy problematizes the procedural unfolding of becoming in an immanent ontology, and his philosophical works contain the solution. It is up to us to make the *implicit* ontological processes subtending his elaboration of concepts *explicit* through a dramatization of becoming.

1

The Conceptual History of
Becoming in Deleuze

The process of becoming is the creative force at work in Deleuze's differential ontology. The concept of becoming populates Deleuze's works and is expressed in myriad masks; different conceptual features are emphasized in different texts, and there are terminological variances that can result in conceptual obfuscation. Upon analysis, however, certain intensive features surface, and these features are condensed into one concept of becoming. As we will see, however, a concept is complex in Deleuze's philosophy and all concepts undergo the processes of becoming themselves. It is often the temporal processes enacted in any given text that provide a roadmap to the intensive features of Deleuze's concept of becoming. Hence, in order to preclude ontological conflation resulting from diverse expressions of the concept of becoming in Deleuze's works, we must map its intensive components. Since concepts are not 'things' but processes in Deleuze, we must catch the processes in the act: they must be dramatized. Employing particular temporal concepts that push the limits of Deleuze's ontology causes the extreme tendencies of the concept of becoming to rise to the surface. The first stage of this conceptual mapping involves an investigation into the conceptual history from which Deleuze draws in the creation of his concept of becoming. This chapter is intended to provide a preliminary sketch of the concept of becoming in Deleuze, the details of which will be fleshed out in subsequent chapters.

One must not take the meaning of becoming as given. So often it is the case that becoming is identified with change, and change defined through mechanistic motion and individuated substance. Deleuze's concept of becoming addresses this concern while he simultaneously distances himself from other attempts to reformulate becoming, particularly the one offered by G. W. F. Hegel. Deleuze's own conceptual history is crucial in the elaboration of a systematic concept of becoming as it appears in his thought; otherwise, his opponents are prone to misread the notional nuances of what will be shown to be a tripartite ontology in Deleuze.[1] Unfortunately, the lack of an explicitly stated theory of becoming in Deleuze results in inconsistent readings of the concept, from both critics and Deleuze scholars.[2] Without a fully explicated concept of becoming, there is a perpetuated ambiguity that becomes dogmatized.[3] We must keep in mind that becoming has a conceptual history in Deleuze, and its intensive features operate differently in the philosophical systems from which these features are extracted.

For Deleuze, becoming is an immanent, counter-actualizing process which individuates actual states of being. Deleuze's concept of becoming has its own developmental history and is a unique collage of Bergsonian and Nietzschean becoming. He re-appropriates the concept of becoming from the temporal projects of these two key thinkers, while splitting the concept of becoming into two registers that are opposed one on key plane: memory. Becoming retains molecular memory in sensation, while it differs in kind in ideation as it enacts ontological forgetting. His re-appropriation of becoming from Bergson and Nietzsche is both distinct from, and integral to, Deleuze's innovative theory of time. This study will then proceed in subsequent chapters by disambiguating the relationship between Deleuze's concept of becoming and his theory of temporal synthesis. Therefore, to adequately apprehend the temporal processes of the concept of becoming in Deleuze's ontological system, we must first remap the conceptual components that he extracts from the history of philosophy.

The first step in analysing Deleuze's concept of becoming is unearthing its philosophical history. This is not intended to provide a comprehensive history of the concept of becoming, but a history of becoming as it pertains to Deleuze's particular philosophical project. When examining the philosophical history of becoming, we do not intend a chronological progression of events, but the superposition of concepts that communicate across historical periods, lending an untimely feature to the concept.[4] We will be restricting our scope to the history of Deleuzian becoming, which finds its sources in the temporal concepts of Bergson and Nietzsche. Deleuze's concept of becoming is also informed by re-appropriated concepts from other thinkers who will be discussed in the following chapters; however, Nietzschean becoming and Bergsonian becoming revolve around one another in Deleuze's ontologically binary stellar system. The first system to be invested is Bergson's concept of duration as it informs one of Deleuze's modes of becoming in sensation. Next, the counter-notion of Nietzschean eternal return appears as the second mode of becoming to be appropriated in Deleuze's complex concept of becoming. Within each system the corresponding components of Deleuze's history of becoming in Bergson and Nietzsche will be dramatized to illustrate how the two orders of becoming interact to form Deleuze's new concept of becoming.

As we will see, Deleuze's texts reveal a consistent tendency to refer to becoming in two distinct ways: either as 'becoming' (in the singular form) or as 'becomings' (in the plural form).[5] What appears to be a classification of the concept of becoming according to universality and particularity is in fact a distinction between the infinite, ideational unfolding of the concept of becoming, on the one hand, and its finite, sensory unfolding on the other. We will examine these two different conceptual registers as they appear in Deleuze's texts and begin to map his concept of becoming through the re-appropriation of temporal concepts in the history of philosophy. We argue that 'becomings' express a re-appropriation of Bergsonian duration, while 'becoming' expresses Deleuze's re-appropriation of Nietzsche's eternal return. The divergence of becoming and becomings is dramatized in a multiplicity of becoming, where the force of the eternal return (becoming) enacts a constellation of singular durations (becomings) in its subversive relationship with the lived present of Being. The concept of becoming that re-appropriates the infinite process of Nietzsche's eternal return will be referred to as 'absolute becoming', and the diverse becomings that exhibit Bergsonian duration will be referred to as 'sensory becoming'. Both notions of becoming diverge according to their milieus of incorporeality and corporeality, respectively.

The guiding thread of this initial chapter is to identify the re-appropriated concepts within the history of philosophy and map them onto Deleuze's concept of becoming. Having located the two temporal frameworks that correspond to Deleuze's dually expressed notions of becoming – sensory and absolute – we are able to bring their inherent temporal processes to the surface. From the outset we discover that the split between sensory and absolute becoming occurs at the interstice of ontological memory and ontological forgetfulness. What is the relationship between ontological memory and sensory becoming? What is the relationship between ontological forgetting and absolute becoming? The solution to this problem rests in the reconstruction of the processes of sensory becoming according to Deleuze's interpretation of Bergsonian duration and absolute becoming as it arises in Deleuze's speculative reading of Nietzsche's eternal return. Once the two notions of becoming have been extracted and explicated from their philosophical histories in Bergson and Nietzsche, Chapter 2 will demonstrate how Deleuze creates an immanent causality to dramatize them in his ontological system. His notion of quasi-causality reveals how the redoubling of the concept of becoming occurs, including its effectuation on the lived present in Being. As we will see, particularly in Chapter 2, Deleuze is not a philosopher of the One, as argued by his opponents, but his ontology is tripartite.

Becoming-Bergson

In *Bergsonism* Deleuze explicates the Bergsonian concept of duration against *and* through the concept of becoming. The way in which Deleuze distinguishes the concept of Bergsonian becoming from duration reveals the influence Bergson had on Deleuze's concept of becoming. It is in *Bergsonism* where Deleuze notes that duration is a *type* of becoming when he states that duration is 'a becoming that endures, a change that is substance itself'.[6] By combining an enduring becoming and substance, Deleuze redefines the materiality of the present according to the Bergsonian model of internal change, and consequently, he redefines substance as a *relationship* in the process of becoming. Not only is becoming the vehicle that produces what we perceive as substance in the lived present, but Deleuze leaves us a clue pertaining to the multiplicity of becoming by writing 'a becoming'. As we will discover upon further examination, the plurality of becoming does not denote discrete pluralities but is indicative of a non-numeric virtual network of becomings. Deleuze's use of 'a becoming' illustrates the influence Bergson's concept of duration, as a continuous virtual multiplicity, had upon Deleuze's formulation of the concept of becoming. Bergson explains,

> An infinite multiplicity of becomings variously colored, so to speak, passes before our eyes: we manage so that we see only differences in color, that is to say, differences of state, beneath which there is supposed to flow, hidden from our view, a becoming always and everywhere the same, invariably colorless.[7]

Like Bergson, Deleuze often switches terminological registers, sometimes speaking of becoming as an absolute individuating process (i.e. becoming, absolute), and sometimes as a relative, fragmented process (i.e. a becoming, or becomings, sensory). We need to be careful not to misinterpret this phenomenon through the schema of the universal and particular, imposing representational thought to an immanent ontological process. New concepts need to be created in order to accommodate the immanent unfolding of becomings.

The implicit, nebulous interconnection between duration and becoming in *Bergsonism* is articulated more explicitly in works such as *The Logic of Sense* and *A Thousand Plateaus* which re-appropriate duration as points of becoming,[8] and blocs of becoming. The distinction between becoming versus becomings that arises in Bergson's writings collapses the one and the many by creating a virtual multiplicity of heterogeneous relations. In a continuous multiplicity the *one* (absolute becoming) differentiates itself across *many* heterogeneous lines (sensory becoming), resulting in an immanent stream of many becomings folded into one becoming. It is clear, however, that Deleuze's concept of becoming is expressed in the same terms of heterogeneous, continuous multiplicity that we see in Bergsonian duration – an internal relationality or change that replaces our traditional notion of substance. The collapse of the one and the many in a theory of continuous multiplicity does not necessitate a subordination of heterogeneity to homogeneity, or a falling back into transcendence. In this chapter, we will examine how newly conceived temporal and causal processes retain heterogeneous sensory becomings within the ideational process of absolute becoming in Deleuze's ontology of difference.

The first notion of becoming to be explicated from Deleuze's ontology is sensory becoming, which maintains the characteristics of Bergsonian duration at the molecular level. Opposed to what he calls 'molar subjects' – individuated forms in representational Being – the differenciated becoming in sensation (sensory becoming) is a pre-subjective molecular collectivity and is consistent with Deleuze's re-appropriation of the multiplicity of duration.[9] The temporal logic of sensory becoming differs in kind from Deleuze's appropriation of Nietzsche's eternal return (absolute becoming) on the axis of memory. When Deleuze speaks in terms of *a* becoming, or becomings, he is speaking of a notion of becoming that unfolds serially along the points of molecular duration. Deleuze's re-appropriation of several key Bergsonian concepts, such as multiplicity, change and duration and ontological memory contribute to the formation of one notion of becoming that will later link up with its counter-notion in the re-appropriation of Nietzsche's eternal return. These two notions of becoming engage in the proliferation of multiplicities which inform the ontological innovation of Deleuze's philosophy. And while there are two registers of becoming – a distinction we have made in terms of notional difference – that correspond to their respective milieus (corporeal versus incorporeal), they form a continuous multiplicity as one concept. It is a relationship marked by divergence that fuels the processes of these two notions of becoming. The notions of sensory becoming and absolute becoming interact primarily through a process of divergence, wherein all forms and states of being are produced. As will be shown in Chapter 2, the virtual and the actual simultaneously produce one another as the two notions of becoming collide in the lived present.

A key concept that enables us to map the influence that Bergsonian duration had on Deleuze's formulation of becoming is that of change. For both Bergson and Deleuze the states perceived in encounters of Being, via representational thought, are real illusions that are produced through becoming and these perceived states obfuscate what it means to change. The ontological misappropriation of becoming as a derivative offshoot of Being in the materiality of the present is inexorably connected to misconceptions of change in the history of philosophy. Throughout much of the history of philosophy change has been understood as the passage through the static moments of Being. Deleuze and Bergson, on the contrary, address the production of change without using the static forms of Being as a reference point. Deleuze's understanding of change is integral to the development of sensory becoming. With Bergson's help in redefining change in terms of internal difference, Deleuze begins to sculpt a new concept of becoming.

Change

The relationship between change and that which undergoes change retains its Bergsonian imparted immanence in Deleuze. Becoming is often very simply defined in terms of change. Is it satisfactory to conceive of becoming as 'active transformation?'[10] Or is becoming more complex? For Deleuze and Bergson, virtual becoming is serially distributed into multiplicities of becoming with singular durations of unique spatiotemporal dynamisms, and these becomings undergo substantial changes derivative to the very movement of the whole of becoming.

Representational thought defines change through discrete states of perception, but change itself, as Bergson and Deleuze contest, is perpetual, and nothing can elude its force, including states, methods and agents. Change is continuous and does not move in discontinuous leaps; it is not created externally but is internal to that which is undergoing change. How might we understand change without appealing to static, transcendental entities? As Cliff Stagoll notes,

> This is not to say that becoming represents a phase between two states, or a range of terms or states through which something might pass on its journey to another state. Rather than a product, final or interim, becoming is the very dynamism of change, situated between heterogeneous terms tending towards no particular goal or end-state.[11]

This change occurs internally through the productive relations of becoming and is not a derivative movement created abstractly as a connection between elements. Pure change, which is synonymous with duration for Bergson, is thusly defined as being absolutely indivisible.[12] That is to say that even if the becoming of change can be measured in time, that time is merely a spatial representation and distortion of said change. We may note that Bergson's own example of sonority in music and its indivisible non-pulsed time reappears in several of Deleuze's texts addressing the dynamism of becoming. The sonorous whole of a melody, for Bergson, exemplifies that change is the thing itself; nothing escapes its force – no subject, measurement or method. The qualitative indivisibility of change connects 'things' through relative speeds analogous to two passing trains that at the moment of encounter seemingly stop motion in the observing train car. The appeal to sonority resurfaces in Deleuze's writings, in particular with the sense of the in-between of becoming. Music is able to maintain its expression of internal change by creatively drawing a diagonal between the verticality of harmony and the horizontality of melody. The example of change in music underscores Deleuze's identification of becoming (sensory) with duration.

> Moving along this transversal line, which is really a line of deterritorialization, there is a *sound block* that no longer has a point of origin, since it is always and already in the middle of the line; and no longer has horizontal and vertical coordinates, and measure, like a drunken boat that melds with the line or draws a plane of consistency.[13]

The sound bloc is a type of becoming that exhibits structural duration which is not transcendentally fixed to any state of being in perception but unfolds in a continuous multiplicity of what Deleuze calls non-pulsed time. This sonorous dynamism, reminiscent of expressed duration in Bergson, is characterized by the infinite transformation of becoming where territories are destroyed in the creation of new networks of sound. The sensory becoming exemplified by the movement of music in Bergson and Deleuze destabilizes identities and all forms through its restlessness: 'a little lost boat, in swirling debris'.[14] Like the landscape that differenciates glaciers, silver suns, waves of pearl and fiery skies in a restless exchange of becoming-other in Rimbaud's drunken boat, the intensive movement of duration/change cannot be divided without changing in nature. Deleuze takes up this understanding of change and becoming as being fundamentally, discretely indivisible in his own works.[15]

Being fundamentally indivisible means that something cannot be divided without changing in kind, which is why Keith Ansell-Pearson connects virtual multiplicity of change in Bergson to Deleuze's account of non-numerical multiplicities understood as indivisibles 'during each stage of the division'.[16] The process of enduring becoming is supported by the definition of change as pure duration and allows for differenciation that is continuous within the virtuality of the real. For Bergson, this intensive, qualitative process of duration is connected to consciousness (of all forms of life). While Deleuze accepts the definition of change as an internal, heterogeneous, continuous multiplicity of duration, he eliminates the (un)conscious element of duration in Bergson and further dissimulates the subject, producing instead, a multiplicity of pre-individualities. According to James Williams, Bergson 'demonstrates incoherence in representational, content-driven and spatial accounts of consciousness and time by showing how they lead to contradictions'.[17] Deleuze resolves these contradictions by ontologizing duration, and thus removing change from the limits of consciousness.

Deleuze relegates the durational character of change to the structure of differenciated-yet-differentiating becomings. In his re-appropriation of duration, Deleuze identifies the notion of sensory becoming with Bergson's notion of virtual memory, as he explicitly states in *Bergsonism*.[18] By bleeding duration into ontological and pre-subjective memory, Deleuze welds his notion of becoming in the sensible along the dictates of self-differentiating memory in virtual coexistence. Therefore, the durational character of becoming is purely ontological in Deleuze and unfolds, in part, through the logic of ontological memory. The re-appropriation of Bergsonian duration does not account for the entire concept of becoming in Deleuze's ontology. In order to carve out a singular concept of becoming as being independent of identity, resemblance, analogy and opposition, Deleuze must distinguish himself from the infamous philosopher of becoming: Hegel.

A rejection of Hegel's concept of becoming

Deleuzian becoming adheres to Bergsonian becoming in the sense that becoming is not the result of a transition between being and non-being. By 'nonbeing', both Bergson and Deleuze take the term to mean negation, or the being of the negative. There is no such negation at the ontological level for them; however, as will be explained later, Deleuze does have his own version of nonbeing ('(non)-being'), which is designates that which is beyond Being, sensory becoming, or what he calls the problematic in *Difference and Repetition*.[19] For Deleuze, (non)-being, or '?-being', is beyond the negative.

Nonetheless, becoming does not begin in the conceptual plane, but arises as the untimely – counter to its time, yet acting upon its time and its future – without beginning or end, in the process of actualization of singular events. A Bergsonian, and then Deleuzian, anti-Hegelianism informs this modification of the understanding of becoming. The criticism that Bergson launches against a dialectical description of becoming, and the Hegelian dialectic in particular, is lauded by Deleuze as the 'finest in his oeuvre'. Deleuze clearly supports Bergson's denunciation of the claim that becoming is produced through the passage of being into nonbeing. He rehashes Bergson's criticism of Hegelian becoming in the exact terms Bergson used to criticize the historical tendency to define change through the artificial reconstructed movement of immobile states.[20] Deleuze proclaims,

> To Bergson, it seems that in this type of *dialectical* method, one begins with concepts that, like baggy clothes, are much too big. The One in general, the multiple in general, nonbeing in general. … In such cases the real is recomposed with abstracts; but of what use is a dialectic that believes itself to be reunited with the real when it compensates for the inadequacy of a concept that is too broad or too general by invoking the opposite concept, which is no less broad and general? The concrete will never be attained by combining the inadequacy of one concept with the inadequacy of its opposite. The singular will never be attained by correcting a generality with another generality.[21]

We can also state that the process of becoming will never result from combining Being with the inadequacy of Hegelian nonbeing. The proliferation of becoming is the dynamic production of relations of the real. Becoming produces the concepts of Being and nonbeing in relations of pure difference: the real. Deleuze follows Bergson in removing the notion of becoming from an alleged formation in the conceptual realm and places it in the midst of the sensible. In *Creative Evolution*, Bergson grounds becoming by stating that 'experience confronts us with becoming: that is *sensible* reality'.[22] In addition to being defined against the inadequacy of purely conceptual movement in dialectical thought, becoming is then posited against representational thought, where mobility is created through the immobilizing, imagistic mechanism of the intellect and the dogmatic image of thought. Becoming, for Bergson and Deleuze, is not the derivative abstraction of static Being. Static Being is the reversal of intensity as an instant of becoming, the effectuated form as an instant of involution, and the projected endpoint as the instant of accomplished action. Pure purposeless movement is restored to becoming against the teleological conception of change seen in what Bergson calls 'the philosophy of Ideas', or the effect of the cinematographic imposition of representational thought onto becoming.[23] The concept of becoming is thus reinterpreted as belonging to the logic of the sensible, and is proliferated in real relations that seamlessly flow between concept and affect.

And while Deleuze remarks on the alleged opposition between becoming and duration in Bergson, he is clearly referring to the abstract concept of becoming in Hegel. The reformulation of becoming that we see in Bergson is compatible with his concept of duration. A distinction is made between becoming and duration because

> duration is a multiplicity, a type of multiplicity that is not reducible to an overly broad combination in which the opposites, the One and the Multiple in general, only coincide on condition that they are grasped at the extreme point of their generalization, empty of all 'measure' and of all real substance.[24]

This is the same critical tool that both Bergson and Deleuze use to level against the Hegelian form of becoming. It is clear that Deleuze's becoming is imbued with the virtual multiplicities attributed to duration. The self-differing features of duration are adopted in Deleuze's concept of becoming, as well as the attribution of becoming to the logic of the sensible. Again, we must keep in mind that sensory becoming only accounts for half of Deleuze's concept of becoming, and there is another logic of becoming that pertains to the realm of pure events, the incorporeal.

Mapping Bergsonian duration onto becoming

Becoming may be expressed as an empty form of time for Deleuze, but it is also an open process.[25] This process mimics many of the characteristics of Bergsonian duration. I am not arguing that Deleuzian becoming is identical to Bergsonian duration, but merely that Deleuze's construction of becoming was heavily influenced by Bergsonian duration, specifically in what concerns becomings, or sensory becoming. For example, becoming does not consist of interpenetrating states of consciousness for Deleuze, but it reflects the continuous heterogeneity implicated in the virtual multiplicity of duration. Becoming is itself a multiplicity, masking a multiplicity of other becomings as they become other while they continue to be what they are. There is not only one empty form of becoming (absolute becoming), but there are also non-discrete multiplicities of becoming that invoke intensive features of duration in sensation (sensory becoming). Becoming is plural; it is a plural monism. Just as Heidegger differentiated between Being and beings, we must make a distinction between pure becoming and becomings; absolute becoming and sensory becoming.[26]

Becoming is univocal in Deleuze's philosophy, and this is not a distinction between the particular and the universal. Rather, becoming is an immanent process that Deleuze discusses in terms of a multiplicity; it is not only an epistemological distinction, but also an ontological distinction. Interestingly, as we survey the concept of becoming across Deleuze's collective works, the differential nature of becoming is witnessed in action, depending on which set of problems is outlined in each text, or each passage. The concept of becoming unfolds quite differently in *Nietzsche and Philosophy* versus *A Thousand Plateaus*, for instance. In *Nietzsche and Philosophy*, Deleuze is concerned with a notion of becoming that will arrive as the empty form of time, the eternal return of difference, as seen in *Difference and Repetition*. In *A Thousand Plateaus*, Deleuze and Guattari are admittedly more concerned with the becomings of corporeal depth, Artaud's body without organs, that is, sensory becoming. Each of Deleuze's (and sometimes Guattari's) works develops conceptual tendencies and defines intensive features of becoming along unique problematics. Focusing on the quasi-causal operator of becoming in *The Logic of Sense* pushes the concept of becoming's potential in his other works, irrespective of publication date, such as *Bergsonism*. As we will see, the concept of becoming itself *becomes* across Deleuze's works, irrespective of chronological publication.

The concept of becoming as such should be understood as a generative process which is fully immanent yet differenciates varying becomings exhibitive of singular durations and temporal combinations as they converge or diverge. The pluralism of becomings is only one piece of the ontological puzzle of becoming. When employing the ontological features of Deleuze's concept of becoming, scholars typically invoke becomings of sensation elaborated in *A Thousand Plateaus*.[27] This line of becoming bears the mark of Bergsonian duration, sensory becoming, and replaces the traditional notion of substance with intensive change. In Deleuze's words, 'Every becoming is a block of coexistence,'[28] mimicking the virtual coexistence we see in Bergsonian duration. Becoming differentiates itself according to the same non-numerical temporal logic of duration, changing in kind as it is divided. This temporality is serial and simultaneous, ordinal not cardinal; it works through a network of virtual coexistence. Deleuze thus sides with Bergson against the criticism of Bachelard's book, *The Dialectic of Duration*, where events are said to be discontinuous and fragmented.[29] How, then, do the processes of Deleuzian becoming reflect those of Bergsonian duration?

The open-ended futurity of duration will help disambiguate the process of becoming in Deleuze. As Elizabeth Grosz iterates, 'It is such a notion of open-endedness that leads Deleuze to seek in Bergson and Bergsonism a concept of duration that is adequate for thinking about all the temporal resonances of becoming.'[30] While not all becomings endure,[31] their functionality replicates much of the productive force of duration. Both replace stasis with pure movement, and this movement is a differentiating force which cleaves paths for new futures. As François Dosse notes, Deleuze's notion of movement borrows Bergson's three tenets of movement: First, Deleuze accepts that movement entails the indivisible act of traversing divisible space. The indivisible act of traversing subordinates movement to the logic of duration. Consequently, the second feature of Bergsonian movement involves an emphasis on ordinary moments in proximity, as opposed to situating and isolating important moments. This revision of movement pushes the inventiveness of time, connecting movement to the production of the new through durational temporality. Finally, Deleuze adopts Bergson's view that movement is a mobile cut of duration, and thus of an open totality. Dosse highlights the inventiveness of durational movement that informs Deleuze's notion of becoming, whereby a-subjective memory unfolds into the depths of time.[32] Anne Sauvagnargues illuminates the primacy of time in movement, and how such a reversal accommodates the temporal invention. She writes,

> 'Movement no longer links time to the cardinal points of the rotation of the stars; it is rather movement that depends upon time. Released from its cosmic hinges, time becomes the condition for the transformation of the whole and becomes emancipated from movement, for which it now becomes the principle.'[33]

Movement is no longer understood according to immobile points in space imposed upon time, but movement refers to the self-differing process of time as its condition.

The following connection between the process of duration and the production of the new appears in Deleuze's differential project of becoming: 'The more we study the nature of time, the more we shall comprehend that duration means invention, the creation of forms, the continual elaboration of the absolutely new.'[34] The continuous destruction and creation of forms in the actual, and blocs of sensation in the sensible, are key features of Deleuzian becoming and mark the mechanism behind the production of novelty. Violently opposed to the status quo, the process of becoming involves '*a reality that is making itself in a reality that is unmaking itself*'.[35] The reality that is making itself is sensory becoming, which is the concept of becoming that retains durational traces at the molecular level. As we will uncover in the investigation of Nietzsche's influence on Deleuze's concept of becoming, there is another concept of becoming that corresponds to a reality that is unmaking itself.

Becoming and aesthetic production

Before proceeding, it would be helpful to discuss briefly what is meant by the production of 'the new' as it relates to Deleuze's aesthetic ontology. The unconditioned movement of becoming produces 'the new', or absolute novelty, in Deleuze, an ontological production that will be articulated in depth in Chapter 2. The new involves Deleuze's subversion of the dogmatic 'image of thought' seen in representational thinking. Following Nietzsche's critique of Reason in *Twilight of the Idols*, Deleuze replaces judgement in Reason with an aesthetic ontology of sensation.[36] The reason he does so is that Reason is premised on the immobilizing mechanisms of the intellect, which freeze the flows of temporality in distortive, chronological time. Accordingly, the concept of the new cannot be subordinated to identity, resemblance, analogy, or opposition; the four branches of representational thought and Reason must be circumvented in the search for the new, which is a qualitative enunciation of sensory becoming. Subordinating the absolutely new to the logic of identity would preclude the actualization of difference in real experience. The new cannot be produced by the logic of the same, which is the time of chronometry and mechanistic causation.

This is why Daniel W. Smith succinctly explains that the new must be distinguished from the categories of transformation, causality and emergence.[37] Transformation merely rearranges the grounding force of ontological memory, that is, in matter,[38] while producing new forms. The ground is not destroyed in transformation, and the virtuality of memory is not overcome. The inadequacy of transformation in producing the new reflects the necessary re-conception of the role of change in becoming, as discussed previously. Correlatively, mechanistic causality, which recomposes movement from static essences or immobile snapshots of time, will fail to produce the new. This conventional scientific causality presupposes successive, linear time where the cause is retroactively constructed according to the image of the effect. As such, the effect is already contained within the cause, privileging numerical novelty rather than intensive novelty. Similarly, emergence is also eliminated in articulating the radically new, as it traditionally comprehends the new as a result of substructive complexity, rather than a primordial ontological process. The absolutely new must be produced at the basic ontological level where representational thought has not corrupted or co-opted the creative force of becoming. It cannot be sought out of fashion for its own sake, nor remodelled after another's invention. The new is the ontological product of becoming, which is unconditioned and internalizes difference in a Deleuzian move where identity is not forged within the logic of the concept. The encounters that will be examined through the confrontation of becoming and the repetition of time will reveal just how the three categorical errors of novelty (transformation, causality and emergence) are trapped within the nexus of the possible-real, as opposed to the virtual-actual. Possibility is temporally bound to mechanistic representational causality, and thus fails as a model for the production of the new through becoming. Any time Deleuze discusses the production of the new he is signalling the intricate processes of becoming in immanence.

Where absolute becoming splits from sensory becoming: Memory

Deleuzian becomings resemble Bergsonian duration in terms of the overcoming of emergence and mechanistic causality. Duration's perpetual transformation is not beholden to the numerical novelty of transformation, as it internalizes qualitative difference, but it is inexorably bound to virtual memory. It is the monumental ground of ontological, virtual memory that forbids the conflation of pure, absolute becoming with duration. Up to this point, we have not yet articulated the difference between the sensory becomings that retain durational features and what Deleuze often uses as an umbrella concept of pure becoming: the empty form of time devoid of duration. While Deleuze often indicates a temporal difference among the two notions of becoming by using the terms 'becoming' rather than 'becomings', or 'a becoming', he sometimes uses the single term 'becoming' when referring to both ontological processes. It is, therefore, necessary to pinpoint when sensory becoming and its molecular duration are being employed, and when absolute becoming and its empty form of time are being employed.

Sensory becoming in Deleuze integrates many of the intensive features of duration; included in this combination of intensive features is memory inscribed at the molecular level. Sensory becoming always exemplifies retention of virtual memory at the molecular level. The reason for this is that duration is a subversion of the chronological, perceived present, but it is not altogether disconnected from individuated objects. It disorients matter through a process of self-differing, yet there is a virtual image that is connected to every actual object through dissemblance. Sensory becoming is also interconnected to absolute becoming, which is void of duration and purges ontological memory. The continuity of Deleuze's concept of becoming, its logic as a multiplicity, means that neither sensory nor absolute becoming remains disengaged from the other. Sensory becoming is constituted by temporally linked singularities that intensively endure *within* a system of becoming.[39] This system forges lines between effectuated being, sensory becoming and the primacy of absolute becoming. The primacy of this system of becoming entails the ontological forgetting enacted by the eternal return of difference. Sensory becoming is the reality that makes itself within the reality of absolute becoming which unmakes it. It forms blocs of sensation in coexistence, which is an effect of convergence in the virtual. Meanwhile, absolute becoming evokes divergence, deterritorializing convergent alliances formed in duration, or molecular memory. The formlessness of absolute becoming distributes sensory becomings while ceaselessly cutting into them, thereby destabilizing their connections of molecular memory.

While absolute becoming is primordially separated from duration in terms of molecular memory, we may safely interpose sensory becoming and duration. Sensory becoming participates in the virtual flux of memory, similar to duration, but sensory becoming is not restricted to psychic life – for this reason, it is not referred to as duration in the subsequent chapters, but is called molecular memory. Furthermore, the virtuality of molecular memory is intensively quantitative and not extensively quantitative, so the perpetual subversion of forms through duration involves heterogeneous continuity, thus making it an open system. These open systems of singular durations populate Deleuze's ontology. Each becoming functions as a network of open nomadological relations, where they interact, destroy and create in simultaneous levels of coexistence. Here we find continuity on the side of Bergson and Deleuze versus the discontinuity posited by thinkers such as Bachelard and Badiou.

The pure relationality enacted by becoming mirrors the interpenetration of moments of duration. Bergson demonstrates the process of interpenetration by saying, 'There is a real duration, the heterogeneous moments of which permeate one another; each moment, however, can be brought into relation with a state of the external world which is contemporaneous with it, and can be separated from the other moments in consequence of this very process.'[40] For Deleuze, the multiplicity of becoming functions in this same manner: sensory becomings heterogeneously permeate one another and are inexorably connected to actuality in the extensive world. This becoming through alliance is logically distinct from the absolute becoming elaborated in the re-appropriation of Nietzsche's eternal return.

Elizabeth Grosz accurately notes that 'becoming is the operation of self-differentiation, the elaboration of a difference within a thing, a quality or a system that emerges or actualizes only in duration'.[41] While sensory becoming and duration function in similar ways, absolute becoming is distinct from duration in terms of its unconditioned actualization through ontological forgetting. We must be aware that the process of becoming is not confined to the virtual alone, but seamlessly cuts into the intermediary zone of the sensible, producing the new in duration. Becomings can involve unfolding sensory blocs of indeterminate duration, as specified by Grosz, but there is also a production of events of '*zero duration* (the operation of the quasi-cause)', according to Manuel DeLanda,[42] which is the absolute becoming of the eternal return of difference. It is the quasi-cause, which Deleuze develops in *The Logic of Sense* as an alternative, immanent causal process that functions as the counter-actualizing operator of absolute becoming. The quasi-cause allows sensory becoming, absolute becoming and the effectuated present to communicate in resonant distance. Untimely in its differential distribution, the quasi-cause causes absolute becoming to diverge from sensory becoming in the process of individuation. It is up to us to elaborate the bifurcating process that splits the two temporal registers of absolute becoming and sensory becoming. Absolute becoming, or what DeLanda calls pure becoming, will be articulated within Deleuze's re-appropriation of Nietzsche's eternal return. For now, we will continue to examine the relationship between sensory becoming and duration (i.e. molecular memory).

Sensory becoming and molecular memory

It is clear that there is a sense of becoming that is a schizophrenic production of internal, perpetual revolution which destroys unities and fixities, and is an empty form of time running contrary to memory. After all, Deleuze explicitly states that '*Becoming is an antimemory*', for becoming breaks away from the arborescent model of thought, and instead is a proliferating rhizome without beginning or end.[43] If becoming is an anti-memory, and 'memory is identical to duration',[44] then how can we claim that becoming is inexorably tied to duration? Before denouncing the equivocation between becomings (sensory) and becoming (absolute) in the philosophy of Deleuze, it is necessary to parse out what he means by memory.

Ontological memory is not arborescent for Deleuze, as it is a virtual multiplicity of the pure past in itself.[45] Memories in this sense do not correspond to a former lived present, but to a present that never was. This is more closely aligned with what Deleuze describes as the confusion of being with being-present, or an intellectual reconstruction of the immediate past, which is the lived present. On the contrary, ontological memory, which is modelled on Bergson's cone of memory in *Matter and Memory*, is a function of the present which '*is not*; rather, it [the present] is pure becoming, always outside itself'.[46] The present that never was, or that never passed through the presence of perception (i.e. the immediate past), constitutes the pure past, thus becoming ontological memory. It is in *this* sense that duration is memory. It addresses the pure past as such, and the multiplicity of relations between levels perpetually revolves as a function of the differential present, i.e. the quasi-cause. Ontological memory – the logic of molecular arrangement in sensation – is without beginning or end but is a virtuality of infinite levels of the pure past that are condensations of one another, and their relationality is in a process of becoming.

The pure becoming of the present transforming into the virtuality of the pure past in memory partially accounts for Deleuze's seemingly contradictory stance on the relationship between becoming and memory. For example, shortly after his statement about becoming being an anti-memory, he chooses to substitute 'memory' with 'becoming'. In the chapter titled '1730: Becoming-Intense, Becoming-Animal, Becoming-Imperceptible...' from *A Thousand Plateaus*, Deleuze and Guattari write a series of sections that name processes of memories that lead up to the substitution of becoming for memory.[47] Why, if becoming is an anti-memory, is the chapter on becomings in *A Thousand Plateaus* structured by sections titled by memories? Deleuze and Guattari state, 'Wherever we used the word "memories" in the preceding pages, we were wrong to do so; we meant to say "becoming", we were saying becoming.'[48] Interesting, however, is Deleuze's (and Guattari's) incitation that we substitute becoming for memory, but 'memories' remain in the text. They actively chose not to edit the text in a way where 'memories' would be erased by 'becoming'. This choice can be traced to two differing aspects of becoming in relation to memory.

First, Deleuze and Guattari are not simply staging an opposition between becoming and memory, but they are revealing the bifurcating process of becoming. While it is accurate to depict becoming as the antithesis of memory, as it decodes, deterritorializes, and destroys everything in its path which is fixed, this is only true of absolute becoming, the repetition of the eternal return. However, sensory becoming (i.e. becomings, blocs of becoming and points of becoming) is inescapably connected to molecular memory – a pure past that is constructed through the non-presence of the quasi-cause.

Secondly, in addition to the distinction between becoming (anti-memory) and becomings (molecular memory), becomings operate within the ontological framework of virtual memory. What Deleuze and Guattari meant to say instead of 'memory' was not 'becoming' but 'becomings', that is, sensory becoming.[49] Becomings possess 'a molecular memory, but as a factor of integration into a majoritarian or molar system'.[50] Since becoming and becomings are not attached to subjects or objects of any sort but are pure relationality, they do not operate within the realm of conscious or unconscious memory. Nonetheless, becomings endure, cohering through ontological memory, which is at the level of the molecular. The memory of becomings is at the sub-representative level, beneath the constituted individuated molar subjects.

The individuating process of ontological memory – the memory of becomings – is expressed by Deleuze in terms of Proustian reminiscence and is a supplemental entrance into Bergson's notion of the pure past. Deleuze writes, 'To remember is to create, is *to reach that point where the associative chain breaks, leaps over the constituted individual, is transferred to the birth of an individuating world.*'[51] The process of creation that arises from ontological memory is the code-breaking logic (or 'antilogos') of sensory becoming whose molecular durations ignite individuation beneath the representation of entities, subjects and objects. This is not the memory of a molar subject, one constructed by an act of re-presentation. Rather, this virtual memory is a differential process involving the passing of the pure present that never is the eluded present of the quasi-cause, into the vortex of the pure past that never was. It is the encounter of a becoming that never is and the pure past that never was that colours becomings with duration. The durational tendency of becomings is run through with the chaotic force of absolute becoming, which is of a separate temporal (dis)order.

Sensory becoming must be seen as both a divergence from absolute becoming and victim of its quasi-causal operator. Though divergent from absolute, ideational becoming, sensory becoming forms continuous multiplicities, and therefore, it is imperative that we apprehend the two ontological registers in accordance with their virtual relationality. The unarticulated twofold movement of becoming, which is the spurious result of the appellation of becomings (sensory becoming) in terms of numerical multiplicity under the banner of one temporal order (absolute becoming), explains the correlative ambivalence of the concept in the secondary literature. It is mistaken to cast all the processes of becoming into a unified temporal landscape.[52] It is our task to learn to negotiate between the various terms Deleuze uses for the rhizomatic process of becoming and to understand how these processes interact. We have differentiated between becoming (absolute becoming) and becomings (sensory becoming) – the latter owing much of its character to the temporal project of Bergson and the re-appropriation of duration in terms of molecular memory. We have yet to elaborate the history of absolute becoming. The following section explicates absolute becoming in Deleuze from Nietzsche's concept of the eternal return.

Becoming-Nietzsche

It is not a surprise that Deleuze's concept of becoming grows out of Nietzschean becoming. He states explicitly in the preface of the American edition of *Nietzsche and Philosophy* that the book is, above all, an analysis of becoming in Nietzsche.[53] For Deleuze, becoming is the force of the eternal return in Nietzsche. Deleuze's concept of becoming adopts the feature of innocence from Nietzsche's appropriation of Heraclitus, as well as Nietzsche's ontological selectivity as it is expressed in his affirmative theory of the eternal return. While Deleuze may use various terms for what has been identified as absolute becoming, the confluence of becoming and the eternal return within Deleuze's philosophy is unmistakable. Very plainly, Deleuze states, 'The Eternal Return is the instant or the eternity of becoming eliminating whatever offers resistance. It brings out, or better yet, it creates the active, the pure active, and pure affirmation.'[54] The eternal return perpetually revolutionizes forms, destroys and creates conceptual arrangments in a frenetic production of multiplicities in chaos. While the multiplicities of sensory becoming exhibit a differential relation to memory, absolute becoming flows through all multiplicities, pulling them out of joint from the actual present. Absolute becoming, which is the work of the eternal return, employs active forgetting thus destabilizing the becomings that emerge in relation to varying durations. As the absolute becoming of the eternal return collides with all emerging forms in its path, the memory nexus of sensory becomings is shattered, creating openings for new forms of thought and life. Deleuze assimilates his re-appropriation of the eternal return into the fundamental processes of becoming. He characterizes the process of absolute becoming according to the interconnected points of Nietzsche's ontology: innocence, selectivity and active forgetfulness. Consequently, we will sketch out the contours of Deleuze's re-appropriation of Nietzschean becoming in order to provide the groundwork for the analysis of the relationship between the eternal return and time in Chapter 4.

The innocence of becoming

Perhaps the most revealing clue to Deleuze's concept of becoming, as well as its eventual formulation as absolute becoming in *What Is Philosophy?*, is his understanding of Nietzschean becoming in *Nietzsche and Philosophy*. At this point in his philosophical career, Deleuze had not explicitly outlined the two orders of becoming of his writings into a comprehensive theory. During the writing of *Nietzsche and Philosophy* Deleuze suggests a single concept of becoming which is fundamentally Nietzschean: selective, innocent and amnesic. It is not until *Difference and Repetition* that we begin to see a more crystallized theory of becoming(s) emerge in his writing. From *Difference and Repetition* onward we see the explicitly developed, divergent account of absolute becoming and sensory becoming in *The Logic of Sense* and *A Thousand Plateaus* and *What Is Philosophy?* At present, we will examine the Nietzschean resonances given in the constellation of ideas condensed by absolute becoming, beginning with innocence, which is synonymous with multiplicity in Deleuze.

What does it mean to say that becoming is innocent? For Deleuze 'innocence is the truth of multiplicity.'[55] And what is the truth of multiplicity? Deleuze adopts the collapse of the One and the Many in the form of virtual multiplicity. Everything is a multiplicity or multiplicities. It is necessary to ask 'how?' rather than 'what?' when questioning the nature of multiplicity. The variety of multiplicity is provided by pure difference, which means that multiplicities are not subjected to a uniform space, temporality, or identity in the concept. Additionally, multiplicity replaces the notion of substance in Deleuze's philosophy. In *Difference and Repetition* Deleuze gives us three conditions of multiplicity:[56]

1. A multiplicity is formless, lacks conceptual signification, sensibility and assignable function. It is ideal and real, but does not actually exist.
2. Multiplicities are intrinsically defined, isolated from outside reference or predetermined spatiality.
3. Multiplicities form differential relations which are actualized in various spatiotemporal dynamisms and produce structures of terms and forms.

Multiplicities are differential relations that are non-localizable, virtual, coexistent, self-referential, purposeless, not presupposing identities, and they are not discrete. The relationality of multiplicities provides the fabric of substantiality for Deleuze, and it is pre-individual. It is the self-referential features of multiplicity that account for innocence.[57] In this sense, they are like Nietzschean forces, referring to their creative potentials. The affirmation of this force of becoming – multiplicities that are immersed in becoming – grants its innocence. The spatially and temporally undetermined differential relationality of multiplicities is enforced by becoming. 'Multiplicity is affirmed as multiplicity; becoming is affirmed as becoming. That is to say at once that affirmation is itself multiple, that it becomes itself, and that becoming and multiplicity are themselves affirmations.'[58] Multiplicity is not a fixed relation, but is in the process of becoming itself and becoming is itself a multiplicity. The innocence of affirmation is in the creative return of becoming in its multiplicity. The aestheticization of becoming as the creative force of the eternal return restores its innocence against representational categories of opposition, analogy, identity and resemblance. Becoming is an aesthetic process and the absolute novelty produced through the syntheses of the eternal return creates the innocence of affirmation.

The truth of multiplicity also involves the denial of transcendent entities, such as God, Self, World, as well as cause and effect. Nietzsche claims, 'As soon as we *imagine* someone who is responsible for us being thus and thus, etc. (God, nature), attributing our existence, our happiness and misery to it as its *intention*, we corrupt for ourselves the *innocence of becoming*. We then have someone who wants to achieve something through us and with us.'[59] Once we allow the proliferation of becoming without trying to fix it with representational thought all identities and intentions dissolve. The appeal to mechanistic laws of nature or any form of teleological cause attempts to limit and restrict the chaotic proliferation of becoming in its heterogeneous multiplicities.

The innocence of becoming is corrupted by the attempt to fix it with immobile, transcendental structures. While becoming supersedes such fixity, its proliferation is denied from without and its multiplicities are territorialized. Essentially, stupidity and fictitious appeals to static being obscure the multiplicity of becoming. As Deleuze reiterates, 'Whatever is opposed to becoming – the Same or the Identical – is not, rigorously speaking.'[60] The only being is that constituted by the return of becoming, and the Same and the One are merely illusory productions within the ontological system described by Deleuze. Therefore, the innocence of becoming denotes its affirmative primordial, sub-representative process of multiplicities. Any structure of thought that attempts to cage becoming in the name of being via the Same and the Identical is not affirmative but negative, and thus disfigures the innocence invoked by the immanent multiplicity of becoming.

The selectivity of becoming

The affirmative multiplicity of innocence is directly tied to the selectivity of becoming – only the affirmative returns. Deleuze quite clearly connects his speculative theory of the eternal return to pure, absolute becoming. He takes the selectivity of thought inherent to the Nietzschean doctrine, which asks the individual to will something in such a way that s/he wills its eternal return, and places it in the realm of becoming. Only extreme forms of being return, which we find out is the unconditioned, or absolute becoming itself. In order to apprehend the eternal return in terms of becoming Deleuze asks, 'How does the thought of pure becoming serve as a foundation of the eternal return?'[61] The question insists that we stop opposing being and becoming, and instead see being as the production of selective becoming. Deleuze cleverly points out that fixed Being of the same is an illusion, and the only being that is selected in the eternal return is becoming. What this means is that only the affirmation of life returns, and this selective return is what constitutes 'being'.

Identity is produced through the differential syntheses of the eternal return – the cast of the die – which is the mechanism of becoming. 'The Negative does not return. The Identical does not return. The Same and the Similar, the Analogous and the Opposed, do not return. Only affirmation returns – in other words, the Different, the Dissimilar.'[62] What returns is the act of returning itself. It would be mistaken, however, to think the eternal return is merely the being of becoming, or the surface effects of becoming; it is also the destabilizing, differential machine that synthesizes untimely moments by disrupting time, pulling it out of joint. That uncanniness of time is the work of becoming. Deleuze goes further to refute any claim of prior identity one might ascribe to becoming. The process of becoming is an eternal returning of that which affirms life:

> [The eternal return] is the selection of Being (Nietzsche's ontology): what returns, or is apt to return, is only that which *becomes* in the fullest sense of the word. Only action and affirmation return: Being belongs to becoming and only to becoming. Whatever is opposed to becoming – the Same or the Identical – is not, rigorously speaking. The negative as the lowest degree of power, the reactive as the lowest degree of form, these do not return, because they are opposite of becoming, and becoming constitutes the only Being. One can see how the Eternal Return is tied not to a repetition of the Same, but to a transmutation. The Eternal Return is the instant or the eternity of becoming eliminating whatever offers resistance. It brings out, or better yet, it creates the active, the pure active, and pure affirmation.[63]

The eternal return simulates identities and forms through the surface plane of selective being. What appears as a conscious production of forms through the act of willing is reformulated by Deleuze in terms of becoming. Univocal through and through, the selection of the unconditioned applies to all forms of life, including structures, multiplicities, pre-individualities, ideas, concepts, 'things', etc. It is in the shift from the thought of the eternal return to the being of the eternal return that Deleuze is able to create an ontological principle out of an ethical moment in Nietzsche. By elevating Nietzsche's thought of the eternal return to the procerity of being, Deleuze is able to shed light on the intensive processes that define an ontology premised on pure becoming. As such, he demonstrates how the selectivity of becoming reinforces the internal difference of being. He declares that "'one' repeats eternally, but 'one' now refers to the world of impersonal individualities and pre-individual singularities'.[64] It is the multiplicity of becoming, the internal identity of chaos, which is affirmed in the eternal return.

The affirmation of the multiplicity of becoming characterizes the selectivity of being; this process of the eternal return reflects the active/reactive poles of Nietzsche's ontology. Deleuze draws out the double movement of becoming from Nietzsche's affirmative ontology: becoming-active and becoming-reactive. The selection of becoming, or difference, is expressed by Daniel W. Smith as the immanent evaluation of power taken to the limit.[65] The immanent criterion revolves around differential power and not a correspondence of truth. The extreme limits that survive the eternal return are affirmative of life. Pushed to the extreme limits, forms are revolutionized and their power is immersed in the capacities of becoming-active. Becoming-active is the only form of becoming that returns as being. According to Deleuze, it would be contradictory for becoming-reactive to constitute the being of becoming, as it is nihilistic.

> The Eternal Return teaches us that becoming-reactive has no being. In fact, it only teaches us the existence of a becoming-active of force. It necessarily produces the becoming-active of force in that it reproduces becoming. But the universal being of becoming calls for a single becoming. Only becoming-active has any being, which is the being of becoming as a whole.[66]

The single becoming that is called for evokes the primacy of absolute becoming, the becoming of the eternal return. However, absolute becoming is an intricate network of sensory becoming in multiplicity, or as Nietzsche describes, 'A play of forces and force-waves simultaneously one and "many", accumulating here while diminishing there, an ocean of forces storming and flooding within themselves, eternally changing, eternally rushing back, with tremendous years of recurrence.'[67] The intensities recurring through the play of forces affirm the production of heterogeneous multiplicities, which defy the bipolarity of the one and the many. The multiplicities of sensory becoming correspond to the 'many', while absolute becoming corresponds to the 'one'; both are folded together in a continuum of intensive temporality collapsing the two into one another, without admixture.

Absolute becoming, in its de-actualizing movement, creates the only identity of the world – chaos – and chaos is the simulating factory of the multiplicity of becoming.[68] The multiplicity of becoming is self-affirming, which makes Deleuze's ontology selective. Absolute becoming is posited differentially amid sensory becoming at the divisive, ontological point of memory and forgetting. The selectivity of absolute becoming requires ontological forgetfulness enacted by the eternal return.

Absolute becoming and ontological forgetting

Deleuze accentuates the necessity of forgetfulness in the dissolution of identities through becoming. He takes note of Pierre Klossowski's interpretation of the eternal return, which moves from the act of willing to becoming-other.[69] The chain of duration (molecular memory) is broken through the movement of the eternal return, which is the dissimulation of absolute becoming. Deleuze implicates the forgetfulness of absolute becoming when he states that the eternal return constitutes the only unity of the world in its repetition and is 'the only identity of a world which has no "same" at all except through repetition'.[70] Deleuze agrees with Klossowski's assessment that the death of God necessarily implies the death of the Self, which is revealed through the active forgetfulness of becoming. Unlike Klossowski, as James Williams notes, Deleuze's reading of the forgetfulness of the eternal return does not rely on the creative will, but the passive synthesis of the future, the return of difference.[71] The dissolution of identities ignites the break of durational becoming through active forgetfulness at the ontological level. Ontological forgetfulness is not restricted to consciousness, or to the selectivity of thought, but is an integral aspect of becoming. Klossowski claims that 'forgetting thus raises eternal becoming and the absorption of all identity to the level of being'.[72] The forgetfulness of becoming is a necessary condition for the enactment of the eternal return, as well as its dissolution of forms and identities. Deleuze appropriates the representational forgetfulness on the surface level of forgetting in Klossowski and injects it into the pre-individual movement of becoming.

The way by which Deleuze makes forgetfulness ontological is by posing it against the category of negation in representational thought. The eternal return escapes the trappings of negation through the force of active forgetting. The positing of forgetfulness against the memory complexes of duration enables Nietzsche, and therefore Deleuze, to sidestep the act of negation, which relies upon the identity of essence in its operation. Without memory, there is nothing, or no 'thing', to negate.

Joan Stambaugh illuminates the resistance of duration established in Nietzsche's doctrine of eternal return. In her book, *Nietzsche's Thought of Eternal Return*, Stambaugh argues that Nietzsche's concept of time, which was not systematically developed, resisted the thought of time as duration. Instead, she claims that Nietzsche supported a temporal theory of disparate instants without duration.[73] That is to say that eternity and time are not held outside one another transcendentally, but are immanently connected. Thus, according to Stambaugh, the resistance Nietzsche had to duration emerged out of his critique of enduring substance. While it is debatable as to whether Nietzsche truly did resist the concept of time as a continuous flux, as claimed by Stambaugh, there is no doubt that he would decry any concept of duration predicated of the ontic 'now'.[74] A true Heideggerian, Stambaugh ascribes an ecstatic conception of time to Nietzsche that resists the linear succession of 'now' points. However, when understood as a continuous multiplicity, duration is no longer weighed down by the unifying structure of substance, but is a dynamic relationality.[75] This conception is consistent with Nietzsche's understanding of the forces of the eternal return. The aspect of Stambaugh's interpretation of Nietzsche's resistance to duration is the replacement of ontological, molecular memory with active forgetting. The divergence from molecular duration in the absolute becoming of the eternal return involves the undoing of mechanistic causality, to be demonstrated in Chapter 2. The anti-memory of absolute becoming also unhinges all mechanistic causation within the realm of sensory becoming. Active forgetting is a function of the immanent causality of the eternal return, inscribing difference into the act of creation. Forgetfulness is the differential alternative to negation, or contradiction, by breaking the principle of identity.[76] This point is reiterated while Deleuze explains,

> The genius of eternal return lies not in memory but in waste, in active forgetting. All that is negative and all that denies, all those average affirmations which bear the negative, all those pale and unwelcome 'Yeses' which come from 'Nos', *everything which cannot pass the test of eternal return* – all these must be denied.[77]

Active forgetting, for Deleuze, is not at the level of representational thought, but is a process within thought, within becoming. The eternal return undoes formed identities and thereby eliminates all molar traces of memory. The process of absolute becoming via eternal return destroys memory traces, and appropriately overcomes the relegation of creation to the negative. Instead, the eternal return genetically produces new 'forms' which are purely different from all that came before.[78] Becoming does not produce new forms by denying prior forms in contradiction, but rather, forgetfulness enables becoming to produce absolutely new forms through its self-affirmation.

The movement of becoming, as it unravels identities, necessarily avoids the stasis of Being. For this reason, the former identity becomes eternally separated from itself by the becoming-other that produces the new identity. In this sense, we see Deleuze mimic the process of forgetting in Klossowski's vicious circle, but on the level of pre-individualities. This re-appropriation is perhaps best understood through an exposition of Klossowski's analysis of forgetting in the eternal return. The willing involved in the eternal return for Klossowski is the re-willing of the non-willed, invariably creating an infinite series of alternative identities. Thus, the act of willing fragments the self, making it other, and then necessarily forgets the willing performed by the former self. Klossowski explains the role of active forgetting in the becoming of the eternal return as follows,

> The moment the Eternal Return is revealed to me, I cease being my own self, *here and now*. I am capable of becoming innumerable others, and I know that I shall forget this revelation once I am outside my own memory. This forgetting forms the object of my own limits. Likewise, my present consciousness will be established only in the forgetting of my other possible identities.[79]

The identity established by the coming back of the eternal return operates in its dissimulating movement, which is the ontological forgetting of forms, identities and histories.[80] Just as memory is not tied to consciousness for Deleuze, he does not restrict the forgetfulness of becoming to the conscious subject. The pre-individualities non-representationally will the return of the unconditioned, all of which happens at the level of intensities in becoming.[81] The molecular memory ties of becomings are cut by the forgetting of absolute becoming in the eternal return. It is through the absolute survey of the eternal return that enables becoming to escape the categories of universality and particularity. Deleuze states, 'The form of repetition in the eternal return is the brutal form of the immediate, that of the universal and the singular reunited, which dethrones every general law, dissolves the mediations and annihilates the particulars subjected to the law.'[82] The eternal return is not a law of nature, but it transgresses laws and forges sensory and absolute becoming into a heterogeneous multiplicity, or rhizome. Absolute becoming of the eternal return is entangled with the multiplicities of sensory becoming, forming one heterogeneous multiplicity. In turn it dissolves all identities, particularities and forms constructed in duration, while producing new heterogeneous constellations of thought.[83] The eternal return affirms chaos, but this chaos is perpetually rearranged in sensory blocs of becoming, producing an endless game of destruction and creation, divergence and convergence. How blocs are formed in sensation is interconnected with the notion of ontological selection. Deleuze places the eternal return within the realm of selective ontology rather than the ethical realm of a regulative law: 'It is no longer a question of selective thought but of selective being; for the eternal return is being and being is selection.'[84] We could say that the concept of becoming is the activity of thought thinking itself, and this activity is inseparable from the varying arrangements in sensory becoming.

As has been stated previously, one difficulty in deciphering the concept of becoming in Deleuze's ontology is terminological variance. We have been able to distinguish the multiplicities of molecular memory of sensory becoming from the infinite dissimulating process of the eternal return in absolute becoming, yet there is another term Deleuze often uses interchangeably with becoming (absolute) and the eternal return: Aion. What is the relationship between Aion and absolute becoming? The significance of this term provides another clue to discovering the history of Deleuze's notion of absolute becoming.

Aion and the eternal return

In *The Logic of Sense*, Deleuze begins to refer more readily to the figure of becoming as Aion, a concept Nietzsche draws from Heraclitus. On the surface it would appear that Aion is understood essentially through the Stoics, but we intend to bring light to the latent source of Aion as it relates to the innocence of becoming in Nietzsche. We see Deleuze use the term Aion periodically in his earlier works, but it symbolizes the temporality of the eternal return in *Nietzsche and Philosophy*.[85] Nietzsche echoes the innocent play of becoming expressed in the thought of Heraclitus, which appears in his early Basel lectures on the pre-Socratic philosophers. Deleuze's use of the term Aion in reference to the eternal return, despite being attributed in *The Logic of Sense* to the paradoxical nature of time in the Stoics, reveals a markedly Nietzschean influence in his conception

of becoming. Aion denotes the innocence of becoming – the affirmation of
multiplicity – and Deleuze retains this association by employing the term in his
own writings. Nietzsche describes Aion as the symbol of becoming in Heraclitus,

> He [Heraclitus] conceives of *the play of children* as that of spontaneous human
> beings: here is innocence and yet coming into being and destruction: not one
> droplet of destruction should remain in the world. The eternally living fire,
> αἰών [Aion, boy-god of the zodiac], plays, builds, and knocks down: strife, this
> opposition of different characteristics, directed by justice, may be grasped only
> as an aesthetic phenomenon.[86]

The eternal creation and destruction of becoming in Heraclitus, which Nietzsche
extracts in his creation of the doctrine of the eternal return, is rearticulated
in Deleuze's work under the banners of 'becoming', 'eternal return' and 'Aion'.
Terminological variance is to be expected, as concepts draw contours in
expression related to their concrete arrangements in sensation. In Aion's game of
innocence, a fragmentation of identity occurs at the hand of the eternal return.
Deleuze picks up on this thread and uses Aion to signify the fragmentation of
identity in *Difference and Repetition*: 'The fracture or hinge is the form of empty
time, the *Aion* through which pass the throws of the dice. On one side, nothing
but an I fractured by that empty form. On the other, nothing but a passive self
always dissolved in that empty form.'[87] Through the passage of Aion, or the
eternal return, the double movement of becoming is laid bare. That which one
becomes is subjected to becoming just as the one that becomes is simultaneously
subjected to becoming. The 'I' is dissolved in the double process of absolute
becoming of Aion, a process that underscores the restlessness of the creative, or
'aesthetic phenomenon'.

   In *Difference and Repetition*, we see Deleuze posit the eternal return of
difference as the third synthesis of time. One might ask how becoming – the
untimely – which splits the present into the always already and eternally not-yet,
can be identified with the synthesis of the future. However, it is clear that this
identification is explicitly outlined in Deleuze's text.[88] It is our task to resolve this
apparent temporal paradox of Aion. The resolution will lie in the relationality
between the absolute becoming of the eternal return and the sensory becoming
of molecular memory. The interstices of these two concepts of becoming account
for the untimely nature of Aion, which is counter to time and acts upon time.
Aion acts upon time insofar as it is integrated into the third synthesis of time, yet
it is also the process that unwinds the cycle of the past. It is both out of joint and
the productive process of the future.

The exact formulation of the eternal return in *Difference and Repetition* is repeated in Deleuze's later works in terms of becoming or Aion. The eternal return and Aion represent the same temporal order enacted by absolute becoming that displaces, dissimulates and differentiates everything in its path. In order to unmask the same process of becoming operating under both the eternal return and Aion we will look first at Deleuze's expression of the eternal return. Next we will compare the intensive features and definition of the eternal return to those characterizing Aion. Of the eternal return, Deleuze writes,

> For if this third time, the future, is the proper place of decision, it is entirely likely that, by virtue of its nature, it eliminates the two intracyclic and extracyclic hypotheses; that it *undoes* them both and puts time into a straight line, straightening it out and extracting the pure form; in other words; it takes time out of 'joint' and, being itself the third repetition, renders the repetition of the other two impossible.[89]

The future, or the eternal return, is the untimely ungrounding of the past and present, and is the pure empty form of time: the unconditioned. In *Desert Islands* Deleuze explains that the only predicates of the eternal return are becoming and the multiple.[90] The same affirmation of becoming and multiplicity appears in his exposition of Aion. The following passage is a perfect replication of the formulation of the eternal return from *Difference and Repetition*:

> Aion stretches out in a straight line, limitless in either direction. Always already passed and eternally yet to come, Aion is the eternal truth of time: *pure empty form of time*, which has freed itself of its present corporeal content and has thereby unwound its own circle, stretching itself out in a line.[91]

Deleuze uses the expression 'the pure empty form of time' to define both the eternal return and Aion. Aion, the symbolic boy-god of Heraclitus's and Nietzsche's innocence of becoming frees itself from the material repetition of the present, as well as the virtual ground of the past. The unwinding of the circle into a line of Aion is the same temporal process we witnessed in Deleuze's analysis of the third synthesis of time: the eternal return.

In a final attempt to unmask the eternal return in terms of becoming, Deleuze states that Aion is 'the time of the pure event or of becoming, which articulates relative speeds and slownesses independently of chronometric or chronological values that time assumes in other modes'.[92] Aion, or the eternal return, is the temporal process of becoming which destroys all forms in an eternal creation of new arrangements of simulacra. One of the forms left in the wake of the eternal return is representational time, a time that arises out of a spatialized representation of temporality into measureable, equivalent units. The eternal return affirms intensive quantity, inequality, and it washes away all formalized and conditioned expressions of time. This is the movement of becoming which fractures the always already from the eternally yet to come through a present that *is* not. And this apparent presence in absence of becoming, of the eternal return, of Aion, is put into question by Deleuze.

Deleuze reasons that the Aion would seem to not have a present at all, since it ceaselessly divides the past and future into the present that is not, subverting the quantitative present.[93] However, Deleuze argues that this pure present of becoming in Aion must be presented somehow. The paradoxical feature of becoming, an operative present that is not, is presented in terms of the instant:

> In fact, the instant as the paradoxical element or the quasi-cause which runs through the entire straight line must itself be represented. ... This present of the Aion representing the instant is not at all like the vast and deep present of Chronos: it is the present without thickness, the present of the actor, dancer or mime – the pure perverse 'moment.' It is not the present of subversion or actualization, but that of the counter-actualization.[94]

Aion is without content and operates as a quasi-cause, which is the time of the pure event; yet, is this the same function that is responsible for the differential undoing of the representational present at the hands of sensory becoming? Deleuze reveals a clue about the dual nature of becoming in *The Logic of Sense* when he speaks of Aion in relation to two ranges of Chronos: depth and surface. What he is revealing is the separate concepts of becoming: absolute and sensory. This revelation is discovered when Deleuze articulates the power of the instant to pervert the 'now' of the measured present. He says,

> The essential difference is no longer simply between Chronos and Aion, but between the Aion of surfaces and the whole of Chronos together with the becoming-mad of the depths. Between these two becomings, of surface and depth, we can no longer say that they have in common the sidestepping of the present.[95]

While becoming-mad of the depths (one mode of becoming) already overturned the representational, spatialized present of Chronos, Deleuze wonders if there is yet another difference between the infinitely subdividing tendency of Aion and the 'bad Chronos' that operates finitely without limitation. While he does not directly address the two modes of becoming announced in *The Logic of Sense*,

James Williams warns of the confusion likely to arise when a reader attempts to reconcile the two times of Chronos and Aion in *The Logic of Sense*, which may appear as 'separate containers or states'.[96] He dispels potential criticisms of two irreconcilable registers of time by detailing the interdependence of Chronos and Aion. The solution to the false problem of irreconcilable temporal dualism can be sought in an examination of sensory becoming, 'bad Chronos'.

Aion of surface is the voice of the eternal return and unfolds on the line of the eternal return repeating difference through the quasi-cause. The 'bad Chronos' of depth evades the present through the force of an intensive 'now' which opposes itself to quantitative, representational and measured time. 'Bad Chronos' is sensory becoming and the former is absolute becoming. The becoming-mad of the depths is the involutionary power of sensory becoming, thus posing its molecular memory against the static measuring devices of Chronos, or representational time. The Aion of surfaces evades all possible division in absolute becoming, permeating the 'bad Chronos' of depth and corporeality, which is subject to division, as its shape-shifting nature is closely tied to duration. Deleuze signals these two branches of becoming when he claims, 'Nothing ascends to the surface without changing its nature'.[97] In this passage Deleuze has effectively disclosed the two orders of becoming: absolute becoming of surface and sensory becoming of depth. These two moments of becoming necessarily differ in kind, each participating in distinct temporal logics. Absolute becoming opens up onto the eternal return, while sensory becoming invokes the pathology of duration. Ultimately, what drives sensory becoming to madness, or pathology, is the differentiating machine of the quasi-cause, the perverse moment.

Another key for decoding the bifurcating process of becoming is found in Deleuze's description of the movement of the eternal return, or Aion. 'It is the law of a world without being, without unity, without identity. Far from *presupposing* the One or the Same, the eternal return constitutes the only unity of the multiple as such, the only identity of what differs: coming back is the only "being" of becoming'.[98] Becoming is without being, as it moves in infinite speed and is formless. Unity is the consequence of the selectivity of absolute becoming of the eternal return. The transgressive law of the eternal return arises out of its selective becoming. Absolute becoming is the chaotic, formless force that produces a multiplicity of becomings in sensation. What returns is the different, the affirmative, which portrays the formless, de-centred multiplicities of becoming (e.g. becoming-woman, becoming-animal). These becomings in turn produce varying spatiotemporal dynamisms that are perpetually destabilized by the ungrounding destructive-creative process.

The double movement of becoming corresponds to the two orders of becoming. 'That which one becomes [sensory becoming] becomes [absolute becoming] no less than the one that becomes [sensory becoming].'[99] The multiplicity of becoming corresponds to the interstitial relationship between the molecular memory of sensory becoming and the pure and empty form of absolute becoming. The constellation of innocence as multiplicity; ontological selectivity as affirmation; active forgetting as the mechanism of new forms and Aion as the alter ego of the eternal return dramatize the historical import of Nietzsche's ontology within Deleuze's concept of becoming. Absolute becoming is the eternal return of becoming. It destroys identities, creates new forms in simulacra and breaks all memory traces while simultaneously producing a multiplicity of sensory becoming. The following passage from *The Will to Power* exemplifies the interplay of the absolute becoming of the eternal return amid the sensory becoming of molecular memory:

> A monster of energy, without beginning, without end; a firm, iron magnitude of force that does not grow bigger or smaller, that does not expend itself but only transforms itself; as a whole, of unalterable size, a household without expenses or losses, but likewise without increase or income; enclosed by 'nothingness' as by a boundary; not something blurry or wasted, not something endlessly extended, but set in a definite space as a definite force, and not a space that might be 'empty' here or there, but rather as force throughout, as a play of forces and waves of forces, at the same time one and many, increasing here and at the same time decreasing there; a sea of forces flowing and rushing together, eternally changing, eternally flooding back, with tremendous years of recurrence, with an ebb and a flood of its forms; out of the simplest forms striving toward the most complex, out of the stillest, most rigid, coldest forms toward the hottest, most turbulent, most self-contradictory, and then again returning home to the simple out of this abundance, out of the play of contradictions back to the joy of concord, still affirming itself in this uniformity of its courses and its years, blessing itself as that which must return eternally, as a becoming that knows no satiety, no disgust, no weariness: this is my *Dionysian* world of the eternally self-creating, the eternally self-destroying, this mystery world of the twofold voluptuous delight.[100]

The twofold voluptuous delight mirrors the eternal crashing of absolute becoming and sensory becoming. The 'one and many' of the forces denotes the process of becoming as a multiplicity where the categories of one and many are collapsed into a heterogeneous flux of becomings. Absolute becoming flows through the sea of molecular memory, pulling time out of joint. It affirms its innocence through the production of multiplicities in sensation. The returning of the unconditioned undermines the branches of analogy, opposition, resemblance and identity within representational thought. The selectivity of becoming employs active forgetting to create new forms thus de-historicizing sensation and concepts. Deleuze effectively takes the doctrine of the eternal return and draws out its process as absolute becoming. The selectivity of thought becomes a selectivity of being, and only life-affirming processes of Aion return. Absolute becoming does not create order out of chaos, but is an affirmation of chaos. The chaos affirmed by the eternal return of absolute becoming dissimulates the memory traces of sensory becoming in a repetition of difference.

Becoming in Deleuze is a twofold process that integrates two inexorable notions of becoming which are univocal but that differ intensively. Absolute becoming is often referred to as pure becoming and is spoken of as an absolute, infinite survey in Deleuze's philosophy. The unity enacted by the lines of absolute becoming is a multiplicity and does not presuppose the similar or the same; it links up with the logic of sensation to produce individuated forms as an effect of difference. Composing the multiplicity of absolute becoming are singular durations of sensory becoming. These becomings are also disjunctively connected to the pure and empty form of absolute becoming through the quasi-cause. The singular becomings in sensation give rise to spatiotemporal dynamisms and are contingently subjected to the dissolution of memory traces by the active forgetting of absolute becoming. This interplay between the active forgetting of absolute becoming and the molecular memories of sensory becoming make up the relational network of the concept of becoming in Deleuze's ontology. By re-appropriating temporal concepts in Bergson and Nietzsche Deleuze is able to create a novel concept of becoming that redefines our understanding of being, causality, evolution and transcendence. The result is an ontology predicated by internal change, multiplicity, quasi-causality and immanent relations. The shift from static Being to dynamic becoming in Deleuze's philosophy undermines the history of substance metaphysics.

Chapter 2 will address the interstitial relationship between absolute becoming (i.e. the eternal return, or Aion) and sensory becoming (i.e. molecular memory, blocs of becoming, or points of becoming). The internalizing processes of becoming display the way in which Deleuze revolutionized causality, theorized a process of ontological involution and accounted for a proliferation of immanent spatiotemporal dynamisms in relational materiality. Given the historical import of Nietzsche and Bergson towards a Deleuzian formulation of the concept of becoming, we will be able to explicate the immanent causal process that connects Deleuze's univocal concept of becoming.

2

Quasi-causality

Having established the conceptual history of Deleuzian becoming along the lines of Bergson and Nietzsche, we can now dramatize the notions of sensory becoming and absolute becoming in process. Both sensory becoming of molecular memory and absolute becoming of eternal return create a multiplicity of becoming that ignites a revolutionary form of causality which subverts formal, material, efficient and final causality. The innovative theory of immanent causality that Deleuze develops addresses ideal events rather than actualized entities, that is, how heterogeneity is produced between the actual and the virtual. Instead of dismissing causality as an illusory production in representational thought that expels difference, Deleuze seeks to reconstruct causality according to the heterogeneous features of becoming.[1] What is the relationship between the counter-actualizing causality of ideal events and the linear causality of simulated objects in the realm of Being? Does Deleuze construct a double causality that mimics that of Whitehead? Does the simulated Being of the actual contradict the becoming of the virtual at the moment of inception? How does quasi-causality operate, and can it defeat criticisms of dualist ontology?

By examining the immanent causality of becoming in Deleuze, we begin to understand how two notions of becoming (quasi)-causally counter-actualize the lived present. Looking primarily at *The Logic of Sense*, we will remap the break between Aion and Chronos onto the intermediary realm of becoming-mad (the subversive, measureless present), and the immanent mechanisms at work begin to reveal themselves. On our journey into the processes of becoming we examine two conflicting, predominant interpretations of Deleuze's double causality, as well as their corresponding consequences. The controversial and ill-understood quasi-cause, which holds the two orders of becoming together as a hinge to the actual, has been interpreted as both a phenomenalized final cause (Shaviro) and a pseudo-cause that connects two incompatible ontologies (Žižek). Both of these readings of quasi-causality exhibit structural weaknesses, and as we expose those weaknesses we can move towards creating a more sound theory of quasi-causality. We will synthesize Daniel W. Smith's distinction of quasi-causality from medieval causality with Jay Lampert's reading of quasi-causal history in order to illuminate the quasi-causal processes which link absolute becoming, sensory becoming and effectuated Being.

The quasi-cause effectively releases ideal events of becoming from the shackles of the actual through the depths of sensory becoming. Sensory becoming has one foot in the door of the materiality of the actual and one foot in the door of the ideality of the virtual. Sensory becoming as molecular memory bears the markings of infinite masks of fragmented identities – the photographic solarization of the actual present has literally gone mad. The quasi-cause, which is modelled after Nietzsche's Moment, as will be shown, strikes the expressivity of sensory becoming with the two opposing directions of absolute becoming, crystallizing the history of infinitely fragmented identities in the form of singularities. The crystallized singularities and their corresponding molecular lines of subversive (non)sense are then distributed along the perpetually displaced line of absolute becoming, the Aion. Ultimately, we will argue that the actual is split by sensory becoming, an emergent nebula that floats between the lived present and the invisible line of absolute becoming – in sensation – and operates according to the disjunctive syntheses of incompossible events which hail down into the actual. A composite sketch of becoming is fleshed out through the complex interstices of these two concepts of becoming.

Double causality in Deleuze

In Chapter 1 we witnessed Deleuze's assertion in *The Logic of Sense* that there are two forms of becoming: becoming-mad of depths and the pure becoming of surfaces, or Aion, often referred to in *Difference and Repetition* as the eternal return. He stated that we are mistaken to simply posit Aion, or the eternal return, against the measured, homogeneous time of actual bodies and forms, Chronos. There is a third element that runs between Chronos and Aion: bad Chronos. This third element is crucial to understanding the processes of becoming in Deleuze, as well as to his concept of the quasi-cause. The becoming-mad of depths is the subversive present that resists measurement and is a qualitative, and not qualified, becoming. This becoming is the molecular insistence – it forms alliances with non-filial singularities extracted from matter – of the pure past in the subversive present of sensory becoming. Like an mischievous alter ego of Chronos, becoming-mad operates through a molecular memory that is not ordered by representation, form, sequence or corporeal sense. This durational presence is characterized by its disorganization of a measured present but still retains the molecular memory trace in its embodied becoming. Becoming-mad perpetually destabilizes the successive, linear time of actualized bodies. Deleuze calls this form of becoming a 'bad Chronos', or the becoming-mad which is

> opposed to the living present of the good Chronos … . The pure and measureless becoming of qualities threatens the order of qualified bodies from within. Bodies have lost their measure and are now but simulacra. The past and the future, as unleashed forces, take their revenge, in one and the same abyss which threatens the present and everything that exists.[2]

We can be certain that Deleuze is not talking about the production of simulacra through the eternal return, for the eternal return does not evoke the becoming of qualities.[3] On the contrary, Deleuze has introduced another order of becoming that engages with the becoming of the eternal return, and this is the subversive, durational becoming-mad. 'Becoming-mad' is what we have been calling sensory becoming up to this point. The shape-shifting self-evasive present of sensory becoming differs in kind from absolute becoming of Aion in that it is the intensive becoming of qualities and is the virtual counterpart to the living present in actuality.

The two orders of becoming mobilize ideal events in a subversion of actualized forms, calling for a new formulation of causality that is not dependent on properties of extension. Deleuze proposes a counter-actualizing causality that does not operate according to the classical categories of formal, efficient, material and final causality. The quasi-cause, which is the causality ascribed to the multiplicity of becoming, does not operate according to the dictates of modern causality – namely efficient and material causality. On the contrary, the quasi-cause is the hinge between absolute becoming of the eternal return and sensory becoming of molecular memory. Sensory becoming is another term for becoming-mad in *The Logic of Sense*: they are one and the same. While this alternative causality defies the traditional categories of cause and effect, it still interacts with its exclusive double, the causality of the corporeal present in actuality. The causal production of actualized forms produces efficient causality, but this illusory causality masks the quasi-causality of becoming. Unmasking the quasi-causal processes of becoming from the surface effects of physical causality will allow us to discover how the quasi-causality of becoming intersects with the efficient causality of actualized forms.

Is the double causality in Deleuze another version of the Kantian distinction between efficient causes of phenomena and final causality of moral freedom, as argued by Steven Shaviro? We will investigate the dynamics of double causality in Deleuze and articulate the inner mechanics of the quasi-cause. Ultimately, the instant will serve as the central clue to uncovering the immanent mechanism operating between the two concepts of becoming and the lived present.

Deleuze, Whitehead and Kant on final causality

Deleuze announced the double causality of his ontological system in *The Logic of Sense* by introducing the concept of quasi-causality. Delineating the immanent causal mechanisms of becoming requires us to understand the processes of the quasi-cause. One possible reading of quasi-causality is an immanent final causality as seen in the process philosophy of Alfred Whitehead. A leading Deleuze scholar provides such a reading. Steven Shaviro interprets Deleuze's double causality in terms of a phenomenalized Kantian double causality where the quasi-cause is masking as a final cause of the new. Is this interpretation accurate?

In his essay 'Novelty and Double Causality in Kant, Whitehead, and Deleuze' Shaviro attempts to lay bare the complicated causal processes of Deleuze's ontology.[4] Shaviro accurately describes the emphasis both Whitehead and Deleuze place on a metaphysical system premised on novelty. Absolute novelty requires a temporality that is future oriented, and this is where Shaviro begins his comparison of Deleuzian and Whiteheadian double causality. Both thinkers, he states, follow Kant in introducing time to the production of the subject, as opposed to a prior temporality that stands outside the subject. The internal movement of time does in fact align Whitehead with Deleuze, but is it also the case that Deleuze's creative metaphysics implies a double causality that mirrors that of Alfred Whitehead's philosophy?

Shaviro claims that Deleuze, along with Whitehead and Kant, maintains two separate forms of causality: a linear, mechanistic causality connecting phenomena in the lived present, and a purposive and freely willed causality. The latter is final causality, which is not bound by the efficiency of actualized bodies, but is an ideal causality that is evoked by the categorical imperative and supplements the natural mechanism of efficient causality. Shaviro states that 'for Whitehead, the final cause is the "decision" (1978: 43) by means of which an actual entity becomes what it is'.[5] This creative self-actualization is how the new is introduced into Whitehead's system, according to Shaviro, and by extension, into Deleuze's system. While Whitehead has apparently made the Kantian noumenal final causality phenomenal through the introduction of an autonomous decision, Shaviro has not shown how this phenomenalization accounts for Deleuze's quasi-causality. If you find the attribution of teleology to the quasi-cause of Aion questionable, this comes as no surprise.

The only connections Shaviro makes between the double causality of Whitehead and Deleuze involve the acknowledgement that both professed to have a double causality, that both privilege a futural temporality in the production of novelty and that both temporal theories move from the virtual/potential to the actual. While it is true that both thinkers have several points of connection, it is not evident that both advocate final causality as the creative ontological movement. Shaviro equivocates between basic conceptual similarities, rather than exploring the depth of their processes. For example, Shaviro cites Whitehead as saying, "'The past is a nexus of actualities" (Whitehead 1978, 214); it is still actual, still a force in the present, because it is reproduced as "datum", physically prehended by each new actual occasion.'[6] However, this characterization of the past does not represent the ontological pure past of Deleuze. Shaviro has described a past constituted by former presents of perception, that is, the measured present of actuality. The pure past is virtual, not actual, in Deleuze, and while it insists and coexists alongside the present of actuality, there is a differential cause between the virtual and the actual whereby the virtual does not become 'what it is', but becomes-other. The contraction of the infinite, virtual levels of the pure past in the actualization of the present is absolutely *not* the physical prehension, or individual appropriation, of the datum of the past. Whitehead explains his use of prehension in the following passage,

> A certain immediate individuality, which is a complex process of appropriating into a unity of existence the many data presented as relevant by the physical processes of nature. ... I have, in my recent writings, used the word *prehension* to express this process of appropriation.[7]

Whitehead's description of the prehension of data, or quantified qualities of the past, along the lines of physical processes of nature highlights the incongruence between his understanding of causality in the production of novelty and that of Deleuze. The pure past has not been experienced, but is composed of the eluded present of becoming. The causality of the quasi-cause does not perform according to the dictates of physical processes of nature, nor is it an appropriation of the past. The pure past has not passed through perception, has not been experienced in the present, and it is not actual. The internal difference contained in each level of the pure past contracts in the lived present, but it does not do so by way of efficient causation. This is the key error in Shaviro's analysis of Deleuzian causality. He states that 'the past remains active within the present by means of the "vector transmission" or efficient causality', but the past is virtual, differential and does not operate according to a causal principle that mechanically connects actual forms with other actual forms.

Additionally, Shaviro's employment of Kant's version of final causality contradicts the autonomy of virtual multiplicities that aid in the process of actualization. Kant states,

> For a thing to be a natural purpose [final cause], in the first place it is requisite that its parts (as regards their presence and their form) are only possible through their reference to the whole. For the thing itself is a purpose and is comprehended under a concept or idea which must determine *a priori* all that is to be contained in it.[8]

Shaviro agrees with Kant that final causality is the causality of freedom, and its release from the laws of mechanistic, efficient causality is ascribed to the production of the new via the quasi-cause. Accordingly, the 'thing' in the previous passage from *Critique of Judgment* corresponds to the actuality of the new. The new is not comprehended under a concept or idea, in a fate worse to tell, the new would be subordinated to identity within the concept or idea. Deleuze opposes this interpretation of novelty, since the disjunctive process of becoming which operates through the quasi-cause, only brings back the unconditioned in the product when creating the new. There is not any idea or concept or whole to which the new is referring or to which it owes an *a priori* determination; the ground of the pure past is ungrounded. 'What is expressed has no resemblance whatsoever to the expression.'[9] Freeing the new from efficient causality is not enough to free it of the logic of identity. The new is a genetic production that differentiates itself without reference; it is not the actualization of a potential within an idea or concept. On the contrary, it is absurd to ascribe final causality to the ontological production of the new in Deleuze, which is why DeLanda rightly states, 'In a Deleuzian ontology final causes would have to be replaced by quasi-causes in order to avoid ascribing teleological or goal-seeking behaviour to physical systems.'[10] Although Shaviro erroneously identifies final causality with quasi-causality, he managed to recognize the double causality functioning in Deleuze's ontology; beneath the mechanistic, efficient causality of actual entities is the quasi-causality of becoming, a novel immanent causal theory that needs to be articulated.

Immanent causation in *The Logic of Sense*

While Deleuze does not supplement the efficient causality of actual bodies with the final causality of ideas, he does create a causal theory that is not bound by the necessary causes of efficient causation. Deleuze employs an immanent theory of causality to explain the communication of ideal events in the virtual. The quasi-cause is the causal process operative at the joint of absolute becoming of the eternal return and sensory becoming of molecular memory. What distinguishes quasi-causality from other forms of causality is its distributive power of difference and its ability to create an ultimate divide of between the cause and the effect. Quasi-causality does not function along the lines of material causes, formal causes, efficient causes or final causes. Furthermore, as pointed out by Daniel W. Smith,[11] quasi-causality also differs from the medieval categories of emanative and transitive causalities. Carving out the causal process of becoming from other forms of causality allows us to study the interaction between becoming and the simulated forms of being in actuality.

The quasi-cause is the link between the paradoxical time of becoming, where that which just happened becomes at the same moment as that which is about to happen becomes. The quasi-cause is the differential connection between ideal events in becoming, eluding the efficient causal connection of bodies. Deleuze describes the need for two causal processes hinged upon two separate interpretations of the present:

> Briefly, *there are two times, one of which is composed of interlocking presents; the other is constantly decomposed into elongated pasts and futures.* There are two times, one of which is always definite, active or passive; the other is eternally Infinitive and eternally neutral. One is cyclical, measures the movement of bodies and depends on the matter which limits and fills it out; the other is a pure straight line at the surface, incorporeal, unlimited, an empty form of time, independent of all matter.[12]

The time of interlocking presents is the time of Chronos, or the homogeneous clock time of measure. This temporal framework is cyclical and is responsible for the eternal return of the same. The latter present is figured by the instant of becoming in the eternal return, absolute becoming. Aion, or the becoming of the eternal return, escapes the present in an unlimited split between the past and the future. The quasi-cause belongs to this temporal order and allows events to communicate through resonating auto-unifying singularities, always escaping actuality and corporeality. While Deleuze states that there are two times – the derivative time of actuality within static being versus the becoming of the Aion within the virtual – it is his bifurcation of becoming into sensory becoming and the absolute becoming that accounts for the encounter between becoming and the lived present. In order to depict the causal connection between becoming and actuality we must first investigate the causal processes in events.

The quasi-cause that connects events into the one event (Aion) is immanent, and this immanence reflects the univocity of becoming throughout Deleuze's system. Borrowing from Spinoza, Deleuze brings immanent causation into play in his philosophical system. Daniel W. Smith explains this appropriation when he says, 'In Spinoza's immanent causality, not only does the cause remain in itself, but its effect remains "immanent" within it, rather than emanating from it. The effect (mode) remains in its cause no less than the cause remains in itself (substance).'[13] However, as Smith points out, Deleuze eliminates Spinoza's substance, making ontology purely modal. A modal, or differential, world forces Deleuze to re-conceptualize the content of immanent causation. In Deleuze's picture, there is no God, but difference relates to difference without mediation, without subordinating the effect to the identity of the cause (God). Eliminating all transcendence in immanent causation, Deleuze paints a universe that repeats the unconditioned of the cause in the effect.

'The autonomy of the effect is thus defined initially by its difference in nature from the cause; in the second place, it is defined by its relation to the quasi-cause.'[14] The effect is synonymous with the Event and is bestowed full autonomy by the operation of the reversible quasi-cause. There are no longer real causes in the virtual, only effects. As the effect differs in kind from corporeal bodies in mixture, it is independent of cause in the classical sense and is impenetrable, impassive, neutral and is devoid of qualitative distinction. Despite the impassibility of singularities-events, they are perpetually in movement, resonating with other singularities-events through the series of effects produced in the nexus of becoming. The paradoxical series, or lines, proliferated through absolute becoming of Aion fragment the separation between past and future where the quasi-cause nomadically distributes singularities in no fewer than two temporal series. These temporal series of events, which resonate through the paradoxical side-stepping of the present in becoming, will later be referred to as a rhizome in Deleuze and Guattari's writings. The ideal singularities are bound to their quasi-causes, but fully independent and dissimilar from any molar past, and are produced through the schizophrenic virtual bifurcation of becoming.

The resonation of the divergent and convergent series produced through the proliferating force of becoming is Deleuze's speculative attempt to outline the inner mechanics of a virtual, immanent plane. The quasi-cause was created in an attempt to demonstrate what a system connected through difference would look like. Events are not causes of one another, and the process of becoming produces simultaneous series of multiplicities that allow the events to communicate not through admixture but through the distribution of nomadic singularities in difference. Events do not form a heterogeneous continuity that internally mixes together, for this would ultimately result in a homogeneous state. The ideal events produced through becoming must maintain their crystallized features, yet not form ideal essences like those in Plato. The temporal detracting force of becoming pulls each event apart, driving it, like two temporal arrows of infinite speed, into the already and not yet. Subsequently, these new series of events are then automatically run through with the force of becoming, thus producing further series connected only through the differentiating bifurcation of becoming in Aion. It is the connection of difference between the ideal singularities-events in the perpetually proliferating series that Manuel DeLanda designates as the first function of the quasi-cause.

> In short, the first task of the quasi-cause operator is what Deleuze calls a *condensation of singularities,* a process involving the continuous creation of communication between the series emanating from every singularity, linking them together through non-physical resonances, while simultaneously ramifying or differentiating the series, ensuring they are linked together only by their differences.[15]

This first task of the quasi-cause – to connect events through difference – is a function of absolute becoming, or pure becoming. Pure becoming has zero duration and is the paradoxical side-stepping of the present in its nomadic distribution of singularities throughout the virtual. The subversive becoming-mad that splits off Chronos through the disruptive force of pure becoming in Aion appears in the second moment of the quasi-cause. The quasi-cause is the conceptual link between the actual, the in-between of sensation and the virtual. The question arises as to whether a 'materialization' of becoming in the actual depends upon two separate ontologies. Does the quasi-cause simply mask the incompatibility of the virtual and the actual, becoming and Being? Before we thoroughly address the causal mechanisms at work in the processes of becoming, we will address this concern.

Žižek and the critique of dualist ontology

Does an ontological system that attempts to account for the product of the forms of Being through the immanent processes of becoming fail from the outset? The quasi-cause, as the link between these two realms, problematizes the interstitial relationship between molar forms and molecular processes of becoming. In *Organs without Bodies* Slavoj Žižek refers to the quasi-cause as the nonsensical meta-cause accommodating the incompletion of causal efficiency in corporeality. The problem, argues Žižek, is Deleuze's use of the quasi-cause (a 'pseudo-causality') to fill in the gaps of corporeal causality.[16] There is an excess that arises in materiality and this cannot be accounted for by mechanistic causal processes. The dualistic picture of becoming versus Being reveals a break in the ontological system, for Žižek. The dualistically 'inconsistent' representations of becoming in Deleuze are not matters of two separate perspectives, he insists, but indicate real systemic differences. What Žižek is calling the incompatibility between Being and Event, materialism and idealism, finds its solution in sensory becoming. Žižek's complaint of dualist ontology in Deleuze is as follows:

> Perhaps the first step in this problematizing is to confront this duality with the duality of Being and Event, emphasizing their ultimate incompatibility: Event cannot simply be identified with the virtual field of Becoming that generates the order of Being – quite the contrary, in *The Logic of Sense*, Event is emphatically asserted as 'sterile,' capable only of pseudo-causality.[17]

Žižek's complaint about the simultaneous sterility of the multiplicities of becoming alongside its elaboration as a generative process reveals an ontology that is simultaneously materialist and idealist, and therefore systematically incompatible. How can a virtual field of becoming produce actualities at the same time that actual bodies produce the virtual? Žižek views the project as fundamentally flawed; a marriage between Hegel and Marx that is possible only through a supplemental causality of excess. Žižek does not directly criticize the creation of a quasi-cause to grant autonomy to virtual processes beyond corporeal causes – in fact, Žižek delights in its apparent similarity to the Lacanian *objet petit a* which orients desire.[18] On the contrary, he uses the quasi-cause to highlight what he deems an unconvincing attempt to 'fill the gap' left open by mechanistic, corporeal causality. Here, the quasi-cause, which Žižek alternatively calls 'pure difference', appropriating Deleuze's central concept, as he did with 'repetition' and the Lacanian non-All (against Deleuze's 'One-All'), is both the object-cause of desire and absolute lack in Žižek's estimation.

As Deleuze rejects the Hegelian Dialectic, as well as ontology premised on negation, the two thinkers' philosophical projects form mirrored images that diverge with respect to *nothing*. Both Deleuze and Žižek

> describe difference as infinite self-differing. Thus, as the term for the ontological in-itself, 'difference' is the key concept for both Deleuze and Žižek, as an empty cause and a dissimulative effect. Despite the similarity between the function of the quasi-cause and *l'objet a*, the meaning of 'difference' within their respective philosophical systems is determined by the concept's corresponding temporal logic. Deleuze's difference is pure, continuous relation, while Žižek's difference operates through discontinuity. It appears that through two sides of the looking glass, both versions of difference eternally repeat as the function of their respective philosophical systems, without mediation or accretion.[19]

Pure difference, the perverse moment, can only be said to express lack from the perspective of representation; it is not ontologically constituted by lack. As a pure differentiating process without duration, quasi-causality is positively, not negatively, generative. The quasi-cause grants autonomy to events but at the expense of making the virtual populated with these impassible, sterile 'objects', and Žižek asks how such a statically generative process that resists admixture consistently produce effects within materiality. Žižek's claim that Being and Event, Actual and Virtual, form two incompatible ontologies is based on a fundamental temporal error.

Žižek's analysis of the quasi-cause and the two seemingly contradictory sides of becoming – generative on one side, sterile and impassive on the other side – unknowingly supports Deleuze's project, rather than damning it. The two contradictory sides of pure becoming that Žižek finds problematic are not two conflicting processes but two complementary logics of becoming which differ in kind. Sensory becoming is closer to materiality, as it emerges like a fog from the tempest of absolute becoming upon the actual, bridging ideational events and individuated forms through durational multiplicities. Absolute becoming differs in kind from the becoming-mad of the depths of sensory becoming and exhibits zero duration, giving rise to surface effects. The project of connecting the surface of absolute becoming with the depths of sensory becoming is part of the project Deleuze undertakes – an attempt to demonstrate the compatibility of a truly immanent ontology of becoming. Daniel W. Smith defends Deleuze against Žižek's criticisms, stating that *The Logic of Sense* is the very attempt to investigate the mechanisms at work in such a system. The dualist accusations borne from the analysis of Being and Event turn out to be reductionist and neglectful of the third term: sensory becoming. Daniel W. Smith provides a Deleuzian response to Žižek's implication that the virtual and the actual cannot be co-constitutive.

> The dynamic genesis thus finds its *real* condition in what Deleuze calls the *static genesis*, which resolves what Deleuze considers to be one of the fundamental problems of the logic of sense: 'How can we maintain both that sense *produces* even the states of affairs in which it is embodied, and that it is itself *produced* by these states of affairs or the actions and passions of bodies?' (LS, 124). On the one hand, the question of the dynamic genesis concerns the means by which sense is produced from the depths of bodies and their states of affairs – that is, sense is the means through which sounds are separated from bodies and organized into propositions (the expressive function); on the other hand, it is only through sense itself that states of affairs are constituted and attributed to bodies (e.g., the battle of Waterloo). Although Žižek sees these two conceptions of sense as 'fundamentally incompatible' (OwB, 20), the entire goal of the *Logic of Sense* is to elucidate the exact nature of their relation and their ultimate compatibility.[20]

As Smith points out, *The Logic of Sense* is an attempt to synthesize the virtual and the actual, nonsense and sense, through the disjunctive synthesis of the quasi-cause. One key feature of his system is the instantaneity of absolute becoming. There is not a chronological sequence accounting for the production of the new alongside the same, and these two poles of becoming are not mutually exclusive. As Deleuze maintains in *The Logic of Sense*, the concepts of becoming-becoming-mad and Aion-are entirely different. The sterile, impassible elements of the virtual, or events, are not identical to *the* event, or Aion. Pure becoming, or absolute becoming, like the Moment in Nietzsche, repeats. In its repetition, it bifurcates into two fundamentally different planes of becoming. The impassible events gather together in the event of the eternal return, but they converge to form becomings of molecular memory in sensation. Hence what Žižek described as two contradictory functions of one becoming are really two supplementary, divergent logics of becoming, differing in kind.

Arguably, in the years since *Organs without Bodies*, Žižek has become more and more Deleuzian,[21] reading the Dialectic through modified conceptions of Difference, Repetition and the non-All: all concepts that mirror Deleuze's own pivotal concepts of Difference, Repetition and the One-All. In *Less Than Nothing: Hegel and the Shadow of Dialectical Materialism*, published in 2012, it looks as if Žižek is finally going to reckon with the complexity of two logics of becoming in Deleuze. In the book, he finally addresses sensory (becoming-mad of depths/corporeal) and absolute becoming (Aion/incorporeal), which provided Žižek the opportunity to explore Deleuze's tripartite ontology, rather than portraying it as a dualistic ontology given to us by Deleuze, the so-called philosopher of the One. Instead, Žižek says, 'This difference between the two becomings, the becoming-mad of depths of the primordial formless Chaos and the surface of the infinite divisibility of the Instant, is almost the difference between the second and the third hypotheses of *Parmenides* – that of the "now" and that of the "instant."'[22] The key word in this passage is 'almost'; the difference between sensory becoming (becoming-mad) and absolute becoming (Aion, or instantaneous becoming) is *almost* that of the 'now' and the 'instant', were becoming-mad not the subversion of the 'now'. However, becoming-mad (sensory becoming) is not of the temporal register of the 'now', but that of molecular duration in sensation, as has been discussed.

Even beyond his Badiouian reading of multiplicity and Event[23] against that of Deleuze, which contributes to the misreading of Deleuze as a philosopher of the One, it turns out that Žižek's reading retains the failure to account for the logic of sensory becoming.[24] He continues to reiterate a fundamental incompatibility between the virtual (Event) and the actual (Being). In a telling gesture, however, Žižek immediately takes a step back to point out the two different concepts ('models') of becoming in *The Logic of Sense*, and asks, 'Is Deleuze's oscillation between the two models (becoming as the impassive effect; becoming as the generative process) not homologous to the oscillation, in the Marxist tradition, between the two models of "reification?"'[25]

If briefly, Žižek acknowledges the two formulations of becoming in *The Logic of Sense*, which he has conflated as absolute, duration-less becoming. Rather than pursue the implications of two temporal logics of becoming, his analogous example of the theories of reification in Marx and Lukács serves to justify his prior conflation of absolute and sensory becoming, while reaffirming his claim that Being (the actual) and Event (the virtual) are ontologically incompatible. In his comparison, absolute becoming resists attributing an immaterial affect to the bodily product from whence it is connected, while sensory becoming is the hidden process that generates the 'reified' realm of Being, the actual. However, not only are the virtual and the actual co-constitutive (the virtual is not the cause of the actual), but Žižek also glosses over the intermediary role sensory becoming plays in processes of individuation, wherein the quasi-cause subverts the actual present by arranging blocs or envelopes of becoming in durational sensation. Unlike the bifurcating process of absolute becoming, which expels all memory traces, sensory becoming retains molecular memory in the form of non-filial arrangements, such as the Proustian example of the wasp and the orchid.[26] Diverse spatiotemporal dynamisms characterize the realm of sensation, which defies the logic of identity without being completely ungrounded by the ontological forgetting of absolute becoming. Being and Event might be incompatible were it not for the intermediary realm of sensory becoming, where the shards of former identities, in molecular memory, are reassembled as pure relations of speed by the quasi-cause. The becoming of sensation disorients and destabilizes the present of the actual, infinitely fragmenting identity, and completely subverting the passing present. This account of becoming is missing in Žižek's works and perpetuates the conflation of the two logics of becoming in the secondary literature on Deleuze. The quasi-cause does not simply link Being and Event (Aion), but passes through the madness of nonsense in the depths of bodies as well.

As a corrective to the misreadings of Deleuzian ontology via the quasi-cause, the question then becomes: How does the quasi-cause order (or disorder) surface becoming with deep becoming, along with the actual present? In order to answer this question, first we must elaborate the immanent mechanisms at work connecting blocs of events in sensation with the event of chaos affirmed by absolute becoming in an eternal return.

As has been hinted, the plurality of events involves the becomings of molecular duration that are precipitated through the electric shock of pure becoming, or *the* event. By looking at the way in which events are created and distributed within the plane of immanence, including the construction of a theory that relates becoming-mad of depth (sensory becoming) with the becoming of surfaces, the Aion (absolute becoming), the quasi-causal process becomes clearer. The two interlocking, inter-differentiating processes of becoming are confused by Žižek as a singular becoming that is both generative and impassive in itself. However, the two orders of becoming, once thematized causally, will elucidate the complex ontology that accounts for reciprocal, disjunctive syntheses of production. Žižek's inscription of the Being/Becoming dichotomy within the virtual itself will be addressed in our discussion of the relationship between the quasi-cause and events.

Absolute becoming and event: Surface

What is an event for Deleuze? An event is ideal and should not be confused with a happening, or a final state evidenced in the actual lived present. In order to create an ontological system premised on becoming, Deleuze inverts the Platonic realm of essences which supports an ontological portrait of static being. The Event is Deleuze's purely immanent response to the transcendent essence in Plato. Events do not correspond to the model/copy distinction, and events themselves converge to form sensory blocs in the continuous flux of becoming. Therefore, events are not subordinated to the logic of identity but are the impersonal assemblages that produce and undo identities. About events Deleuze writes,

> Events are ideational singularities which communicate in one and the same Event. They have therefore an eternal truth, and their time is never the present which realizes them and makes them exist. Rather, it is the unlimited Aion, the Infinitive in which they subsist and insist. Events are the only idealities. To reverse Platonism is first and foremost to remove essences and to substitute events in their place, as jets of singularities.[27]

Deleuze distinguishes events from accidents in the present, as well as from essences. Events are produced immanently through the resonant forces of the virtual. The vehicle responsible for the production and communication of events is absolute becoming. 'Events are changes immanent to a confluence of parts or elements, subsisting as pure virtualities.'[28] Events are fragments of the one Event that is the open totality of Aion. 'But the paradoxical instance is the Event in which all events communicate and are distributed.'[29] Unlike a transcendent entity, the Event is the paradoxical instance, which is the representation of the paradoxical present of absolute becoming.

The 'One' in which all events participate is the differentiating machine of becoming, which distributes singularities, causing events to resonate through their internalized difference in series. The events that synthesize the a-logic of the paradoxical instant dissimulate molecular lines formed in sensory becoming. These becomings are non-localizable, particular constellations of singularities that are destabilized and distributed by the paradoxical instance of absolute becoming. Events are represented by phantasms of the collision between becoming-mad and the line of Aion. The phantasm demarcates the point at which sensory becoming is placed into the ideality of the pure event. Events are phantasmal in the sense that they echo the disordered sense of the simulacra on an immanent plane of ideation. In his investigation of the role of quasi-causality in an immanent conception of history, Jay Lampert offers a concrete example that illustrates how the quasi-cause turns actual occurrences into phantasmal events. He says,

> We might think of a quasi-cause as the moment at which Joan of Arc becomes a phantasm that anyone can live through. Such a moment begins with a particular Joan of Arc action, yet operates by way of variability. Qua phantasms, hinge-events co-exist at all times, without regard to their original manifestation.[30]

The 'hinge-event' of the Joan of Arc action is the simultaneous splitting of the action into the past and future. Thus, it is not a matter of becoming Joan of Arc, the actual person, but of actualizing a Joan of Arc effect. The phantasmal, duration-less Joan of Arc effect is distributed in divergent series that may or may not converge with other effects to form blocs in sensation. This means that actions predating Joan of Arc's actual existence, as well as actions postdating her existence, can be ascribed to the Joan of Arc effect, irrespective of subjective or objective positioning. Quasi-causes operate through simultaneity, not succession. The Joan of Arc effect is statically distributed in virtual, divergent lines of absolute becoming, mapping an interconnected world of incompossible presents (eluded presents) on the line of Aion. As Lampert explains, 'The argument that incompossibles co-exist is surprisingly simple. If two series converge, that is a real feature of the world; if one series diverges into two possible series, that is just as real.'[31] If a person who is not Joan of Arc activates a path that was not chosen by Joan of Arc, we have an instance of real incompossibility. While the Joan of Arc effect does not intermix with durations in sensation, its proximal arrangement with other variations in sensation forms blocs of coexistence that expand its conceptual tendencies. Accordingly, the Joan of Arc effect is not fixed in essence but arranges sensation in unique, indeterminate expressions, or else it is actualized in new forms of life. By placing the Joan of Arc effect in varying neighbourhoods of thought and sensation new lines connect it to other virtual series, expressions in sensation and structures in the actual. The Joan of Arc effect is a multiplicity defined by the lines it proliferates. For that reason, the effect (singularity) should not be confused with unchanging, eternal essences. Convergent and divergent lines that form the network of an effect are constantly being drawn, erased or redrawn. Since these singularities communicate at a distance, they are not at risk of merging into one undifferentiated mass. The interconnected world of incompossible presents portrayed by Lampert, where Deleuze reads Leibniz through Borges, rests on the power of the false. As Jon Roffe notes, the language of the simulacra and phantasmal events falls away in Deleuze's writings, but its meaning persists. 'The simulacra contains a genuine creative power that Deleuze will later go one to call the power of the false: the capacity to integrally *produce* reality without any recourse to a transcendent model, rather than represent what are apparently the most profound elements that exist *in reality*.'[32] Thus, how does the creative power of simulacra rise into phantasmal events?

The eternal return creates fissures in molar forms, and becoming-mad, that is, sensory becoming, becomes cloaked in the simulacra arising from the corporeal present. Sensory becoming is the logic of time created through the subversion of the actual present, and when intersected by the quasi-cause its expression is pushed into the virtual past and the future. According to Deleuze, becoming-mad (i.e. sensory becoming) splits into two directions at once; a feature he draws from the pathology of duration in Bergson.[33] The infinite contraries of fragmented identities revolve around one another, wear the masks of becoming-mad, and are subjected to the quasi-causal operator. This drives sense into two directions simultaneously, exchanging one for the other. The process of sensory becoming is the fortuitous moment when becoming-mad is struck by the differentiating mechanism of Aion which occurs *in perpetuum*. Each of the two directions of sensory becoming 'subdivides itself into the other, to the point that both are found in either. Two are necessary for being mad; one is always mad *in tandem*.[34]

An example of this bifurcating direction of sensory becoming through absolute becoming is the Hatter and the Hare from *Alice in Wonderland*. Both change places, running in opposing directions either too late or too early, but never on time. Their orientation is perpetually displaced as their identities are fragmented. The Hatter and the Hare are the phantasms of the depths rising to the surface of Aion. They represent the fissures of the actual as it is subverted then bifurcated. The substitutability of the Hatter and the Hare exemplifies the retention of the infinite identities that each passes through in the madness of measureless, qualitative, sensory becoming. The phantasms of events correspond to the crystallization of dissolved forms in simulacra and are eternal ghosts of their future destruction, eternal ghosts of their disorienting sense. Phantasms are effects of the quasi-cause's freeing of singularities from their formal prisons of static representation. As a result, the phantasms of events are displaced in the transcendental field of becoming, or the plane of immanence. Deleuze states,

> The phantasm recovers everything on this new plane of the pure event, and in this symbolic and sublimated part of that which cannot be actualized; similarly, it draws from this part the strength to orient its actualization, to duplicate it, and to conduct its concrete counter-actualization.[35]

The quasi-cause operates in the mode of the infinitive, which connects the transcendental field of sense with the depths of bodies, or the subversive present. As the modality of the quasi-causal operator, the infinitive is central to the compatibility of becoming-mad and the line of Aion. The infinitive form of the verb in French expresses the pre-individual becoming of sense more adequately than the infinitive in English, simply because the infinitive form of a verb is often used when the gerund is used in English. For example, '*devenir*' can mean both 'to become' and 'becoming' in French. Deleuze seizes upon the infinitive expression of the phantasm, or link between events, using the verbal both/and to signify the bridge between Being and becoming, respectively. As an infinitive, the phantasm escapes subject or object attachment; expresses itself as process; contains a status as a verbal midpoint; denotes neither beginning nor ending, and operates in the midst of becoming. Being of the infinitive form, the phantasm reflects the distribution of events from the extractions of the actual present. Simulacra created by the subversion of fixed forms are rendered phantasmal as they ascend into absolute becoming. Phantasms are the symbols of change itself within the event. Deleuze explains the passage of simulacrum to phantasm on the line of becoming:

> Earlier, there have been only simulacra, idols and images, but not phantasms, to represent events. Pure events are results, but results of the second degree. It is true that the phantasm reintegrates and retrieves everything in the retrieval of *its own* movement, but everything is changed. It is not that nourishment has become spiritual nourishment, and copulations gestures of the spirit. But each time a proud and shiny verb has been disengaged, distinct from things and bodies, states of affairs and their qualities, their actions and passions: like the verb '*to green*', distinct from the tree and its greenness, or the verb '*to eat*' (or 'to be eaten') distinct from food and its consumable qualities, or the verb '*to mate*' distinct from bodies and their sexes – eternal truths. In short, metamorphosis is the liberation of the non-existent entity for each state of affairs, and of the infinitive for each body and quality, each subject and predicate, each action and passion.[36]

The infinitive is the connective moment of sensory becoming and absolute becoming and indicates the crystallization of a given fold of sensory becoming. Sensory becoming initially disorients the materiality of the present, and in this nebulous cloud of infinitely fragmented identities, folds, condenses and expresses its contents in novel ways within the infinite speed of absolute becoming. Sensory becoming is a perfect haecceity, always in the middle, defined by lines, clouds and fogs of refracted light. The quasi-cause then strikes a given expression like lightning and crystallizes its singularities. The singularities guard their fragmented, molecular memory, and are thrown into various assemblages in the virtual across divergent lines.

The infinitive expresses the order of absolute becoming, while the infinitive-proper name designates any series of sensory becoming. Deleuze says,

> In the first place, the verb in the infinitive is in no way indeterminate with respect to time; it expresses the floating, nonpulsed time proper to Aeon, in other words, the time of the pure event or of becoming, which articulates relative speeds and

slownesses independently of the chonometric or chronological values that time assumes in the other modes.[37]

The infinitive is a-subjective and expresses the time of the 'pure event', which is, the Event of the eternal return, or absolute becoming. When paired with a proper name, the infinitive expresses a bloc of becoming, or two or more molecules converged in indeterminacy. Once attached to the infinitive, the proper name is detached from any subject, form or class and is an agent of the undetermined. The hyphenated infinitive + proper name combination denotes multiplicities of the virtual and helps expose the counter-actualizing effect of the quasi-cause through the depths of sensory becoming. Where we see a proper name we witness a zone of proximity that catalyses the bifurcation of absolute becoming and sensory becoming along the lines of the past and future. The disoriented, displaced and fragmented identities of madness are extracted along the line of absolute becoming. The virtualization of the actual is described in *A Thousand Plateaus*:

> Starting from the forms one has, the subject one is, the organs one has, or the functions one fulfills, becoming is to extract particles between which one establishes the relations of movement and rest speed and slowness that are *closest* to what one is becoming, and through which one becomes.[38]

In this passage 'becoming' denotes the comprehensive process of both notions of becoming. The subject, form, organ and class in the actual are subverted by the 'bad Chronos' of the measureless present, forming a cloud of undetermined madness that is expressed in a myriad ways. These expressions are then subdivided *ad infinitum* into the past and future directions of absolute becoming. The molecular memory of becoming-mad draws a zone of proximity around a bloc of singularities. For 'becoming is to emit particles that take on certain relations of movement and rest because they enter a particular zone of proximity. Or, it is to emit particles that enter that zone because they take on those relations'.[39] Sensory becoming subverts the measured present and fragments the four branches of representational thought, thereby delimiting a nebulous zone of proximity and folding two or more singularities together in expression. The emission of particles results from the quasi-cause's encounter with matter. The molecular memories of sensory becoming designate a zone that is defined by a fragmented history of emitted singularities. The zone of proximity is a site of convergence between events in sensation independent of subjectivities and forms. Zones of proximity are created through the relationality of molecular becomings and their singular histories outside of chronological time. Of course, the molecular histories of sensory becoming may be subjected to the paradoxical instance of Aion at any time.

The paradoxical instance of Aion is where all events assemble and produce change, perpetually splitting into two directions at once. The coming together of all events in *the* event of absolute becoming triggers the quasi-cause, which creates the communicative effect. This is the moment where

> death turns against death; where dying is the negation of death, and the impersonality of dying no longer indicates only the moment when I disappear outside myself, but rather the moment when death loses itself in itself, and also the figure which the most singular life takes on in order to substitute itself for me.[40]

The quasi-cause rushes through events like a storm, dismembering any molar memory traces, all forms are pulled from the subject, and the Self, God, World and necessary causation all dissolve into a nomadic distribution of singular points along the surface of absolute becoming.[41] Death as a final state is detached from its static form and is plunged into the de-centred, impersonal and pre-individual chaos of becoming. The fait accompli is dislodged at the aleatory point of becoming, and its singularities are extracted and redistributed through the event producing mechanism of the quasi-cause.

We must keep in mind that the quasi-cause is an operator of contingency, and the coup de dés determines which forms are dissimulated. Realizing that the present is de-actualized in contingency helps answer the question, 'Why now?' Asking why a particular event is actualized implies a causal necessity of chronological time.[42] To ask why ancient Greece was the birthplace of democracy imposes efficient causation onto the becoming of events.[43] The question attempts to naturalize the concept of democracy, which, in its present form, postdates the time of ancient Greece. The selfsame process described by Bergson in the cinematographic, stop-motion mechanisms of the intellect – where, for instance, the movement of an arrow is understood through immobile points in space – is invoked when asking why an effect is actualized in successive time. Events operate through an untimely logic of coexistence; therefore, to inquire about the necessity of an actualized effect ignores the logic of the quasi-cause. Why, might we ask, does the monumental effect of Combray arise from the depths of the past when the narrator of *In Search of Lost Time* takes a bite of the tea-soaked madeleine? Chance. The narrator did not *will* the return of Combray, did not *seek* the return of Combray in recollection; its effect was purely contingent. A better question would be, 'How did Combray rise up from the depths of ontological memory in the present moment of sensation?' In an untimely return, counter to its own time, the effect of Combray is driven to the future in the nonnumeric present of sensation. This is how becoming moves: in communes.[44] When we ask why ancient Greece was the birthplace of democracy, we must understand that we are retroactively imposing conceptual tendencies that were not active during ancient Greece. Deleuze never strays far from Bergson in his understanding of creative movement; unless we place ourselves within the streams of becoming, then we are reconstructing quasi-causal processes through the efficient causation of representational logic. Contingency is the mode of the quasi-cause, and asking why an event was actualized at a particular time presupposes a conscious arrangement of history. In the immanent processes of becoming, conceptual components fold in unique expressions that could have proceeded otherwise.

The nonsense of sensory becoming is distributed on the line of Aion and forms a transcendental field where no reference is made to consciousness, subject or object. The transcendental field is absent of all transcendent entities and its pre-individual, anti-generality connects the actual to the virtual. The transcendental field is the plane of immanence in Deleuze's ontology. Deleuze explains that 'immanence is not related to Some Thing as a unity superior to all things or to a Subject as an act that brings about a synthesis of things: it is only when immanence is no longer immanence to anything other than itself that we can speak of a plane of immanence.'[45] The resonance of events through the quasi-cause defies the logic of representational thought, and through the forgetting function of absolute becoming singularities break with memory traces.

Absolute becoming is devoid of memory, history and duration, but the fragmentary blocs of becoming produced through absolute becoming retain a pre-individual history of singularities. Deleuze claims, 'Metamorphoses and redistributions of singularities form a history; each combination and each distribution is an event.'[46] In this passage Deleuze draws a clear distinction between events and *the* event. The events that participate in the event are the becomings of molecular memory produced at the quasi-causal moment of extraction. Roffe explains how the singularity of the event creates the new in sensation: 'It is not from the bones that lie in the depths of bodies that an avenger arises; the event itself provides the genetic kernel that every revenge, every act of war expresses. It is that certain *aliquid*, that some*thing* that, like the grain of sand in an oyster, engenders the production of novelty in these depths.'[47] The dice throw of chance finds the oyster producing a pearl in a fortuitous expression of materiality.

Singularities have a history of combinations in actuality, and this history is fragmented through the extraction and distribution of the quasi-cause as molar memory shatters into molecular memory. The memory of Klossowski's moment of forgetting in the experience of the eternal return remains within the singularity – the Artaudian, schizophrenic copula of all worlds and subjects simultaneously passing together in an instant informs the singularities, and therefore their corresponding events.[48] Singular events function as an immanent nomadology, where God is replaced by the single event of absolute becoming: chaos. The system is thereby de-centred and in perpetual movement, while each element retains its self-referential nature and does not mix with other elements. Events relate through distance and form a disjunctive synthesis that adopts the compossible/incompossible distinction provided by Leibniz.[49]

The surface of becoming is possible through the disjunctive synthesis of series. Deleuze de-centres Leibniz, and events are defined in a-logical terms of compossibility and incompossibility. 'Two events are compossible when the series which are organized around their singularities extend in all directions; they are incompossible when the series diverge in the vicinity of constitutive singularities.'[50] The distribution of singularities determines whether events are compossible or incompossible. The incompossibility of events arises from evaluating contraries through an operation of identity, but rather, their incompossibility results from the affirmation of internalized difference. The Deleuzian appropriation of incompossibility involves the affirmation of differences through distance. This topology developed by Deleuze employs a positive distance which does not appeal to a transcendent god, nor does it integrate negation.

An example is given whereby Nietzsche's perspective of sickness creates concepts of healthiness in the affirmation of distance between these two affective zones. Perhaps the clearest explanation of how events communicate through disjunctive syntheses can be found in Deleuze's take on Nietzschean perspectives, expressed in terms of towns and worlds. Rather than run perspectives through exclusion by way of convergence, having the same perspective on a town, Nietzsche endows each perspective with an affirmative distance.

> With Nietzsche, on the contrary, the point of view is opened onto a divergence it affirms: another town corresponds to each point of view, each point of view is another town, the towns are linked only by their distance and resonate only through the divergence of their series, their houses and their streets. There is always another town within a town. Each term becomes the means of going all the way to the end of another, by following the entire distance. Nietzsche's

perspective – his perspectivism – is a much more profound art than Leibniz's point of view; for divergence is no longer a principle of exclusion, and disjunction no longer a means of separation. Incompossibility is now a means of communication.[51]

Rather than building a spherical model of convergence where all events converge in order to communicate, forcing out incompossible worlds in communicative functions, Deleuze provides his own immanent monadology (nomadology) with the infinite, incompossible perspectives that resonate through their affirmative distance. As opposed to reeling through an infinite number of predicates, as occurs in the becoming of depth, or sensory becoming, the becoming of Aion has severed all ties with identity and operates through the impersonality of the infinitive. On this plane, then, only the crystallized *effects* of becoming-mad and the simulacrum-become-phantasm enter into the series. Sensory becoming corresponds to the identity-breaking mechanism of the eternal return as described by Klossowski, where each moment is the instantaneous passage between all predicates, worlds, as well as god and self, in a connective process. The surface of absolute becoming is not weighed down with qualities or infinitely fragmenting identities; it has already passed through this moment and arrived in the universe of divergent singularities. Events arise out of the nonsense and the cutting of the paradoxical instant, or quasi-cause. The very moment becoming-mad is displaced along the de-centred line of absolute becoming it creates events that mobilize to produce unique resonances that express in actualization.

When speaking of the quasi-causal relationship between the surface of sense and the depth of nonsense, Deleuze emphasizes the interstitial link between sensory becoming and absolute becoming. He describes the surface of events as the receptacle of 'mono-molecular layers'. These layers represent the singularities extracted from the present, coated with the infinite masks of being that are extracted further through the infinitive of the quasi-cause.

Sensory becoming and bodies: Depth

The quasi-cause functions on two levels, both levels are intersected by the aleatory point of absolute becoming. It is imperative that the quasi-cause connect ideal events, as well as extract elements from the actual present, in order for Deleuze's ontology to remain purely immanent. We have studied the immanent mechanics of quasi-causality as relates to events, now we must unveil the quasi-causal processes that connect events with actualities in the lived present. The sky of the eternal return draws points of moisture from the ground of the actual present, creating a thick fog between the two realms: the becoming-mad of molecular memory. As the singular points of mist transform through the groundless, formless aleatory instant of the eternal return, a third realm is created – not quite pure becoming – and not quite corporeal duration. This monstrous cloud layer is sensory becoming, as a moment of abstraction of singularities from the actual present. The paradoxical instant, which is the quasi-cause, runs through the actual present, disturbing it in two registers of becoming. The quasi-cause splits the actual corporeal present into the time of states of affairs and its subversive counterpart of intensive becoming. The intensive, subversive becoming is abstracted from the actual present and is absent of any molar memory, yet it keeps the faint trace of molecular memory and continuous multiplicity. Events are the singular becomings of pure becoming. Each event is composed of redistributed singularities that are extracted from the actual present. They are constantly being redistributed through the distant resonation of the Event of all Events: the eternal return. Instantaneously passing through the brumes of sensory blocs, the becoming of the eternal return then rains down constellations of singularities like a tempest into the actualized present. This is the very process of the interstitial quasi-causal operator that Deleuze describes in the following passage:

> Between the eternal return and the simulacrum, there is such a profound link that the one cannot be understood except through the other. Only the divergent series, insofar as they are divergent, return: that is, each series insofar as it displaces its difference along with all the others, and all series insofar as they complicate their difference within the chaos which is without beginning or end.[52]

The simulacrum is the subversion of molar forms within the actual, corporeal present. The quasi-cause of becoming does not simply apply to the ideal events within the plane of immanence, but also reaches into the actual present. Were this not the case, then we would be left with strict dualism cut definitively between an immanent causality of events and an efficient causality of bodies. The quasi-cause links the forms of actuality with the eternal return of the plane of immanence, producing a counter-actualizing effect. As from an actual image, the quasi-cause extracts points of light and colour and redistributes them in novel combinations, creating constellations of closed colour points that disperse; in turn, they form new constellations while moving through ever-changing galaxies of light. The movement of the quasi-cause is not unilateral; for certain excessive rays of singularities are then actualized through the productive becoming of the eternal return. This is not a top-down ontology where virtuality is prior to actuality; they are co-productive. While the quasi-cause resonates ideal events in distance, it also perpetually divides the present into two opposing streams of the always already and eternally not yet. The distribution of the divisions and subdivisions of the subversive present and the actual present is supplemented by the extraction of singularities from the simulated forms of individualities and worlds within the lived present. The extractions of the lived present constitute events as crystallized sensory becomings which are struck by the disordering lightning bolt of pure, absolute becoming. Singularities-events are in perpetual flux in sensory becoming without intermixing, creating a truly heterogeneous field of spatiotemporal dynamism.

While it is clear that the virtual and the actual must be causally understood through the other, is there still a contradiction in the claim that the virtual creates the actual and vice versa, as argued by Žižek? Deleuze draws our attention to the vaporous realm of sensory becoming, the depths of bodies, as the connective between the virtual and the actual. The actual would have to presuppose the sense of the surface in order to create the virtual, and this is clearly not what takes place. The depths, the infinite masks at once, tend towards a folding and expressing that creates the singular events of the virtual. Žižek fails to acknowledge what Lampert calls the mélange, which is the meeting of quasi-causality and mechanistic causality in a bloc of sensation. As Lampert states,

> Series 23 [from *The Logic of Sense*] thus argues that causality depends on quasi-causality, and vice versa. The causal chain as a whole is distributed throughout the mélange of bodies, but each actual causal sequence [mechanistic causality] depends on distinguishing parts of that mixture, and on measuring alterations. But the measured division into parts is a subversion of body (Argument 4a in chapter 3). It might look as though body is stable before the past and future dissipate it, before divergence contradicts it, before sense interprets it. But body would have been from the start an undifferentiated mass unless discontinuities were already subverting it. The smooth time of simultaneity [quasi-causality] and the measure of rigid succession [mechanistic causality] co-exist as soon as there is a mélange. The quasi-cause is the unstated presupposition in causality, a differentiation of meaning that will have been operating before anything can have become present. The presence of quasi-causes in regular causes is what allows the Stoic sage to 'identify with the quasi-cause even though the quasi-cause itself is lacking from its own identity' (196). The quasi-cause lacks identity precisely because it becomes causal the moment it divides up a body.[53]

The mélange that Lampert says connects mechanistic causality to quasi-causality is the indeterminate zone of a measureless becoming-mad in sensation. Earlier in his book he provides a brief argument for the dependence of successive bodies on undifferentiated materiality.[54] He explains that

> 'temporal succession depends on the way that bodies are always in the process of being blended. But if bodies are in flux, no body can explain the successive states of it or any other body. Succession yields an infinite regress of appeals to objects, a system of causes that cannot form a unity. Orderly succession ultimately lies in disorder'.[55]

This argument mimics the one Deleuze uses to argue for a temporal model of coexistence that grounds the passing present of succession. He calls on Bergson's cone of memory to explain that succession in the actual is impossible without the insistence of a virtual past that allows the present to pass.[56] It is the logic of representation that repeats the indeterminacy of sensation in homogeneous, discrete units of measure, as Bergson and Deleuze demonstrate.

Lampert's argument signals an infinite regress in efficient causation. When an object is said to be caused by another object, we must follow the chain infinitely without solution. The quasi-cause is thus built into bodily causes. Likewise, the quasi-cause is inoperable without the materiality of the actual present. Actual presents provide the embedded singularities to be extracted in a simultaneous constitution of the virtual. The depth of bodies in nonsense serves as the intermediary link between successive and simultaneous causalities. The measureless present of becoming-mad holds the key to both the effectual production of forms and the counter-effectual production of divergent series. Symbiotic causalities keep Deleuze's ontology from falling into either strict idealism or materialism.

The unmeasured, qualitative becoming of sensation subverts the actual and produces the singular events of the surface. The measureless sensory becoming is divided by the quasi-cause of absolute becoming and driven into the simultaneous series while side-stepping the present. This operation of the affecting quasi-cause then lifts becoming-mad from the depths of matter which results in the displaced memory trace of molecular duration. The singularities drawn through the descent of becoming-mad have an eternally displaced molecular history; this is the process of sensory becoming, as its nebulosity is divided from all molar materiality and placed into the resonating universe of events. The expressivity of becoming-mad is the moment of sensory becoming, and its distribution along the divergent lines of becoming-past and becoming-future creates a fragmented and de-centred memory trace that corresponds to events in the virtual. This process of condensation of the depths of becoming through expression accounts for the movement from the actual to the virtual. Deleuze explains,

> The question is now about bodies taken in their undifferentiated depth and in their measureless pulsation. This depth acts in an original way, *by means of its power to organize surfaces and to envelop itself within surfaces*. This pulsation sometimes acts through the formation of a minimum amount of surface for a maximum amount of matter (thus the spherical form), and sometimes through the growth of surfaces and their multiplication in accordance with diverse processes (stretching, fragmenting, crushing, drying and moistening, absorbing, foaming, emulsifying, etc.).[57]

The depths of sensory becoming are expressed in a multitude of ways, providing material for divergent series disjunctively synthesized in incompossible events. Sensory becoming expresses in infinite ways; the spherical expression evokes the convergent sphere of actual compossibility of maximal materiality; the surface expression evokes the divergent series of incompossibility in the virtual.

Whether the depths of sensory becoming give expression according to the sphere or surface depends upon the aleatory point of the quasi-cause. The expression of sensory becoming is driven by the dice throw of the eternal return, where the quasi-cause counter-actualizes a given expression. The singular points of an expression are then resonated along the differential machine of absolute becoming. Events become serialized in a chaotic fashion, their singularities open to the process of actualization. The continuum of individuation moves from chaos to form, and back again in the order: actual form; sensory bloc; ideal events; Event of all events and chaos. Individuation occurs transversally; a combination of the horizontality of mechanistic causality and the verticality of quasi-causality. Differential networks of the virtual are created through the mobilization of the actual, and the actual is simultaneously created through the return of these divergent networks. The actual and the virtual are co-constituted while passing through the intermediary realm of sensory becoming. The symbiotic relationship between sensory and absolute becoming can be understood as two liquids of differing viscosity, chemistry and physical tendencies in the following passage:

> Being a theater for sudden condensations, fusions, changes in the states of extended layers and for distributions and reshufflings of singularities, the surface may indefinitely increase, as in the case of two liquids dissolving into each other. There is therefore an entire physics of surfaces as the effect of deep mixtures – a physics which endlessly assembles the variations and the deep pulsations of the entire universe, enveloping them inside these mobile limits.[58]

The events of the virtual arise out of the expressivity of becomings, where the becomings subvert the actual, destabilizing forms and identities while preserving a map of this fragmentation. The displaced molecular memory of sensory becoming in all its varying expressions creates the landscape where singularities are emitted and absorbed into the surface of events. The quasi-cause is behind the scenes in the crystallization of expressions of sensory becoming in events, as well as their distribution along the line of Aion. Sensory becoming is the intermediary realm between the virtual (Event) and the actual (Being), and as such, this third term reveals criticisms of dualist ontology to be the consequence of posing a false problem. How does the quasi-cause disjunctively synthesize sensory becoming and absolute becoming? We will articulate the interstitial quasi-cause through an analysis of the Moment in *Thus Spoke Zarathustra*.

The gateway of the moment and the quasi-cause

To better understand the operation of the quasi-cause we can map the concept onto Deleuze's re-appropriation of the Moment from Nietzsche's *Thus Spoke Zarathustra*. It is the Moment that repeats the aleatory point, the paradoxical instant of the quasi-cause in absolute becoming. Reading the passage on the gateway of the Moment in 'Of the Vision and the Riddle' through a Deleuzian lens illuminates the quasi-causal process between the eternal truth of pure events and the present of actuality. Zarathustra says,

> 'Behold this gateway, dwarf!' I said. 'It has two faces. Two paths meet here; no one has followed either to its end. This long lane stretches back for an eternity. And the long lane out there, that is another eternity. They contradict each other, these paths; they offend each other face to face; and it is here at this gateway that they come together. The name of the gateway is inscribed above: "Moment." ... "Behold," I continued, "this moment! From this gateway, Moment, a long, eternal lane leads *backward*: behind us lies an eternity. Must not whatever *can* walk have walked on this lane before? Must not whatever *can* happen have happened, have been done, have passed by before? And if everything has been there before – what do you think, dwarf, of this moment? Must not this gateway have been there before? And are not all things knotted together so firmly that this moment draws after it *all* that is to come? Therefore – itself too? For whatever *can* walk – in this long lane out *there* too, it must walk once more.'[59]

The Moment in Nietzsche is the quasi-causal operator for Deleuze. There are two conceptions of eternity that are indicated in Nietzsche's passage. One of the two eternities includes the cyclical conception of eternity which is predicated of the measured present. In this conception, we have a homogeneous succession of now points, and the future and past are dimensions of this measured present. Of course, this first, manifest understanding of eternity operates according to efficient causality of concrete bodies. The other conception of eternity, according to a Deleuzian reading, is the eternal return of Aion. Where the first form of eternity is produced in the forms of static being, the alternative account of eternity is the chaotic proliferation of forces in becoming. It is not a surprise that Deleuze picks up on the 'long lane' of the latter interpretation of the eternal return. The long lane of eternity is not one of measured, identical units of time, but the line of Aion, which stretches out, intersected by the paradoxical quasi-cause through its length of zero thickness. Passing through the gateway we have the two interpretations of time linked by the Moment. The first is the manifest level of the eternal return; the cyclical return of the same that is produced as an effect of becoming in molar forms. The second interpretation involves the eternal return of difference, which runs backward. This backward movement does not occur along the successive linear time of efficient causality, but along the ideational line of events. The backward movement of the eternal return is the catalysing effect of the quasi-cause, which is *counter-actualizing*.

Two forms of eternity that are supposed to contradict one another collide at the gateway of the Moment, the paradoxical instant. Two parallel interpretations of the eternal return are given in Nietzsche's passage. All that has happened has happened before and will do so again and again for an eternity. Clues about the two interpretations of the opposing lanes of the eternal return can be found in the form of the spider in *The Gay Science* and *On the Genealogy of Morals*. In the infamous passage where Nietzsche presents the greatest weight of the eternal return, it reads as a return of the same on the surface. He asks how we would react if a demon were to tell us that we would live this exact life innumerable times, with every joy and sadness returning in the exact succession, 'even this spider and this moonlight and this moonlight between the trees, and even this moment and I myself'.[60] Nietzsche then deconstructs the appearance of the repetition of the same in reference to the spider in *On the Genealogy of Morals*. He reveals that 'hubris is our stance toward God, that is to say toward some alleged spider of purpose and morality behind the great snare-web of causality'.[61] Nietzsche's use of the spider to signify the hubris of presuming the metaphysical veracity of causality, specifically mechanistic causality, casts the reading of the eternal return in *The Gay Science* in a new light that shatters cause and effect, and thus the manifest reading of the eternal return.[62]

The manifest reading of this occurrence is that all forms will repeat identically as they have previously in successive, linear, homogeneous time. However, what Deleuze designates as the latent interpretation of the eternal return is the unlimited division and subdivision of each present by the paradoxical instant of the quasi-cause, which is Deleuze's appropriation of Nietzsche's Moment. If we compare the aforementioned passage from 'On the Vision and the Riddle' to Deleuze's distinction between the present of Chronos and the instant of Aion, we witness the reflection of Nietzsche's Moment. Deleuze proclaims, 'This present of the Aion representing the instant is not at all like the vast and deep present of Chronos: it is the present without thickness, the present of the actor, dancer or mime – the perverse "moment". It is the present of pure operation, not of the incorporation.'[63] The present of Artaud's actor, Nietzsche's dancer and Mallarmé's mime represent the perverse Moment in Nietzsche which extracts the singular points of the actual in a counter-actualization that is hinged by quasi-causality. It is the instant without thickness which subordinates each form, each action, each present to the broken circle of absolute becoming. That which is unconditioned in the present recurs eternally through the untimely Moment.[64] The two opposing readings of time cannot be understood without reference to the other. The latent quasi-causality of becoming is reached alongside the manifest, causal chain of bodies and vice versa. A more sustained analysis of the role of the Moment in Deleuze's concept of becoming is elaborated in Chapter 4.

Instantaneous time and nomadology

Deleuze forecloses the possible reading of quasi-causality along transcendental lines. Anti-Platonic events do not pre-exist the actual present, and the actual present does not predate events. We do not have an empirical understanding of becoming as the reintroduction of movement through immobilizing mechanisms, nor do we have a transcendental understanding of becoming as autonomously separated from the enduring present. The virtual and the actual are inexorably connected, creating a universe in true heterogeneous multiplicity. DeLanda explicates the intersection of the virtual and the actual in the quasi-cause, accounting for the production of multiplicities, or constellations of singularities. He says,

The time of a pure becoming, always already passed and eternally yet to come, forms the temporal dimension of this impassibility or sterility of multiplicities. But I also said that the quasi-causal operator, far from being impassible, is defined on the contrary by a pure capacity to affect, acting in parallel with physical causality in the production of the virtual. In particular, the quasi-cause must be capable of weaving multiplicities into a heterogeneous continuum and to do so constantly so as to endow the latter with a certain autonomy from corporeal causes.[65]

The time of pure becoming, or absolute becoming, is the instantaneous. The instantaneity of absolute becoming is able to operate through quasi-causality, which is at the point of zero duration. The quasi-cause rejects the Newtonian concept of a self-sufficient temporality, or space-time, and does not depend upon the inherence of the transcendental ego to produce time. Being free from the corporeal forms and causes, its temporal function of becoming is not weighed down by an enduring substratum. Interpreting eternity according to the backlighting of the instant provides a dimensionality to repetition. Each instant takes every form through an infinite number of identities while they simultaneously walk the line of efficient causation in the corporeal present. Actual bodies do not proceed by a simply horizontal movement of effectuation, argues Deleuze, but through a spiralling movement through the virtual.

The quasi-cause extracts singularities from the passing present and distributes them in a double movement that constructs events. Since absolute becoming functions according to the logic of the paradoxical instant, it is simultaneously more contracted that the smallest unit of actual time and more elongated than the entire circle of actuality. The present instantaneously gives rise to the event, and the truth of the event doubles: first, as a phantasm of the broken present, and second, as the constellation of singularities that may be actualized in the present. That is not to say that the event, once actualized, resembles its virtual counterpart; however, its movement is automatically doubled in the extracting moment of the quasi-cause.

The singularities extracted from the present are haunted by the phantasms of their impersonal history along the line of pure becoming. Deleuze remarks on the distancing mechanism of the quasi-cause when he writes, 'But the event nonetheless retains an eternal truth upon the line of the Aion, which divides it eternally into a proximate past and an imminent future. The Aion endlessly subdivides the event and pushes away past as well as future, without ever rendering them less urgent.'[66] It is important to recall that the pure event *never* happens but is a confluence of forces, jets of singularities that are perpetually displaced by the instantaneous machine of becoming. Just as Derrida describes the untruth of truth in *Spurs*, the eternal truth of the event is never locatable, is veiled and is always deferred.[67] The reason for this is that the desire to seek the event is characteristic of an ontological system of fixed being, or what Derrida calls the metaphysics of presence. It is hopeless to measure the event according to the standards of physical mechanics, imposing representational categories to sub-representational processes, for the time of the event defies this metaphysical register. Our tendency to judge becoming according to the dictates of molar form results in what Bergson calls a false problem. By creating a new image of thought we can begin to think immanent mechanisms.[68]

The positive distance of the divergent series of becoming apprehends becoming in its complex internal movement. The double causality of becoming announced by Deleuze in *The Logic of Sense* dramatizes the interstitial relationship between the virtual and the actual through the fog of molecular, sensory becoming. The subversion of all actual sense through the differential molecular machine of becoming-mad subdivides itself endlessly along the line of the eternal return. Blocs of becoming create zones of proximity that differentiate singularities and crystallize their internal, fragmented history. Identities thrown into eternal flux are expressed and folded in various ways through sensory becoming. Then absolute becoming takes on the temporal logic of the Moment: instantaneity. The quasi-cause envelops becomings in accordance with their zones of proximity, driving them into the multiplicities of becoming-past and becoming-future. The process of identity fragmentation, where sense becomes infinitely other in sensation, is the repetition of the eluded present of quasi-causality. As a result, subjects and objects are replaced with pre-individual singularities on the plane of immanence; blocs of becoming resonate across divergent lines of incompossibility. Through the immanence of the quasi-cause, Deleuze has inverted incompossibility in Leibniz and created a nomadology, or heterogeneous monism. He is neither a philosopher of the One, nor the Many.

The quasi-cause apprehends the becoming-mad in its subversion of the actual present, which is already spinning out of the efficient causality of bodies. Contingent in its movement, the quasi-cause operates as the dice throw of chance, subdividing the present into divergent series of the past and future. The quasi-cause is not a final cause, as it does not exhibit any resemblance between 'itself' and the effects of events, for its only identity is its absence of identity. Having elaborated the tripartite ontology in Deleuze, we can safely reject the assertion that quasi-causality is a 'pseudo-causality' linking Being to Event, holding two incompatible worlds together. The intermediary mist of sensory becoming is the landscape where the counter-actualizing causality of absolute becoming forms blocs of singularities in coexistence. *The Logic of Sense*, through its elucidation of two concepts of becoming, effectively connects the efficient causation of material bodies with the quasi-causality of the eternal return. The actualization of bodies through the virtuality of events is in a perpetual process of involution, where forms are unfolded into the chaos of pure becoming. Sketching the quasi-causal operation of absolute becoming, or the line of Aion, and the subversive present of sensory becoming allows us to better articulate the relationship between the concept of becoming and time. The line of Aion is only one example where the figure of the line connects becoming [Aion] and time [eternal return]. Deleuze invokes the figure of the line in several of his works to express the becoming of temporal syntheses. Chapter 3 examines the many lines in Deleuze's works in order to tease out the relationship between time and becoming.

Lines and Becoming

The counter-actualizing causality of the two notions of becoming symbiotically relates concrete bodies and virtual series. The ability to extract singularities from forms in actuality and redistribute them along new, divergent series within the virtual does not happen outside of time. What, then, is the relationship between becoming and time? Is time an interpretation of becoming for Deleuze like it was for Nietzsche?[1] At various points in his writings Deleuze may speak of becoming as a subversive, mad present; an untimely process; blocs of molecular memory; as the force of Aion, or the Eternal Return, which identifies becoming with the future. In fact, the frequent identification of becoming and temporality in Deleuze's works is no accident. In response to Jean-Noël Vuarnet's question about his then book project investigating the notion of repetition, or what would become *Difference and Repetition*, Deleuze replies, 'Yes, I finished the book – on repetition and difference (they're the same thing) as the actual categories of our thought.'[2] The parenthetical remark that Deleuze makes is most significant. Difference, which is another term for becoming, and Repetition, which signifies his theory of temporality, are pronounced to be the same, collapsing the distinction between becoming and time.[3] This chapter investigates the relationship between becoming and temporality by analysing the function of *the line* in Deleuze's works. No matter which expression becoming or becomings may take in Deleuze's writings, a figure that keeps recurring is the line. The line figures prominently in Deleuze's analyses of becoming and is often used to describe time itself. Following the line between becoming and time in his works will lead us to a better understanding of how the two fit together.

From the abstract line in *Difference and Repetition* to the northern line in *Francis Bacon* and *What Is Philosophy?*; from line of Aion in *The Logic of Sense* to lines of flight in *A Thousand Plateaus*, the figure of the line connects becoming(s) to the three syntheses of time: past, present and future. All of the various incarnations of the line in Deleuze form one line that is constantly being broken. We will see how the line itself is in a process of becoming within Deleuze's works, and as he says in *Francis Bacon*, 'By constantly being broken, the line becomes more than the line.'[4] In this chapter, we uncover the various lines in Deleuze's philosophy and argue that despite its permutations from one work to another, there is one line in Deleuze, a line that is 'constantly being broken'. The line starts as a figure of time in *Difference and Repetition* and moves towards a figure of becoming in *A Thousand Plateaus* and *What Is Philosophy?* In the process of being broken from text to text, the line becomes more than itself and expresses the figural connection between time and becoming. The becoming of the line in Deleuze's writings forms a temporal synecdoche of becoming as such. This chapter analyses the temporal logics of the line through a sampling of creative works from Odilon Redon and Jackson Pollock. Pulled from the artistic works it informs, the figure of the line depicts the aesthetic nature of becoming in Deleuze's philosophy.

The abstract line

In *Difference and Repetition* the abstract line fractures the 'I' and introduces difference within thought, and this is accomplished through the empty form of time: the eternal return, or the future. 'It is this form of time which distributes throughout itself an "I" fractured by the abstract line, a passive self produced by a groundlessness that it contemplates.'[5] Right away we are struck by the temporal inference of the abstract line in thought. The groundlessness that is contemplated by the passive, larval self is the formlessness of the eternal return, the third synthesis of time. As Deleuze notes, groundlessness is a 'universal ungrounding which turns upon itself and causes only the yet-to-come to return'.[6] By turning upon itself, the eternal return enacts the abstract line, deforming the ground through a contemplation of the groundlessness of the future in the present. The abstract line fragments all identities in its wake. Contemplation is not a mental act of reflection in transcendental unity but a pre-subjective, sub-representational contraction that occurs in the present of habit. The abstract line is thus posited against a representational model and engenders thought within thought through the present contraction or contemplation of the future. In a perpetuation of non-representational violence, the abstract line produces the conditions under which thought and action are possible. Between the determinate and the indeterminate is the abstract line.

Deleuze borrows the figure of the abstract line from the chiaroscuro of Odilon Redon,[7] and against representation, the line is invoked to revolutionize the image of thought. Deleuze explains, 'The theory of thought is like painting: it needs that revolution which took art from representation to abstraction. This is the aim of a theory of thought without image.'[8] As Deleuze understands the abstract line operating in the works of Redon, it abandons the model, and in a minimalist gesture distinguishes itself from the ground by dissolving forms. The ground no longer lurks below but rises up as an autonomous existence while not distinguishing itself from the abstract line. It is as if the abstract line in its mark of determination pulls the ground from the abyss of pure indeterminacy. The balance of light and dark in chiaroscuro which creates difference does so by combining the determinate with the indeterminate in one stroke. At this precise moment, the human face and all forms reflected in the rising ground of indeterminacy are deformed by the abstract line. This occurrence entails Redon's use of the abstract line to break through the indeterminate without representing naturalistic forms. Redon states, 'Suggestive art cannot produce anything without resorting exclusively to the mysterious play of shadow and rhythm of mentally conceived lines.'[9] The mysterious play of shadow and rhythm expresses what Redon calls 'the indeterminate', and piercing the indeterminate is the abstract line of the de-forming work of art.

Deleuze takes Redon's abstract line – an agent that comes out of the depths and acts upon the spirit – and imbues the concept with temporal significance pertaining to becomings. In *Difference and Repetition* Deleuze restates Redon's journal passage almost verbatim but changes the word spirit (*esprit*) to soul (*âme*).[10] Deleuze writes, 'The rising ground is no longer below, it acquires autonomous existence; the form reflected in this ground is no longer a form but an abstract line acting directly upon the soul.'[11] The subtle shift in Deleuze's reformulation of the abstract line from *esprit*, which can be translated in English as either spirit or mind, to *âme*, which is translated as soul, indicates a temporal function in Deleuze's use of the abstract line. The soul to which Deleuze is referring is not the beautiful soul of Hegel, or the soul of Platonic reminiscence but is the Humean contemplative soul in the synthesis of the present, or habit. He says, 'A soul must be attributed to the heart, to the muscles, nerves and cells, but a contemplative soul whose entire function is to contract a habit.'[12] To contemplate, Deleuze says, is to draw something (i.e. difference, or the new) from repetition, and the contemplative soul draws difference from its object by contraction in the present. The self has countless contemplative souls that are adjacent to the self or the subject, and they function as pre-individual selves at the molecular, rather than the molar, level. The contemplative souls that contract habits in the present operate through passive syntheses at the sub-representative level. Their connection to molecular becoming is attributed to their synthesis of binary cases (tick-tock, tick-tock), whose succession is contractively fused in the contemplative soul. This fused succession of cases, however, is fragmented by the abstract line when the 'object' of contemplation is the groundlessness of the future. Habit takes successive elements and cases and in fusing them through passive syntheses produces an 'I'. This 'I' self-modifies according to that which it contracts, thereby defining itself through possession.[13] With the future, however, there is nothing to possess, there is no ground, and so the contemplative souls of habit distribute this groundlessness into the 'I'. The abstract line is a sub-representational figure that emerges when the groundlessness of the future is contracted by the enduring present in habit.

The 'abstract line acting directly upon the soul' subverts the present, or what Deleuze calls the present present, which is the present that represents the former present while reflecting itself. The representation of the passing present fragments and de-forms as the groundlessness of the future is contemplated and contracted: this is the work of the abstract line. The abstract line is an abstraction of the 'lines of fact' that Bergson traced to the conversion point of the insertion of thought into matter. Deleuze strips thought of the subjective consciousness seen in Bergson's analysis, but the temporal resonance of Bergson's lines of fact and Deleuze's abstract line is unmistakable. In 'Life and Consciousness' from *Mind-Energy* Bergson seeks to explain how consciousness bridges the gap between what has been and what is to come, and his pursuit follows what he calls *lines of fact* – speculative directions that converge upon the same point. Lines of fact are posited against mathematical deduction, and as Bergson states, mathematical deduction is insufficient in revealing truths of mind and matter. Therefore, if we follow various lines of fact that emerge from separate realms of experience and lead towards a point of convergence, that will reveal desired knowledge. Deleuze knew *Mind-Energy* well, and the conversion point of Bergson's lines of fact will seem eerily similar to the exposition of the contemplative souls in *Difference and Repetition*. Bergson states,

> All I wish to say is that this new line of facts leads us to the same conclusion as the former line. Whether we consider the act which consciousness decrees or the perception which prepares that act, in either case consciousness appears as a force seeking to insert itself in matter in order to get possession of it and turn it to its profit. It works in two complementary ways: – in one, by an explosive

action, it liberates instantly, in the chosen direction, energy which matter has been accumulating during a long time; in the other, by a work of contraction, it gathers into a single instant the incalculable number of small events which matter holds distinct, as when we sum up in a word the immensity of history.[14]

The second way mind inserts itself into matter, by contraction, is echoed in Deleuze's exposition of the pre-individual selves, or contemplative souls. Does the contemplative soul not contract the duration of its object in the instant of the present? There is a functional parallel between Bergson's consciousness and Deleuze's contemplative souls; both define themselves through a contractive encounter with an object, and as the object escapes, consciousness, or contemplative souls – the passive self – becomes unhinged. The moment of contraction, however, is the moment of possession and the successive and entire history of the object contemplated is fused in an instant. The coherence of the self is intimately connected to the compressed duration of that which it contemplates, and the lines of fact sketch the process of the present as it becomes embedded into the past.

The possession resulting from contraction in the present creates an ontological memory within the larval self (or consciousness, for Bergson). A history of distinct events and sequences are synthesized into the present moment of contraction, which provides a ground for the present to reflect upon itself as it splits into the pure past. There is no present of perception, as Bergson reminds us, and the pre-individual self is a 'continuity of creation in a duration in which there is real growth; – a duration which is drawn out, wherein the past is preserved indivisible; a duration which grows like a plant, but like the plant of a fairy tale transforms its leaves and flowers from moment to moment'.[15] Bergson contrasts the durational character of consciousness with what Leibniz called 'a momentary mind': matter. We see that without the grounding force of an object, the self becomes unhinged from the past and future and exhibits the primordial forgetfulness of matter. As the contemplation of the larval selves contract the groundlessness of the future, they become disconnected from memory and durational content, fragmenting identity. The experiential lines of fact that converged at the point of definition through possession transform into an abstract line. The lines of fact in duration are abstracted, content-less, and formless as soon as the future is contracted by the passive self in the present. Lines of fact are those lines that articulate, define, differenciate and demarcate, but the abstract line, on the contrary, diverges, disfigures, de-forms and destroys boundaries. We can say that the lines of fact draw the edge around the tree, with its ever-changing branches and blooms. Meanwhile, the abstract line dissimulates the edge, causing the form of the tree and all of its parts to disappear against the groundlessness of the future. Lines of fact invoke dynamic genesis while the abstract line invokes static genesis that contracts through contemplation, rather than action, as seen in Bergson.

When Deleuze speaks about the abstract line being an agent that is directed towards the soul, he is referring to the contractions of the present synthesis of time performed through pre-individual souls in contemplation. Deleuze opposes contracting a habit through contemplation to the psychological presupposition that habits must be acquired in action, or in motion. The abstract line, however, operates out of a synthesized present that fuses successive binary cases not through movement in action, but through the static contemplation of groundlessness. The system of dissolved selves, whose splintering results from the abstract line acting upon the contemplative soul, reveals a temporally based deformation in becomings (sensory becoming). As it is developed in *Difference and Repetition*, the abstract line arises through the contemplation of the groundlessness of the future in the passing present. The line is an abstraction of the forms successively fused in the passing present through habit. Subversive duration of the present, which is contracted into an open series of closed binary cases, disperses the souls contemplating it, cracking the surface of identity, or the 'I'. This is the effect of contracting the groundless, empty form of time – the future. The abstract line is a deforming weapon of absolute becoming, and when it reaches into the actual it causes the measureless present of sensory becoming to dissolve forms along the way. The deforming effect of the abstract line is a product of the contemplative soul contracting the yet-to-come, groundlessness. And what do contemplative souls have to do with becoming? Contemplation is our entry point into processes of becoming. As Deleuze and Guattari boldly state, 'We are not in the world, we become with the world; we become by contemplating it.'[16]

While the lines of fact in Bergson are grounded in experience, the abstract line is not altogether divorced from experience in Deleuze. On the contrary, the abstract line acts on the percepts and renders imperceptible forces perceptible. The abstract line effectively connects the virtual with the actual through temporal dissonance. In the conclusion of *Difference and Repetition*, Deleuze states, 'Time must be understood and lived as out of joint, and seen as a straight line which mercilessly eliminates those who embark upon it, who come upon the scene but repeat once and for all.'[17] Is this straight line the very same abstract line? If we want to understand more about the relationship between becoming(s) and time, then we must continue to trace Deleuze's lines.

The northern line

Art continues to be an influential source in Deleuze's concept of the line. The abstract line in *Difference and Repetition*, abounding with temporal processes, destroys the contours of forms while the larval selves contemplate the groundless future. As the eternal return of difference unwinds the circle of time into a straight line, as lines of fact become an abstract line, this straight line then lands in *The Logic of Sense* under the name of Aion. But before going back to the line of Aion, we shall explore the artistic aspect of the abstract line as it becomes the northern line, which features markedly in Deleuze's discussions of art in *Francis Bacon* and *What Is Philosophy?*

As Deleuze's exposition of becoming/s undergoes a radical process of involution and complication in his later works, so does his exposition of the line. He moves from the chiaroscuro-inspired abstract line to the abstract northern line in modern art, seen in the works of such painters as Bacon, Kandinsky, Pollock, Mondrian and Kupka, where the line serves to render the intangibility of becomings tangible. As Deleuze and Guattari move towards building a body without organs, the line (without contour) is the figure that makes the virtuality of time and becomings sensible. Deleuze ascribes the possibility of expressing the imperceptible forces of time to modern art. In *What Is Philosophy?* we see Deleuze connect the percepts of art to the concepts and affects of becomings and time.

> Is this not the definition of the percept itself – to make perceptible the imperceptible forces that populate the world, affect us, and make us become? Mondrian achieves this by simple differences between the sides of a square, Kandinsky by linear 'tensions', and Kupka by planes curved around the point. From the depths of time there comes to us what Worringer called the abstract and infinite northern line, the line of the universe that forms ribbons, strips, wheels, and turbines, an entire 'vitalized geometry', *rising to the intuition of mechanical forces,* constituting a powerful non-organic life.[18]

The abstract line folds in on itself, forming whirls, a dynamic spinning universe that emerges from the straight line of time. As the line is expressed in percepts, it attains the reeling movement of simultaneous forces being expressed like pirouettes of light and sensation. The northern line deterritorializes, forming a non-organic universe that is self-referential, a percept. A percept is not attached to an object but expresses the becomings of landscapes and nature. Percepts reflect the two notions of becoming, as their sensory becomings, however brief, are instantaneously extracted by the quasi-cause of absolute becoming and distributed eternally into divergent series of the virtual. Meanwhile, the life of a work of art resonates through the infinite layers of the pure past at the same time that the circle of time is broken by the future. Deleuze and Guattari use the sensation of art to provide another distinction between becoming (absolute) and becomings (sensory). The abstract line, which becomes the northern line, infiltrates both notions of becoming. What we have understood as becomings of molecular memory is characterized in *What Is Philosophy?* as sensorial becomings, and they are posited against the becoming of zero-duration that extracts singularities from actuality through the quasi-cause, or what Deleuze and Guattari call absolute becoming.

> Sensory becoming is the action by which something or someone is ceaselessly becoming-other (while continuing to be what they are), sunflower or Ahab, whereas conceptual becoming is the action by which the common event itself eludes what it is. Absolute becoming is heterogeneity grasped in an absolute form; sensory becoming is otherness caught in a matter of expression. The monument does not actualize the virtual even but incorporates or embodies it: it gives it a body, a life, a universe.[19]

The straight line of Aion's static genesis is animated in expression, not able to occupy infinite series in actuality. The northern line pushes into as many directions as it can while remaining one, and the product is the 'vitalized geometry' of modern art. For instance, the abstract line that conveyed indistinctness of form in the chiaroscuro of 'Below, I Saw the Vaporous Contours of a Human Form' becomes the indistinctness of the line in 'Ophelia'. Zones of indiscernibility characterize the northern line and operate by means of a realism of deformation.

Although Deleuze contrasts the northern line with the abstract line of chiaroscuro, both were defined by their deforming effect. Forms disappear when cast against the groundless future, a phenomenon of the abstract line. Deleuze pulls the abstract line out of chiaroscuro, but just as in *Difference and Repetition*, the northern line dissolves forms and eliminates the ground. Luminous disaggregation of the abstract line takes on an expressionistic quality in *Francis Bacon*. The brushstrokes exhibit animalistic or anthropomorphic traits that do not recover forms but express the intense mass of the line alone. The northern line does not trace contours, and the sole entity that it outlines is itself, its infinite variations.[20] It perpetually encounters accidents and countless obstacles that cause it to constantly change direction and integrate these changes with itself. The abstract line in *Difference and Repetition* ran into the problem of pure optics, where the tactile expressivity of the line is absent. Optical disintegration does not go far enough to express the haptic qualities of non-organic vitality. Thus the abstract line disintegrates forms in the moment of determination and straightens itself out through the contemplation of the future, whereas the northern line denotes the expressivity lacking in the abstract line of chiaroscuro. An intensive luminosity of the abstract line in chiaroscuro breaks and abstracts forms, subjecting them to its optical code of black and white.

The northern, or Gothic, line, on the contrary, expresses an intensive power that is beyond the control of the hand. In his explanation of the northern line's break from antique art Wilhelm Worringer compares the measured, uniform, balanced lines you would see in someone's calm doodling, which is not divorced from the artist's will, to the frantic a-subjective line that is formed under duress. As soon as the person doodling experiences rage or distress the line leaps from the artist's hand and becomes unmeasured, jagged, with acute asymmetrical angles and repetitive broken lines. These lines then race through every form and are inexorably implicated in their identity. In *Deleuze on Music, Painting, and the Arts* Ronald Bogue explains that 'plant and animal motifs appear in Goth ornamentation, but they are absorbed within a maze of lines, products of a linear fantasy rather than a close observation of the organic forms of nature'.[21] The non-organic life expressed in Gothic art is animalistic (becoming-animal), for the forms expressed are subsumed by the wild, frenetic lines that trace through them. In fact, there are several key concepts within *Form in Gothic,* published in the original German in 1911 that foreshadow Deleuze. We see an intensive line of art that is always in between, a-centric – the line is an abstract machine that defies organic movement and instead is a quasi-causal expression of repetition at work. And while Worringer does not himself demonstrate such a Deleuzian programmatic, reading the constellation of terms in *Form in Gothic* must have been like looking in a mirror for Deleuze. Take the following passage where Worringer compares the northern line against the line of antique art as an example:

> We have already said that the endless activity of the Northern ornament is identical with that which Gothic architecture later wrested from the inanimate masses of stone, and this comparison is but confirmed and made clear by the establishment of a difference. For while the impression of endlessness of line could only be attained if it really had no visible end, that is to say, if it vanished unmeaningly into itself, in architecture the impression of endless movement was attained by the exclusive accentuation of the vertical. ... The difference between the radial movement of antique and the peripheral movement of Northern

ornament is therefore quite similar to that between simple repetition and
repetition with counterchange. In the one case there is quiet, organic movement;
in the other, the uninterrupted, accelerating, mechanical movement.[22]

Here we have the distinction between two types of repetition, one organic and
measured, and one that is defined by counterchange and verticality. These two
forms of repetition can be precisely mapped onto Deleuze's bare repetition and
clothed repetition. The northern line repeats not through the same, equally
measured organic forms, but through the unequal excess of counterchange, which
Deleuze interprets as the clothed repetition of difference. The two repetitions in
Worringer reflect the two repetitions in Deleuze. Deleuze says, 'Returning to itself
is the ground of the bare repetitions, just as returning to another is the ground of
the clothed repetitions.'[23] What is described as the repetition of counterchange
in the northern line is none other than the return of the other. The verticality in
Worringer's exposition recurs in Deleuze's articulation of clothed repetition, along
with the a-centric, peripheral movement that breaks down the boundaries that
define organic form. The endlessness or eternity of repetition lies in its in-between
status, just as in Worringer's northern line, where beginning and end are absent.

The northern line, as described by Worringer, implies the expression of
difference not mediated through the bare repetition of identity. These implicit
threads that are linked in conceptual constellations from *Form in Gothic* become
explicit when rereading them through the lens of *Difference and Repetition*. It is
striking to read Worringer's passage in its postulation of two different repetitions
– one organic, cyclical, repeating the similar; and one that is unequal, in-between,
a-centric, non-organically repeating otherness through verticality – and realize
that the passage was written fourteen years before Deleuze's birth. The repetition
of terms in Deleuze's own writings creates dynamisms in Worringer's text
which had been formerly unexpressed. Deleuze took the eternal movement of
Worringer's northern line and infused it with temporal significance. Once again,
the repetition of the eternal return is connected to the line.

When explicating the abstract line, Deleuze remarked that it came from
the depths of time. The northern line and its reformulation as clothed or
disguised repetition point to the eternal return of difference. The tendency to
call the repetition of excess, of difference, 'clothed' or 'disguised' harkens back
to the infinite masks of Nietzsche. Behind every mask, we find another mask,
ad infinitum. These disguises of identity reveal the proliferation of difference
without concept in Deleuze's theory of time and becoming. The northern line
in art expresses the imperceptible eternal return of difference through the use of
disguised repetition. From *Difference and Repetition*:

Repetition in the eternal return appears under all these aspects as the peculiar power of difference, and the displacement and disguise of that which repeats only reproduce the divergence and the decentring of the different in a single movement of *diaphora* or transport. The eternal return affirms difference, it affirms dissemblance and disparateness, chance, multiplicity, and becoming.[24]

Clothed repetition reproduces divergence by distributing difference in a single a-centric stroke and is none other than the movement of the northern line in art. Without beginning and without end, reeling in whirls and turbines, or ritornellos, the abstract line reaches into sensation, condensing the unequal. It is a repetition of counterchange and otherness, the eternal return expressed in art. Like Mihály Vig's monstrous and delicate circle dance, the northern line renders the twists and turns of resonant echoes sonorous.[25] The broken circle that becomes the straight line of the eternal return, the synthesis of the future, which was expressed by the figure of the abstract line, applies also to the northern line in sensation. For the northern line is the abstract line having been broken continuously. The becoming of the line itself in Deleuze's works brings us back to the contemplation of the future exhibited by the abstract line in *Difference and Repetition*. Within the folds of time and becoming the riddle of the line rests hidden. That is to say, we become (other) what we contemplate (groundlessness). The northern line is an expression of a contemplation of the eternal return, and the becoming produced by the northern line is an expression of the forces of becoming.

The northern line expresses sensory becoming through the intensity of an asymmetrically, repetitious line that assumes a life of its own. It should be stated that the northern line need not be confined to Gothic art, and it need not resemble Gothic art. Any work of art that employs an abstract line, is autonomous and non-organic and cuts through all forms with its intensive vertical movement can be said to express the northern line for Deleuze and Guattari. Most of the painters to whom Deleuze attributes the northern line are artists working in the nineteenth and twentieth centuries, such as Jackson Pollock and Francis Bacon.

In order to better understand the divergence of the abstract line, we will analyse one artist in particular: Odilon Redon. It was the chiaroscuro of Redon that influenced Deleuze's interpretation of the abstract line as the identity shattering effect of the contemplation of the future. What Deleuze would later characterize as the force of the optical code of black and white in luminous artworks refers to chiaroscuro, which creates zones of indiscernibility in regard to forms. Redon's lithograph, 'Below, I Saw the Vaporous Contours of a Human Form', is a perfect example of this effect.[26] The chiaroscuro lithograph depicts a seated figure whose ghostly form is absent of locatable line. The contrast between black and white in varying intensities creates gritty patches of light against shadows that blend into the figure itself. As the abyssal ground rises to the surface, it is undone, and in this Redon masterpiece the abstract line actively deforms the figure. The forms in the piece are in the process of becoming indiscernible. It is unclear if it is a woman or man seated, and the cloudy spattering of light above the table is obscured. The title of the lithograph suggests that the 'I' of the composition floats above, which is identified by only a pair of disembodied eyes. Like the smile of the Cheshire Cat, the eyes are partial objects, detached from any subject or object. The vaporous outline of a human form is without distinct contour, and the play of light and dark illuminates an impersonal figure of indeterminate sex. There is not a single classical line to be seen in the work of art, but the interpenetration of groundlessness and the dissolution of forms cannot be denied.

In his diary, Redon explains that his originality 'consists in putting the logic of the visible to the service of the invisible'.[27] This is precisely the same way Deleuze describes the effect of the northern line. The northern line makes imperceptible forces perceptible. While Redon accomplishes this feat in his chiaroscuro drawings and lithographs from the 1880s, his pastels drawings in the early twentieth century infuse a rich colour field with an innovatively disjointed use of the abstract line. In 'Ophelia', for example, there are traces of the chiaroscuro effect in certain edges of forms, and this is in conjunction with a powerful, broken and jagged line that runs through all the forms in the pastel drawing. It exhibits what Ronald Bogue describes as 'a random, manual catastrophe giving rise to a figural becoming that deforms images and subsumes them within a field of nonorganic forces'.[28] These are the traits of the northern line; this new line in Redon's work not only allows one form to become another so that the scattered and broken line creates its own universe through subverted forms, but it simultaneously causes those forms to dissipate into the scattered light and colour of the abstract line. The two apparently diverse lines in fact work together to dissolve forms.

If the optical code of the abstract line is separate from the haptic northern line, why do they appear to share the same deterritorializing, deforming, identity-fracturing effect? It is clear that the abstract line from *Difference and Repetition* bleeds into the northern line from *Francis Bacon*, *A Thousand Plateaus* and *What Is Philosophy?* Certain theorists, such as Stephen Zepke, use the abstract line to encapsulate both the abstract line from Redon's chiaroscuro and the appropriation of the northern line in Deleuze and Guattari's later works. Zepke interprets the abstract line as Worringer's northern line stripped of its transcendental search. 'Deleuze and Guattari's abstract line is neither abstract nor Gothic in Worringer's sense, because its inorganic vitality is immanent to its material, rather than that which attempts to transcend it.'[29] For Worringer, the northern line's geometric vitality is attributed to its inorganic search for a crystalline vision. Deleuze and Guattari take the nomadic form of the line and make it immanent to the materiality of the painting. Is Zepke incorrect in his conflation of the abstract line and the appropriated northern line? Basically, no, he is not incorrect. The abstract line expresses an optical code that disintegrates forms in the luminosity of chiaroscuro, and it is issued from the groundlessness of the future; the straight line of time that is the 'deep source' of the northern line in Deleuze and Guattari's later writings. The difference arises in terms of that which is being expressed. The abstract line expresses the future's fragmentation of identity, while the northern line expresses becomings in sensation and their respective molecular memory. The abstract line is the first moment of the disintegration of forms, and the northern line then expresses the network of becomings that populate the nebulae of lost forms. Having understood how the abstract line figures as the temporal thread that eliminates all who land upon it, it is now time to investigate the role of the northern line in Deleuze's concept of becoming.

'Ophelia', and other works from this period in Redon, successfully express the becoming of the line, as depicted by Deleuze. We witness this from the abstract line, the straight line of time as it is unwound by the future, to the intensive becoming of a northern line that has fully abstracted all forms and cut through them. The northern line has infused forms with a molecular memory which connects to all other becomings through the line itself. The zone of indiscernibility is no longer attributed to forms as the ground rises to the surface. Again, the dissolution of forms on the abstract line in chiaroscuro begins with the abstract line, and these indistinct non-forms are then distributed and scattered by the vicious northern line. There is also a new haptic quality to Redon's use of tonality; he contrasts warm and cool colours, and not just the optic values of dark and light through the abstract line.[30] The haptic use of colour in Redon's later works layers the expression of sensory becomings with the fragmentation of identity. Redon's task of subjecting the invisible to the logic of the visible is successful, and in one pastel drawing we can see how the abstract line is broken and then integrates this breaking into itself, becoming the northern line. What are the temporal implications of line's becoming?

Having examined the interrelation of the abstract line and the northern line in Redon's 'Ophelia' we are able to better articulate what Deleuze means when he says that 'from the depths of time there comes to us what Worringer called the abstract and infinite northern line'.[31] We are struck again by the emphasis on time as the deep source of the abstract northern line.

The northern line is the broken effect of the abstract line, which is the figure that emerges from the contemplation of the future. There is no time without the future, and the future, or the eternal return, determines the figure of time. The circle of time is broken and becomes a line. The line of time is what turns forms into indiscernible nebulae. Like the cloudy figures in 'Below, I Saw the Vaporous Contours of a Human Form' are made indiscernible by the abstract line, with their identities clouded and dispersed, time allows only nebulae to return. The future always has the first and final say in Deleuze, and forms are stripped of identity, their contours blurred by the indeterminacy of the future. Deleuze explains this process in *Difference and Repetition*:

> [The eternal return] allows only the plebeian to return, the man without a name. It draws into its circle the dead god and the dissolved self. It does not allow the sun to return, since it presupposes its explosion; it concerns only the nebulae, for which alone it moves and from which it becomes indistinguishable.[32]

The nebulae contain the birth, life, death, rebirth and virtuality of the sun, as it is stripped of a definite identity. Once the future is contemplated by the temporality of the sun, its form disintegrates and its distinguishing marks disappear. This is the same phenomenon we saw with the vaporous figure, as with the flowers, water and forms of 'Ophelia'. The extraction of singularities from the forms they assemble in actuality is an immanent abstraction, and the connection between singularity and the identity of a form is forever severed. Which expression gathers these singularities instantaneously and distributes them into infinite virtual series? The northern line. Chiaroscuro intermingles with the haptic colourism of the northern line in Redon's 'Ophelia', and this provides the onlooker with a visual clue to the riddle of time and becomings. The eternal return, the third synthesis of time, continues to reappear whenever becomings are expressed. From the emergence of the abstract line in its contemplation of the future, to the northern line's expression of clothed repetition, the eternal return is inexorably connected to becoming and becomings. The connection will become demystified as we examine the other lines in Deleuze's work.

The line-bloc

After *Difference and Repetition* we see the term 'difference' used less and less frequently while 'becoming' is its ubiquitous replacement in later works, such as *A Thousand Plateaus*. The multiplicity of becoming is a difference machine, and the figure that is synonymous with becoming as process of difference in *A Thousand Plateaus* is the line. We see line-blocs, lines of flight and rhizomatic lines scattered throughout the work.[33] All of these expressions of the line describe the same process: becoming. Each term is chosen to demonstrate different tendencies that arise through the processes of becoming. The lines that populate Deleuze's texts are not filial lines that branch off like a linear history, as species, phylum, heritage, genealogy and so on. There is nothing 'linear' about the line for Deleuze and Guattari.[34]

Our analysis of the line began with the consideration of the abstract line in its contemplation of groundlessness, or the eternal return, and now we will examine the line's bifurcating logic between the processes of absolute becoming and sensory becoming in *A Thousand Plateaus*. The first expression of the line to be analysed from *A Thousand Plateaus* is the line-bloc. Line-blocs are molecular becomings; they move beneath the eye of perception as pure affects passing through forms, traits, points or terms and subject them to the processes of becoming, just as the northern line subjected forms to its self-referential movement. Since the line-bloc is exemplary of becomings of molecular memory, we will begin by mapping its inspiration back onto Bergson.

Line-blocs, like all lines in Deleuze, are characterized by speed, by pure movement. Deleuze's characterization of becomings as movement incorporates Bergson's response to Zeno's paradox in *Creative Evolution*. Zeno claimed that for an arrow to move it requires a moment for each locatable point it passes through in its trajectory, which means it is at rest at each point, and therefore never moves. Bergson's critique of understanding change and movement through immobilizing mechanisms of the intellect rested on the differentiation between the creative act and its reification. The duration in which the arrow's movement is created is indivisible, and it is only upon intellectual reflection that we are able to divide that movement into discrete points in space. The movement itself is not a thing, it is a process; it only becomes a 'thing' through the retroactive work of representational thought.[35] The movement of the creative line is not determined by the points through which it is said to pass – this would be a reconstruction of movement under the guise of immobility. The creative line is a process whose speed defies the assignation of localizable points. These traits of duration, movement and the line remain with Deleuze and inform his understanding of lines and line-blocs.

In *A Thousand Plateaus* we are told that 'every becoming is a block of coexistence'.[36] This means that a line of becoming is not composed of two distinct points. Like the movement of the arrow, becoming cannot be divided into discrete localized points in space. It is pure speed prior to any attempts to fix movement in actuality. The line-bloc passes between two points creating a zone of proximity between these two unequal forms. It does not combine or mix two different fixed terms or elements but creates a line of coexistence between them, dislocating them from their respective localizable positions. Points are given new functions and enter into an assemblage; new worlds and systems are created through blocs of coexistence. To make this a little more concrete Deleuze uses the example of the wasp and the orchid.

> The line or block of becoming that unites the wasp and the orchid produces a shared deterritorialization: of the wasp, in that it becomes a liberated piece of the orchid's reproductive system, but also of the orchid, in that it becomes the object of an orgasm in the wasp, also liberated from its own reproduction. A coexistence of two asymmetrical movements that combine to form a block, down a line of flight that sweeps away selective pressures. The line, or the block, does not link the wasp to the orchid, any more than it conjugates or mixes them: it passes between them, carrying them away in a shared proximity in which the discernibility of points disappears.[37]

The wasp and the orchid are two heterogeneous entities whose encounter forms a bloc of becoming – a line-bloc – that releases the two from any sense of individual history. Both the wasp and the orchid construct a becoming of the other, and the becoming-orchid of the wasp is not a filial relationship premised on resemblance or imitation. This is an example of two heterogeneous entities that form an alliance that, in effect, throws their individual temporal sequences out of joint as they form a new bloc of becoming. The line-bloc is another term for becomings in molecular memory (sensory becoming) and the figure of the line describes the freeing of the points between which it moves in order to create a zone of proximity. Tendencies, traits and singularities are dislocated from the actual form and given space to create new alliances and becomings. In this way, the line-bloc breaks linear histories, successive chronologies, and material and efficient causality that regulate forms in actuality. The line-bloc is defined by its anti-memory (anti-molar memory), its dispersal of singular points into various, divergent coexistent series – its ability to remain perpetually in-between. Deleuze and Guattari explain,

A line of becoming is not defined by points that it connects, or by points that compose it; on the contrary it passes between points, it comes up through the middle, it runs perpendicular to the points first perceived, transversally to the localizable relation to distant of contiguous points. A point is always a point of origin. But a line of becoming has neither beginning nor end, departure nor arrival, origin nor destination; to speak of the absence of an origin, to make the absence of an origin the origin, is a bad play on words. A line of becoming has only a middle. The middle is not an average; it is fast motion, it is the absolute speed of movement. A becoming is neither one nor two, nor the relation of the two; it is the in-between, the border or line of flight or descent running perpendicular to both. If becoming is a block (a line-bloc), it is because it constitutes a zone of proximity and indiscernibility, a no-man's-land, a nonlocalizable relation sweeping up the two distant or contiguous points, carrying one into the proximity of the other – and the border-proximity is indifferent to both contiguity and to distance.[38]

We can see elements of Bergson's critique of movement in this passage. Just as one cannot assign a point to the line of the arrow in flight without reconstructing and distorting its creative movement through the immobility of auxiliary space, Deleuze's line cannot be reduced to any number of points. The line, then, is absolute speed that is freed from the fixity of form and structure. No aspect of becoming can be said to resemble actual form, and different sensorial becomings are characterized by their relative speeds. The pure movement of the line-bloc, or the bloc of becoming, dislocates the points between which it moves. The characterization of the line-bloc is a repetition of the northern line from *Francis Bacon*. Deleuze says, 'It is the northern stain, the "Gothic line": the line does not go from one point to another, but passes *between* points, continually changing direction, and attains a power greater than 1, becoming adequate to the entire surface.'[39] The line-bloc remains abstract in the sense that it does not create the contour or boundary to anything or any 'thing'. It perpetually dissolves forms and all determinations that employ the use of auxiliary, stratified space, such as inside, outside, convex, concave, here and there.

As sensory becomings, the abstract northern lines in art, especially modern art, concretize the concept of the line-bloc in Deleuze. The line-bloc is another name for corporeal becoming examined from the point of view of temporal composition. Becomings are characterized as line-blocs for their temporal movements of non-localizability (line) and co-presence (bloc). Sensorial becomings evoke a zone of proximity that allows various particles of different forms to assemble together. The concerned particles of separate forms participate in the process of becoming through coexistence set up by the relative speeds established by zones of proximity. The 'bloc' of the line-bloc signifies coexistence. The coexistent singularities drive a line of becoming that informs the different, actual forms in which they participate. For example, the line-bloc that forms in the alliance between the wasp and the orchid involves their individuated forms while simultaneously diverging from them. The line-bloc of wasp–orchid is an implication of two varying speeds in a particular zone of proximity. The alliance between them is characterized by an externality of relations. The wasp-orchid, which forms this relationality, is a becoming that defies any sort of filial connections premised on genus and species. The line-bloc of the wasp–orchid can be understood as follows: a co-presence (bloc) of two filially unrelated entities – each its own multiplicity – align to form a new multiplicity of external relations (line). The wasp–orchid line-bloc is a sensory becoming that cannot be traced back to the individuation of either of the pair; the species of the wasp did not emerge from the orchid and vice versa. Accordingly, the line-bloc deconstructs the arborescent, or filial, description of individuation, and external relations generate assemblages that undermine actual identities. Its resistance to arborescent, universal-particular organization accounts for the line-bloc's undoing of formal, final, material and efficient causality. Against the model of individuals as forms, the line-bloc is an assemblage of affects and speeds, or what Deleuze and Guattari call a haecceity.

'Haecceity, fog, glare. A haecceity has neither beginning nor end, origin nor destination; it is always in the middle. It is not made of points, only lines. It is a rhizome.'[40] A haecceity is a gathering of different lines, or affects, themselves becomings, and provides an interpretation of individuation that is not reducible to forms and structure, but action, power and spatiotemporal relations. The line-bloc is a haecceity. As Anne Sauvagnargues points out, haecceities are a Deleuzian appropriation of Spinoza's *affectio* in terms of longitude (speeds and slownesses), and *affectus* in terms of latitude (the power to affect and be affected).[41] Deleuze explains, 'You are longitude and latitude, a set of speeds and slownesses between unformed particles, a set of non-subjectified affects.'[42] The cartography of speeds and slownesses that inform a haecceity is described by Sauvagnargues in the following way:

> The *affectio* (longitude) concerns the encounters that subject a body to a punctual instant and the composition of movements that affect it (affection): The effect of the sun, for example, which we know only through the ideas we have of it, can burn us or warm us, harden clay, or melt wax. But 'affection is not

only the instantaneous effect of a body upon my own, it also has an effect on my duration, pleasure or pain, joy or sadness' (*CC*, 173). *Affectus* (latitude) concerns the variations of power that involve the passage from one state to another.[43]

Thus, explains Sauvagnarges, a haecceity is a transversal relationship between extrinsic force relations (longitude) and the corresponding intensive, power fluctuations (latitude).[44] The haecceity individuates not by means of necessity, transcendence and permanence, but by contingency, immanence and flux. Intermittent quantitative alliances effect qualitative changes and reformulations. The individual is not understood as an enduring essence of a particular form, but is a temporal line-bloc, a becoming that exhibits a certain molecular duration (dx), and whose constellation of parts (relations) link up with other haecceities, thus perpetuating a stream of contingent force relations. These series of alliances, or line-blocs, turn formal individuation on its head, revealing individuals as indeterminable becomings dancing in and out of various alliances. The notion of haecceity revolutionizes what is considered an individual. For instance, 'individuals' now include such examples as a weather pattern, five o'clock in the evening, a Norwegian omelette, a galaxy, an equation and so on.[45] The non-subjectified plane of haecceities virtually grounds the chronological field of subjects, forms and things. A line-bloc, the alliance and comingling of affects and speeds, does not function in successive, chronological time, but operates within the two temporal logics of becoming. A line-bloc, or haecceity, is synonymous with the molecular memory of sensory becoming; meanwhile, it is simultaneously dispersed and distributed along the line of Aion, or the empty time of absolute becoming.

Line-blocs, as Deleuze and Guattari explain, move by way of involution, not filiation, evolution or devolution. They say, 'But to involve is to form a block that runs its own line "between" the terms in play and beneath assignable relations.'[46] Intensive, sensory becomings, or line-blocs, are speed without location, and before they can even be assigned any representative meaning, they have already disappeared and moved on. Becomings are inherently nomadic, and through their associations, destructions and dispersals, they form a line of pure motion – that is, pure movement beyond all mobilizing points. The abstract line of chiaroscuro that dissolves forms by raising groundlessness to the surface invokes the empty time of the future, racing through forms like a Jackson Pollock drip painting. Points are disoriented and subjected to the movement of the abstract northern line, breaking contours and forming colour fields. The indefinable lines of pure speed form coalitions that rupture histories and families, forming packs that create new meaning – line-blocs that float between fixed meanings, beneath, over and within 'things'. Against the measured present, line-blocs draw zones of proximity between points that serve as virtual speakeasies, where each becoming is involved in a line of flight.

The line of flight

In the expanded theory of becoming-woman in *A Thousand Plateaus* we see the abstract line characterized as a line of flight. The abstract line *is* a line of flight, and the authors use the terminology of flight to dramatize the intensive features of escape involved in each becoming. And each becoming must pass through the molecular memory of becoming-woman. Becoming-woman is the minoritarian, de-centred, process that is molecularly invoked by every becoming, and is, therefore, not attached to the molar forms of woman. Like in Jacques Derrida's 'Choreographies', the binary of male-female is deconstructed at the hands of difference, or becoming – and in this case, becoming-woman. Using the anarchist revolutionary, Emma Goldman, as a figure for woman, Derrida explains that woman does not have a place – that she is, like in *A Thousand Plateaus*, indiscernible. Woman is in a perpetual dance as other, and she constantly escapes the trappings of essence.[47] Derrida enunciates the process of becoming-woman in the following passage:

> Your 'maverick feminist' [Emma Goldman] showed herself ready to break with the most authorized, the most dogmatic form of consensus, one that claims (and this is the most serious aspect of it) to speak out in the name of revolution and history. Perhaps she was thinking of a completely other history: a history of paradoxical laws and non-dialectical discontinuities, a history of absolutely heterogeneous pockets, irreducible particularities, of unheard-of and incalculable sexual differences.[48]

The other history that is taken up by Goldman is a history that does not express molar forms, such as strict sexual distinction and homogeneous, successive temporal continuity. Her history is made up of the same type of 'memories' we see in Chapter 10 of *A Thousand Plateaus*. Goldman's is a becoming that subtends all of the women's movements and is a 'history' of molecular memory, rather than molar memory understood chronologically and periodically. Her history does not succumb to the trappings of identity politics, and one must beware of misreadings of becoming-woman that bolster identity politics. The history described by Derrida is the anti-history of becomings that are not restricted by static Being, or what Derrida calls the 'metaphysics of presence'. Derrida dreams of a space opened up by woman that goes beyond the established sexual binary, where the individual is swept away by choreographies of sexual multiplicity that overcome the molar forms of man, woman, heterosexual, homosexual and bisexual. He is describing the heterogeneous, placeless becoming-woman we witness in Deleuze and Guattari: the line of flight.

The revolutionary woman's overcoming of binary logic in Derrida repeats Deleuze and Guattari's description of becoming-woman in *A Thousand Plateaus*. Woman is revolutionary in 'her speed, her freely machinic body, her intensities, her abstract line, or line of flight, her molecular production, her indifference to memory, her nonfigurative character – "the nonfigurative of desire."'[49] In order to destabilize and dismantle dualisms, becoming-woman deterritorializes organisms and molar memory, passing through molecular memory in order to align new communes of singularities that are not filially connected. Becoming-woman makes herself a body without organs, slipping between all dualisms while forming a bloc that retains a molecular memory of the dualisms she deterritorializes. This Trost-inspired delineation of woman reveals the becoming of the line in Deleuze's thought.

Becoming-woman is an abstract line, as she forms anomalous borders of multiplicities, a line without contour. In her ontological status as in-between she disengages all forms by disorienting their singularities, allowing them to escape structure; this is her tendency as a line of flight. She is also a line-bloc, as she forms a bloc of becoming that refers to the molecular memory of the dualisms she defies. She produces infinite molecular lines – rhizomes – between dualistic points. Above all, she is action at a distance, she is flight. The line of flight is always a becoming-woman, an infinite speed that evades capture, territorialization and flies beneath the radar of reification. Deleuze and Guattari describe the logic of the line of flight through becoming-woman and the correlative ontological fugue in what is no less a line of *fight*.

> Although all becomings are already molecular, including becoming-woman, it must be said that all becomings begin with and pass through becoming-woman. It is the key to all the other becomings. When the man of war disguises himself as a woman, flees disguised as a girl, hides as a girl, it is not a shameful, transitory incident in his life. To hide, to camouflage oneself, is a warrior function, and the line of flight attracts the enemy, traverses something and puts what it traverses to flight; the warrior arises in the infinity of a line of flight.[50]

Just as thought is always a perpetuation of ontological violence, the line of flight is catalysed through becoming-woman and transgresses all established norms and forms. There is no core self-identity that is being disguised, but rather, becoming-woman is the noma-robot revolutionary invoked in masks. The anti-memory of becoming-woman flees designation, signification, form or structure. As a line of flight, becoming-woman is engaged in a perpetual fight against representation and reification. The power of the line of flight is the ability to use the abstract northern line to subject all content to its empty formalism. If we use an abstract painting as an example of this process, we see the upside to the violence waged against representation. The forms that are disintegrated by the abstract northern line are *freed* from the confines of self-identity – everything pulled into the orbit of the line of flight is released from the logic of transcendence. Everything becomes other, fleeing the capture of representation when traversed by becoming-woman, the abstract line, the line of flight. Despite its deterritorializing function, the very power of the line of flight, which is the power of becoming-woman, may be temporarily and temporally arrested by molar forms. This is the reason Emma Goldman rejected adhering to the representational logic of historic women's movements. Women's movements are on the level of representation and chronological time, and as such, they do not have the infinite speed and freedom afforded sub-representational becoming. It is impossible to be truly free when bound by definition, and definition is work of representation. The identity politics of previous and contemporary women's movements reified woman, stripping her of her ultimate power: f(l)ight.

Flight is a fight against representation. The line of flight which characterizes becomings simultaneously exercises the two temporalities of becoming: the floating, non-pulsed time of Aion; and the inverted duration of Chronos in sensory becoming, or becoming-mad.[51] As forms involve and fold through the line of flight their singularities are simultaneously distributed along the instantaneous series of Aion and are displaced in sensation while infinite masks replace the identity of self. The displacement of sensory becoming is what Pierre Klossowski referred to as the vicious circle of the eternal return.[52] Identity is de-centred through the centrifugal forces of the eternal return. It is not a coincidence that the etymology of centrifugal means 'fleeing the center', and identity becomes defined as perpetual flight. The line of flight de-centres identity, and in doing so causes the individual (form, thing, person, etc.) to pass through infinite masks. Klossowski states,

> The centrifugal forces never flee the center forever, but approach it anew only in order to retreat from it yet again. Such are the vehement oscillations that overwhelm an individual as long as he seeks only his own centre, and cannot see

the circle of which he himself is a part. For if these oscillations overwhelm him, it is because each corresponds to an individuality other than the one he believes himself to be, from the point of view of the unfindable centre. As a result, an identity is essentially fortuitous, and every identity must pass through a series of individualities in order for the fortuitousness of a particular identity to render them all necessary. What the Eternal Return implies as a doctrine is neither more nor less than the insignificance of the *once and for all* of the principle of identity or non-contradiction, which lies at the base of the understanding.[53]

Klossowski's interpretation of the eternal return brought about a sea change in Deleuze's reading of Nietzsche.[54] Although Deleuze removes the vicious circle even further from the realm of subjective experience, the flight from the centre as expressed by Klossowski is an integral feature of Deleuzian becomings and appears in the figure of the ritornello in his later writings with Guattari. Deleuze adopts Klossowski's description of the necessary coexistence of forgetfulness in the experience of the eternal return and the memory of the other selves that were never actualized.[55] Identity is an effect of non-identity. An identity is formed though the repression of former identities which become de-actualized. We forget the divergent series of former selves in order to maintain a coherent sense of self, and we ignore the countless paths opened by the present so as to construct a single, actual identity. The eternal return, on the contrary, is the wilful forgetting of *this* self, de-actualizing the present self and recalling the infinite series of virtual, other identities. It is through those other identities, like a whirring shutter of a camera, that we recollect this identity, and thus resurface from the experience of the eternal return.[56]

This nexus of memory and forgetfulness is ontologically inscribed into the two notions of becoming in Deleuze, where it is no longer a matter of conscious, subjective amnesia or recollection. The forgetfulness of the current identity is appropriated in Deleuze's absolute becoming of Aion, and the memory of infinite, virtual others is the becoming-mad of molecular duration, or the abstract northern line. This Klossowskian forgetfulness and recollection that is inscribed in Deleuze's ontology is done so at the larval, a-subjective level. It is not the individuated subject that consciously forgets about the presently formed self in order to initiate the eternal return but the eternal return plunges all forms into the 'chaosmos' of becoming, which involves conceptual forgetfulness as well as molecular memory of sensation (Boulez-inspired 'blocks of duration'). The divergence between forgetfulness and memory replays the separate sections of the line of becoming, from conceptual event to expressed sensation. It is crucial to remember that these processes of memory and forgetfulness are beyond the matters of fact and rigidified Being, much less empirical experience.

Again, duration is not of the order of successive chronology, but is the subversion and infinite disorientation of the measured, corporeal present. In this re-appropriation through ontological memory, duration is considered molecular memory. Molecular memory and its formulation as a 'becoming-mad' in *The Logic of Sense* is a different becoming than the absolute speed of static genesis we see along the line of Aion, the realm of the pure event. Duration, as Deleuze notes, is a concept Bergson invented to avoid time's conflation with absolute becoming.[57] Deleuze's duration is the becoming of sensation; it passes beyond the reflection and perception of the present, subverting the present. In order to subvert the present, duration rejects molar memory and instead retains a molecular, virtual memory of singularities, as opposed to forms, elements and 'things'. These singularities are then infinitely distributed along the line of Aion, which is an incorporeal division of the past-future, without the content of the present. As such, the line of Aion, the series of events, operate in a space that DeLanda calls 'zero duration', like a mathematical function indifferent to the content it is distributing. Duration, on the other hand, provides the molecular content in terms of arrangement of singularities arising in the being of sensation.

The line of flight is catalysed by the ontological forgetfulness of the eternal return, yet it is able to flee concrete Being into the molecular duration of sensation. The line of flight must retain the molecular memory of that from which it flees, otherwise it would be dissolved in an undifferentiated abyss. However, the singularities extracted from sensation and distributed along the line of Aion keep the line of flight running between the actual and the virtual. The line of flight enables becomings to escape capture via a becoming-woman, keeping identity in a perpetual state of flux. Identity is ungrounded by the contemplated groundlessness of the eternal return via the abstract line. The line of flight underscores the tendency of the abstract line to escape definition. Lines of flight do not trace contours but are abstract lines that make all they touch indiscernible series of lines – a rhizome that recalls Redon's vaporous outline of the human form. A rhizome is a multiplicity, an assemblage, and it is composed of multiple lines. It is able to escape punctual location through its molecular memory, which rejects fixed measure and filial structure. As Deleuze and Guattari note, 'There are no points or positions in a rhizome, such as those found in a structure, tree, or root. There are only lines.'[58]

The abstract line, or line-bloc, forms alliances by contagion, rather than filial reproduction as in a blue spruce tree, and this gives the rhizome a particular freedom, for it is not tied to lines in chronological history. Without the organizing structure of chronology, the rhizome is a continuous multiplicity that does not replicate an ancestry but allows different families, species and singularities to collide and form a communal assemblage. The model of the assemblage and its rhizomatic production is not confined by genetics, or any preordained structure. Assemblages, on the contrary, flee structure by never being permanently bound to locatable points. The assemblage, as a non-organic pack, does not have a definite border, but floats in-between, without subject or object. Its substitution of contagion for ancestry allows it to flee the chain of association and genetic history. In this sense, the assemblage is to the individuated subject what Pollock is to Raphael in painting. Between the segmented lines of the formed individual are the abstract lines of flight. The line of flight takes advantage of the zones simultaneously destructive and creative.

For example, a disjointed line of disconnected drips in Pollock's 'Full Fathom Five' is an expression of the line of flight in sensation. Its abstract line is not formed by ordinary points of structure, but by singular points that are contiguous and operate at a distance.[59] The line is not a geometric line that demarcates a contour or outline but floats between points as pure movement. Pollock's line destroys rigidified structures by freeing singularities and redistributing them in the process of creating new affects in sensation. In his review of the 2006 retrospective at the Guggenheim in New York, 'No Limits, Just Edges: Jackson Pollock Paintings on Paper,' Jerry Saltz mirrors Deleuze's own estimation of Pollock. He writes,

> It is not possible to look at great Pollock drip painting and not know how it was made. Pollock's drip is instantaneously apparent; it is crystalline information, a carrier and the thing carried. It is versatile, complete unto itself, but also a detail. The drip has no history, yet it's been there all along.[60]

Saltz's observation that Pollock's drip, or line, has been there all along highlights the line's in-between status, its anti-molar history. As he remarks, the painting is abstract while possessing incredible detail. Pollock's painting reminds us that abstraction does not need to imply generality. 'Full Fathom Five' both displays and materializes the extraction of singularities from actual forms, then involves them in a self-referential abstract northern line in sensation. There is nothing discernible in the painting in terms of form, but there are blocs of sensation. The structures that are dissolved through the line of flight's involution are the segmented and fixed lines in actuality. The perpetual conflict between the temporalities of these two lines – chronological time and the empty form of time of Aion – demonstrates that they are inexorably connected, constantly undermining the other. The line of flight cannot operate in the pure absence of form, and form would be eternally static without the disorienting logic of the line of flight. Furthermore, the symbiotic involvement of virtual, abstract, deterritorializing lines, and actual, concrete, territorializing lines does not simply rest on the division of Being-as-stasis and becoming-as-change. The involvement of the actual and the virtual depends on the interplay of static Being, chronologically subverted becoming in sensation, and the eternal distribution of singularities in absolute becoming. 'Full Fathom Five' depicts the moment of interaction between these ontological logics, as form is counter-actualized in the abstract line of flight. These various lines – segmented lines and abstract lines – condense to form an assemblage, an alternative model for the traditionally conceived individual. Pollock's painting is an individual in the Deleuzian sense. It is an assemblage of colour and sensation bound through an abstract line that defies formal outline. As Deleuze explains,

> Just as in painting, assemblages are a bunch of lines. But there are all kinds of lines. Some lines are segments, or segmented; some lines get caught in a rut, or disappear into 'black holes'; some are destructive, sketching death; and some lines are vital and creative. These creative and vital lines open up an assemblage, rather than close it down. The idea of an 'abstract' line is particularly complex. A line may very well represent nothing at all, be purely geometrical, but it is not yet abstract as long as it traces an outline. An abstract line is a line with no outlines, a line that passes *between* things, a line in mutation. Pollock's line has been called abstract. In this sense, an abstract line is not a geometrical line. It is very much alive, living and creative. Real abstraction is non-organic life.[61]

Pollock's line is perpetually fragmented and refers to nothing other than itself, creating a new universe of sensation. The drips create a line that is in perpetual flux. His later works, such as 'Full Fathom Five', abstract from actual form, but in doing so, they do not form generalities of actual form and are detailed line-blocs that escape the filial categories of organic life. The abstract line in Pollock is a perfect instance of the line of flight, the line that deterritorializes all segmented and reified lines in its proximity. As a result, we have a visual encounter with sensory becoming.

The becoming-mad in sensation and the identity scrambling effect of the line of flight is a characteristic of Pollock's drip paintings. As mentioned earlier, Deleuze takes Klossowski's cue about the de-centring mechanism of the eternal return with respect to identity. The molecular duration of form is retained in 'Full Fathom Five', not in terms of what is represented in the painting, but in terms of the representational logic that is subverted by its use of the abstract line. The subversion of form is not only a subversion of representation *per se*; it is also a subversion of the time of representation. The chronological, linear, homogeneous time of structure, form and 'things' is unhinged in the sensorial expression of becoming, molecular, differential memory. The infinite becoming-other of molecular memory is sensed affectively in Pollock's paintings. The line that is perpetually in-between, that has no beginning or end, or what Jerry Saltz describes as 'being there all along',[62] is a classic expression of becoming-woman: the anti-logic of the line of flight. All forms are dismembered and rendered anomalous, and encountered points are subjected to the pure speed of the abstract northern line. The freeing of singularities from established forms occurs as the information of the dissolved forms is crystallized in indiscernible detail in sensation.[63] This deterritorialization effectuated by the line of flight is not simply destructive, but it opens up the possibility for new kinds of sensation, and correlatively, the creation of new forms in actuality.

Deleuze's broken line: The rhizome

Deleuze's unconventional account of temporality and becoming continuously invokes the figure of the line in each of his texts. In *Difference and Repetition* we saw the abstract line drawn from the chiaroscuro of Redon as the instance where the groundlessness of the future is contemplated in the present, dissolving all forms in its wake. In *Francis Bacon* and *What Is Philosophy?* Deleuze continues to refine his notion of the abstract line by exploring what happens to the line as it reaches into sensation. It is at this moment that the abstract line emerges as the abstract northern line in Deleuze's work. The northern line, appropriated from Worringer's analysis of gothic art, is applied to the abstract art of Jackson Pollock, Kandinsky and many others. The emphasis now is not strictly on the rising of groundlessness in the contemplation of the future, but the haptic, self-referential repetition in sensation. The northern line is distinctive in its further departure from the contours of form. Its indiscernibility arises not through a play of opposites, light and dark, but through a clothed repetition that inculcates its disorienting otherness in the very representational logic of form itself. This transitional moment where the abstract line reaches from ideational becoming into the becoming of sensation appears in the later pastel works of Redon, such as 'Ophelia'.

Next we mapped the line-bloc, which expresses the figure of becoming in its intensive features of coexistence. Different lines of sensory becoming align to form non-organic, non-filial assemblages that defy representational logic. These assembled alliances combine and disperse in unique temporalities, floating from one another like a bee moving from flower to flower. This enveloping of varying speeds is split into already and not yet and distributed along the line of Aion, the counter-actualizing time of absolute becoming. The line-bloc then re-conceives the individual according to constellations of speed, beyond the radar of the individuated subject. Its creative force can be thus understood as essentially fleeing categories, reification, and the static Being of representation. The line-bloc is a line of flight. Line-blocs flee the static forms of Being marked by points in representation. The detailed abstraction of forms in actuality, or what Deleuze alternatively calls 'extraction', subverts the forms' chronology, plunging their singularities into a chaosmos that undoes representation. As it happens, there is a common thread to these various lines in Deleuze's works.

The line connects absolute becoming with sensory becoming. The line of Aion is the same line as the abstract line, northern line or line of flight just caught at a different moment of either ideation or sensorial expression. The line in Deleuze is, fittingly, a multiplicity. It is serial, moving from the ideational, virtual abstract line in the contemplation of the future to the whirling repetition that glides between forms in sensation. Deleuze takes Bergson's critique of the reconstructed line of the arrow we see in *Creative Evolution* and endows it with absolute conceptual speed and relative sensory speed. The line of Aion is the abstract line that splits into virtual series of not yet and already; this split is what defines the line as a rhizome. As the line of Aion creates a circuit where conceptual series are proliferated in virtual events chronological time is subverted in dizzying repetition in sensation. In a process of de-actualization, the quasi-cause of Aion strikes the abstract line at the moment of futural contemplation at the same time that the northern line in expression undoes identity by creating infinite masks in sensation. A game of chance is initiated, and the quasi-causal moment on the line of Aion sets off an extraction of singularities from actuality. Those singularities simultaneously form coexistent constellations (line-blocs) of sensation (the northern line) and virtual ideation (the abstract line).

These different formulations of the line in Deleuze are really the same line, the rhizome, caught in different moments on the virtual-actual continuum. As coexistent blocs of sensation assemble in the line-bloc, the immobilizing function of representation and the logic of identity are escaped. This constitutes the line of flight. Every degree of expression on the continuum of the line changes the line in kind, breaking it continuously. The line of Aion's temporal splitting drives a repetition of form in sensation, as we see in gothic art, while distributing singularities in different abstract lines within the virtual. This temporal split looks as follows: always already (molecular memory in sensation) ←quasi-cause→ eternally yet-to-come (eternal return of the future in ideation). The virtual lines and the sensory lines do not resemble one another, yet they form a continuum of becoming(s). The sensory lines that allow non-filial alliances to coexist in sensation (the line-bloc) connect to the conceptual series in the virtual. As one continuous line, the rhizome creates a symbiotic complex between the actual and the virtual. Jackson Pollock's 'Full Fathom Five' is a beautiful expression of the various tendencies of Deleuze's line, which is continually broken. The dissolution of form in the abstract line is depicted in the painting, as is the haptic quality of the northern line which subjects all locatable points to its internal logic. The colour blocs created by the dissolution of form, the drips, subvert the logic of identity in a universe that is sub-representative, yet fully sensible. The coexistence of dissolved form and the repetitive broken line that forms the painting open up new possibilities of expression in sensation. And, ultimately, the effect is a line of flight, a flight from the fixity of static Being in a fight against representation.

There is a perfect symmetry between the theory of the line(s) in Deleuze's works and its expression in his philosophy. The abstract line, the northern line, the line-bloc, the line of flight and the line of Aion form a rhizome within his works that dramatizes his theory of the continually broken line. Deleuze's theory of the line is operative in his body of work where the line breaks into its different manifestations according to the specific problematics established in each philosophical work. The result is a seamless flow between thought and sensation that assembles a multiplicity of becoming.

Each of the tendencies of Deleuze's line, in their varying speeds, corresponds to different temporal rhythms that glide between the chronometric corporeality of the actual, to the becoming-mad of molecular duration in sensation (between the actual and virtual), to the absolute becoming of the abstract line which is defined as the empty form of time. As a system, the line is a rhizome that *assembles* segmented lines of territorialized Being and its circuit with the deterritorializing lines of sensory and absolute becoming.

The line explored in Deleuze and Guattari's individual and collective works – in its different speeds, its absolute and sensory encounters – perfectly demonstrates that 'by constantly being broken, the line becomes more than the line'.[64] The line is the systemic figure that connects the actual to the virtual. The efficient causation in corporeal actuality is interstitially related to the quasi-causality of the virtual. By following the twists and turns of the line in Deleuze we arrive at a connection between time and becoming. The contemplative souls of habit in the present take the future as its object in the abstract line, and the eternal return of difference guides the line in simultaneous directions of the absolute line of Aion, as well as the expression of the ritornello in sensation. Molecular memory resonating in sensory becoming, the virtual memory of the never experienced present as past, serves as the intermediary link – a line-bloc – between chronological time and the empty form of time in pure, ideational becoming.

In *The Logic of Sense* Deleuze refers to the line of Aion as both the empty form of time, that which is referred to almost exclusively in *Difference and Repetition* as the eternal return, and also as the infinitely divisible time of an eluded present that splits into simultaneous past and future. The former description of the line of Aion, as the eternal return, is synonymous with the third synthesis of time, the future. The latter description of the line of Aion is a simultaneous and unlimited splitting of past and future. How might we reconcile these two distinct concepts of the line of Aion? How can the eternal return simultaneously be the future and the infinite division of the past and future? How might we make sense of Deleuze's claim that difference and repetition are 'really the same thing'?

To complicate matters, the eternal return is also described as the being of sensation in the form of the ritornello, or what Brian Massumi translates in *A Thousand Plateaus* as 'the refrain'. The ritornello takes on different properties than the property-less eternal return as the line of Aion, which seems incompatible with the notion of the eternal return as the empty form of time. In order to reconcile these differences, Chapter 4 explores the divergent and convergent syntheses of the eternal return as it moves from virtuality to actuality and vice versa. The Deleuzian delineation of the future, the eternal return, bleeds into the two forms of becoming: absolute and sensory. The guiding question of the next chapter is: 'What is the relationship between the future and becoming?'

Time and the Eternal Return

In *What Is Philosophy?* Deleuze and Guattari ask what a concept is and how it operates. Understanding the constitution and mechanism of the key concepts of the eternal return and the ritornello (*ritournelle,* translated as 'refrain' by Brian Massumi in *A Thousand Plateaus*) in Deleuze's (and Guattari's) works will illuminate their trajectories as they relate to Deleuze's concept of the future. The concept of the ritornello is indebted to Guattari and his articulation diverges from that of Deleuze, for Guattari's vision of time and repetition is less metaphysical than that of Deleuze. However, Anne Sauvagnargues remarks that Guattari approaches time from the perspective of becoming, although 'he approaches it on a plane that is practical, pragmatic, clinical and political, asking how we can change our habits, start the revolution, and transform our ritornellos'.[1] Accordingly, Guattari's take on the ritornello is of a becoming embedded in the present of habit. Rather than follow the ritornello along the vector of Guattari's thought, I delineate the concept as it appears in *A Thousand Plateaus* and through the lens of Deleuze's ontology.

For this reason I have chosen to use the alternative translation of the French *ritournelle,* 'ritornello', as it phonically demonstrates the concept's resonance with *l'éternel retour* (the eternal return), the third synthesis of time. The diminutive 'ello' indicates a small return that Deleuze and Guattari directly explicate via Nietzsche, but a Nietzsche dramatized through the intensive features of Bergson: a return of molecular duration in sensation. Unlike the eternal return of *Difference and Repetition,* the ritornello is imbued with and productive of qualitative, intensive properties; it is both territorial and territorializing. The eternal return in *Difference and Repetition,* however, is the static genesis of the line of Aion, the empty form of time, as we saw in the analysis of *The Logic of Sense.* What we discover is that these two formulations of Nietzsche's eternal return, the ritornello and the line of Aion, form a multiplicity of sensory and absolute becoming. If we follow Deleuze's conceptual lines into the eternal return, the temporal syntheses of becoming will arise. Is the complex of becoming simply the future in disguise? Yes and no. Deleuze and Guattari state,

> A concept is heterogeneous – that is to say, an ordering of its components by zones of neighborhood. It is ordinal, an intension present in all the features that make it up. The concept is in a state of *survey* [*survol*] in relation to its components, endlessly traversing them according to an order without distance. It is immediately co-present to all its components or variations, at no distance from them, passing back and forth through them: it is a refrain [*ritournelle*], an opus with its number [*chiffre*].[2]

The concept, say Deleuze and Guattari, is a ritornello; it is both relative and absolute. The concept is relative in its relationality, in its divergence of components, and its relation to other concepts. It is absolute in its systematic co-presence in all its variations and its framing of diverse problems.[3] The concept is analogous to a galaxy composed of different celestial bodies each singular in their unique encounters, contextual envelopment and external relations. Yet, the galaxy is absolute in its collectivity as a single star system, absorbing the diverse expressions in an absolute ordering of events in a whole. When Deleuze and Guattari state that the concept is '*infinite through its survey or its speed but finite through its movement that traces the contour of its components*',[4] they are echoing the logics of absolute and sensory becoming, respectively. Absolute, or ideational, becoming involves the infinite subdivision of past<-->present, while sensory becoming involves the finite dynamism of the subverted present in sensation. Both notions of becoming operate as singular concepts that make up a multiplicity of becoming, which is a complex of both; each becomes the other. Absolute becoming *becomes* sensation through its contours, and sensory becoming *becomes* conceptual in its distribution in static series by the quasi-cause. The multiplicity of the concept of becoming unfolds the eternal return in differing temporal logics depending on whether the plane of immanence or the plane of composition is engaged.

At first blush, there seems to be an inconsistency involved in defining the same concept, the eternal return, as the third synthesis of time; the infinite subdivision of the past and future; a return of the unconditioned; and an expression of qualities. These disjunctive characteristics appear to be at odds with one another, and therefore inconsistent. This is a false problem premised on an understanding of consistency along the lines of representational thought–the idea that each component of the concept must conform to a universal identity and internal resemblance. Consistency, for Deleuze and Guattari, must preserve internal difference and not impose a structural logic upon each of its components in a universalizing manoeuvre. Rather than an adherence to laws of non-contradiction and identity, the concept maintains heterogeneous consistency by tying its variations together through resonance, a refrain, an enveloping rhythm. This is precisely what is meant when the concept is said to be a ritornello. It is this rhythm that repeats in the variations of the concept, lending it its consistency. Therefore, what appeared to be conceptual inconsistency are really levels of difference resonating with one another outside a centralizing model of thought. 'What is primary is the consistency of a refrain, a little tune, either in the form of a mnemic melody that has no need to be inscribed locally in a center, or in the form of a vague motif with no need to be pulsed or stimulated.'[5] The ritornello repeats heterogeneous elements, uniting them virtually in one concept. The variations of the eternal return, as the future, as an eluded present, as being without property and as an expression of property, all cohere conceptually through the resonant movement of the ritornello, granting its heterogeneous consistency.[6]

Upon examining the relationship between the two separate formulations of the eternal return in Deleuze, the temporality of becoming and its constellation of concepts become clear. Absolute becoming is synonymous with the future, while sensory becoming is the disoriented and ungrounded virtuality of the past repeated as the future. As Deleuze states in *Nietzsche and Philosophy*, 'The eternal return is the being of becoming.' This concise yet paradoxical statement (paradoxical because becoming necessarily resists Being) contains the intensive features that are condensed into a constellation of concepts dramatizing Deleuze's theory of temporality. This chapter will, in effect, return to this statement from *Nietzsche and Philosophy* as a point of implication. We soon realize that the quasi-cause splits the concept of the eternal return itself into the virtual past and virtual future. The virtual *past* arises from the dramatization of the eternal return with the intensive features from Proust and Bergson in sensation: the ritornello. The virtual *future*, on the other hand, dramatizes the eternal return with intensive features from Leibniz, Borges and Nietzsche. Taking on two distinct points of view in ideation, the eternal return reflects Deleuze's re-appropriation of the inverse relation between infinitesimal differential (the quasi-causal Moment) and integral (the synthesis of the future) calculus in Leibniz. We will see how Deleuze dramatizes the intensive features of Leibniz and Borges to explicate the 'once and for all' of Nietzsche's eternal return.[7] In combination, the ritornello of the past and the eternal return of the future compose a temporal rhizome for the concept of becoming.

Ritornello: The eternal return and the pure past

'The whole of the refrain is the being of sensation. Monuments are refrains.'[8]

In *A Thousand Plateaus* we are introduced to an extensive examination of the refrain, or the ritornello [*ritournelle*]. The ritornello, as its etymology suggests, is a return. In fact, it is a version of Nietzsche's eternal return. 'Let us recall Nietzsche's idea of the eternal return as a little ditty, a refrain [*ritournelle*], but which captures the mute and unthinkable forces of the Cosmos.'[9] The ritornello is an in-between movement that begins to orchestrate out of chaos. The ritornello territorializes chaos through expression in sensation. Through a rhythmic repetition, it provides a grouping of heterogeneous elements that provide the conditions of possibility for the actual. The act of circularity in the rhythm of the ritornello keeps the horror of chaos at bay. For example, Deleuze and Guattari open the chapter, '1835: Of the Refrain,' with an anecdote about a boy calming his fears with the repetition of a song. 'The song is like a rough sketch of a calming and stabilizing, calm and stable, center in the heart of chaos.'[10] The ritornello draws a circle within chaos, creating a territory. The territory blocks flows within chaos and is an essential pathway leading from the virtual to the actual and vice versa. These territories, like views from nowhere, then resonate with other territories, forming new worlds of sensation and blocs of becoming. The ritornello is the northern line in art, the whirring repetition that conditions sensation.

In keeping with the idea of consistency via heterogeneous resonance, the ritornello's cyclic rhythms engage counterpoints in sensation. This allows for the absolute population of concepts in relative frameworks and singular worlds. The ritornello is this sense creates a relative centre within sensation which resonates with other ritornellos in an anarchic procession. Form and content are not homogenized by the folding over and over by the ritornello but are temporalities ordered within the virtual networks of sensation. The following passage from *What Is Philosophy?* reveals the absolute resonance of the ritornello through its various territories,

> Every territory, every habitat, joins up not only its spatiotemporal but its qualitative planes or sections: a posture and a song for example, a song and a color, percepts and affects. After every territory encompasses or cuts across the territories of other species, or intercepts the trajectories of animals without territories, forming interspecies junction points.[11]

Territories drawn by the ritornello circulate, just as we saw in Pollock's 'Full Fathom Five', and all forms, points and counterpoints are looped in a relationality that affords temporary alliances and new assemblages. The question is to drag sensation out of chaos and maintain consistency among singularities and forms across other singularities and forms. The consistency is effectuated by the molecularity of material in sensation. Consistency goes hand-in-hand with the notion of consolidation for Deleuze. Material expression depends upon the arrangement of molecular becoming arising from the cosmic forces of chaos.

It is at this point that Deleuze inscribes the Nietzschean eternal return, the ritornello, into the ineffable realm of chaos, which is purposefully reminiscent of the final passage from *The Will to Power*.[12] The Nietzschean ritornello is not the eternal return of *Difference in Repetition* but is infused with the Bergsonian-become-Proustian conceptualization of the pure past. The past in-itself is the never experienced, monumental past that employs duration, which is another term for molecular memory, in its constitution of the virtual. We need an ontological, molecular notion of duration in order to territorialize sensation in meaningful ways. Otherwise, if we had pure, systematic ontological forgetting, no connections would assemble, no worlds would be created. At the same time, an empirical or experienced past is inadequate, as it carries the parts of identity from molar forms, producing a logic of the same. The ritornello, as the eternal return in sensation, is partially informed by Proust's monumental past. What separates the ritornello from duration proper is its tension with ontological forgetting from the empty form of time, the eternal return of difference.

The ritornello, as Deleuze indicates, occurs between milieus and is not locatable. It provides the conditions for actions in particular milieus, habitats, houses or anything understood within the purview of place. Interestingly, then, the ritornello cycles like the infinite virtual levels in the cone of memory, levels that also float between milieus. The consistency of the ritornello is like that of the virtual layers of the past, it is condensed like the aperture of the camera. Accordingly, the ritornello implies the mechanism of the cone of ontological memory as reconceived in Deleuze's Proustian appropriation of Bergson. The ritornello is like a dust devil that appears suddenly in one territory, circulates particles from the ground into the air and then dissipates, dispersing those particles into new territories. The ritornello must implicate virtual memory of matter in order to release it from previous forms and to distribute its singularities into new constructions and landscapes. Without the ritornello there would be absolute stagnation at the level of matter; the returning accommodates expression in the realm of sensation and provides the possibility for building new worlds in sensation.

This is not the first time that Deleuze's interpretation of Nietzsche has been thought to be heavily influenced by his studies of Bergson. Giovanna Borradori's article, 'On the Presence of Bergson in Deleuze's Nietzsche,' highlights the current of duration as a transformative and subversive force of time in Deleuze's conception of Nietzschean affirmation.[13] The affirmative is, of course, the only survivor of the centrifugal wheeling of the eternal return. That which is reactive is not and thus does not return. Deleuze's interpretation of the eternal return is highly temporal, something that Keith Ansell-Pearson identifies in the philosopher's works as an expressed affinity between Bergson and Nietzsche.[14] It does not come as a shock to see that Deleuze and Guattari's ritornello, the repetition of sensation, invokes duration as both a subversive force and the molecular memory that provides the organizational structure for territories.

The mark of duration in the concept of the ritornello is made plain in the following passage:

> Debussy ... Music molecularizes sound matter and in so doing becomes capable of harnessing nonsonorous forces such as Duration and Intensity. *Render Duration sonorous.* Let us recall Nietzsche's idea of the eternal return as a little ditty, a refrain [ritornello], but which captures the mute and unthinkable forces of the Cosmos.[15]

The capturing of unthinkable forces of chaos, the cosmos, is accomplished through the repetitive work of duration. The confluence of duration and the ritornello is unmistakable in this excerpt, and the task of the ritornello is to transcribe the becoming-mad of molecular duration with a heterogeneous rhythm. If 'the eternal return is the being of becoming,' then the past in-itself is the being of the ritornello. The disorganization of the identity break that we see in becoming-mad of duration, or in Klossowski's description of the experience of the eternal return, is given a framework by the circuits of the ritornello.

The appeal to music in Deleuze is a callback to Nietzsche as the possibility for expression of the forces of chaos.[16] The previous passage also reveals Deleuze's interpretation of duration as a kind of madness or chaos, which is consistent with his explication of becoming-mad as the subverted present in *The Logic of Sense.* In order for duration to be expressed in material reality, its forces must be repeated in sensation. Music is able to accomplish this by expressing points and counterpoints without subjecting heterogeneous elements to the logic of the same. Music can preserve unique durations by making them dance with rhythms that are impossible without maintaining their internal difference. When Deleuze says that Debussy molecularizes sound matter, he is specifically referring to the tendency of the ritornello to extract singularities from the unthinkable depths of matter and distribute them in rhythmic circles of expression. By molecularizing sound, the ritornello is drawing from the monument of ontological memory. Ontological memory is, after all, Deleuze's appropriation of Proust's pure past – Bergson's duration devoid of subjective or psychic perspective.

The fundamental difference between Proust's notion of reminiscence and the pure past and that of Bergson is that we have access to the pure past in Proust through involuntary memory. This access to the pure past is most famously exemplified by in *In Search of Lost Time* when the narrator tastes the madeleine soaked in lime blossom tea and he remembers the Combray of his childhood, as it was in-itself. It is not through the subjective work of representational thought that the pure past is accessed, an obstacle that Bergson realized and did not transgress. Proust, however, takes the pre-subjective realm of sensation as the bridge between the pure past and the individual. As Proust notes,

> It is a waste of effort for us to try to summon it [the pure past], all the exertions of our intelligence are useless. The past is hidden outside the realm of our intelligence and beyond its reach, in some material object (in the sensation that this material object would give us) which we do not suspect. It depends on chance whether we encounter this object before we die, or do not encounter it.[17]

The pure past, then, is a monument that is connected to experience through sensation, and the virtual levels of the ontological past serve as the backdrop to the ritornello. The role of chance in the encounter of the pure past involves the aleatory point on the line of Aion for Deleuze, whereby the distribution of singularities and their potential actualization are purely contingent and cannot be influenced by the subjective will. The cone of memory that Bergson theorized, and upon which Proust's notion of reminiscence depends, entails infinite circular levels that may be more or less condensed in the realm of sensation. The circularity of the conic levels of the monumental past provides the spiritual repetition of the ritornello in sensation.

Deleuze prefers the Proustian formulation of memory over Bergson's, for it eliminates the stark dualism one might perceive between matter and memory. Sensation is the point of connection between the virtual series and the actual bodies, and accordingly, it has its own type of becoming: sensory becoming. Sensory becoming maintains the trace of the never experienced pure past and a process between actuality and absolute becoming. As Deleuze remarks, the virtual levels in the cone of memory differ in kind from the actualized present, and 'duration is never contracted enough to be independent of the internal matter where it operates, and of the extension that it comes to contact.'[18] Duration is never divorced from matter and it carries the information internal to matter, regardless of its being attached to or divorced from a subject. Within the cone of memory, the pure past is constituted independently of a perceiving subject or a transcendental ego. The pure past is never experienced or perceived by the intellect, making it pre-subjective and inexorably connected to the molecular constitution of matter. We may also remark that the pure past is durational, and as Proust shows us, is the temporality of sensation.

The revolving virtual conic levels of the past produce the ritornello in sensation. Again, this accentuates the seemingly counterintuitive role of memory in the ritornello. It is counterintuitive because becoming and the eternal return are conceived as breaking with the past. We must remember, however, that it is the concrete, actualized past that is broken by the ritornello, as well as by the cone of ontological memory. The singularities of matter in actuality could not be extracted and distributed with any sense without a sub-representative operation of memory. Otherwise, we would never emerge from randomness and chaos of pure difference. The ontological pure past provides the grounding of sense and is repeated in sensation through its durational becoming.

'The whole of the refrain [ritornello] is the being of sensation. Monuments are refrains [ritornellos].'[19] Deleuze and Guattari reveal the Bergsonian influence in their conception of the ritornello, which is, as they have stated, Nietzsche's eternal return in sensation. The ritornello involves the Bergsonian influenced pure past of Proust in its appeal to the virtual levels of duration in sensation, as well as the eternal return of Nietzsche, characterized by ontological forgetting. The forgetting is of molar forms, and this is necessary in order for the activation of becoming that we see in duration, yet it is a remembrance of molecular matter to be repeated. The pure past provides a permeable border to matter that keeps a sensory expression from falling into nonsense or static. 'The material must be sufficiently deterritorialized to be molecularized and open onto something cosmic, instead of lapsing into a statistical heap.'[20] For Debussy to render duration sonorous a conceptual consistency of points and counterpoints must be repeated to produce resonance throughout other assemblages. Matter is released from its molar form in new sensory expression, but this expression enacts an open circuit in order to avoid falling into a black hole of insular self-referentiality. The intensities of matter on the plane of sensation are linked to virtual levels of the ontological past, opening up to contextual integration across temporalities.

When Deleuze discusses the two powers of ontological memory in *Proust and Signs* he does so in terms of difference in the past and repetition in the present, implying an internalized difference that is repeated by the ritornello in sensation.[21] None of the 'four iron collars' in the image of thought return in the condensation of the pure past; Combray arises out of indeterminacy as it was in-itself and bears no resemblance to the Combray which was experienced in the past of perception. There is a molecular resonance that emerges as a result of the repetition of the ontological past, but it evades the logic of representation and is 'monumental' in this sense. It is no coincidence that the ritornello is expressed in the same terms as the pure past in Deleuze's earlier works, such as *Proust and Signs*. The monument is a ritornello, just as ontological memory is monumental.

The monument is the creative force of ontological memory. Deleuze's famous dictum in *Proust and Signs*, 'To remember is to create,' is an expression of molecular memory, as an internalization of difference in the work of art.[22] Ontological memory is effectuated through qualitative connections between the past and the present, yet outside any perceived present or former present. The creative, heterogeneous power of ontological memory, or what is referred to as involuntary memory in *Proust and Signs*, involves a qualitative identity of two moments in sensation. That identity, though, is not at the ontological level, it is a by-product of the subjective encounter. Two moments in time are enveloped in one another in the present of sensation, but qualitative identity only arises when the subject attempts to discover its trans-temporal meaning. The ability of ontological memory to repeat two moments of internal difference in one sensory expression produces the new within the virtual levels of the past. Combray arises as a monument from the past in a novel fashion, as Combray that was never before experienced. Deleuze offers a distinction between voluntary memory, which is bound to a perceiving subject, and involuntary memory, which is the repetition of difference beyond subjective perception. The work of art draws on involuntary memory to produce the new in sensation, as we see in Deleuze's analysis of the madeleine scene in Proust:

> So long as we remain on the level of voluntary memory, Combray remains external to the madeleine, as the separable context of the past sensation. But this is the characteristic of involuntary memory: it internalizes the context, it makes the past context inseparable from present sensation. At the same time that the resemblance between two moments is transcended in the direction of a more profound identity, the contiguity that belonged to the past moment is transcended in the direction of a more profound difference. Combray rises up again in the present sensation in which its difference from the past sensation is internalized.[23]

The rising up of Combray as it was never experienced attests to the immemorial character of the pure past. As internalized difference of durational, virtual levels, the pure past is contracted and condensed in sensation, evoking an uncanny combination of similarity and difference. There is a simultaneous sensing of a past moment and a new truth. For instance, the desire to reread great novels, gleaning new insights and forming new connections with the work, reactivates the virtual levels produced in a work of art itself.

The artist creates a monument, which is 'time in a pure state,' accessed through sensation. Duration differs in kind from others and itself, and this difference is the unthinkable within thought. The artist's task is to take duration and express it in sensation, which is what Deleuze means when he says Debussy makes duration sonorous. Certain artists are able to establish a framework around and from within duration and render it qualitatively palpable to the individual. There remains a past that was never experienced within the work of art that is synthesized in new ways in sensation. Art opens the possibility for the encounter of newness in sensation by capturing the pure past and condensing it in matter. The very idea of connecting the past with the present in qualitative sensory experience arose from the literature of Proust. Without Proust's artistic expression of Bergson's cone of memory, the access to the pure past remained in the realm of the non-signified. By expressing the concept of involuntary memory in *In Search of Lost Time,* Proust pulled the experience of the pure past from the darkness of chaos without subjecting it to the logic of the same. The narrator's folding of the present and the past in the sensation of the tea-soaked madeleine created a monument to the production of the new through the virtuality of the past. This is accomplished not just at the level of literary theme, but also as a qualitative impression that echoes throughout all of sensory experience. The content and form of the novel collapse giving rise to new truths that are not bound by chronological time.

As Ronald Brogue explains, the monumental character of the work of art is its ability to conserve itself in an expression of eternity wrapped in the diverse durations of sensation, or as William Blake writes, 'To see a world in a grain of sand/And a heaven in a wild flower/Hold infinity in the palm of your hand/And eternity in an hour.'[24] The monumentality of the work of art consists of its ability to express the infinite in the finite, expressing time in a pure state and its being 'out of joint' at the same moment. The monument, as Bogue describes, is a construction of a house within sensation, a house understood as a structural organization of forces.[25] Much like Gaston Bachelard's analysis of the house as a concatenation of imagination and memory in *The Poetics of Space,* the monument of art invokes the repetition of the future and the virtuality of the pure past. For Bachelard, the house of our childhood is not an embodiment of an experienced past but is the poetic space for imagination and daydream. The work of imagination extracts the space of the past and gives it a significance that is immemorial.[26] The unreality of time and space that occurs in the memory of one's childhood home is the disjointed time that is eternalized in the work of art.

The expression of eternity in duration is repeated in the work of art. The virtual levels of the pure past are actualized and condensed in such a way as to produce innovation in expression. A poet who masterfully creates spatiotemporal worlds in his writing, and who, like Proust, addresses the resonance of the past in territories drawn around the ineffable, is Rainer Maria Rilke. In 'On the Edge of Night' Rilke thematizes and dramatizes the artist's ability to create a monument which stands alone. The following poem articulates the ritornello's power to resonate with other sensory blocs against the background of chaos.

> My room and this vastness,
> awake over the darkening land, –
> are one. I am a string,
> stretched tightly over wide
> raging resonances.
>
> Things are violin-bodies
> full of murmuring darkness:
> in it dreams the weeping of women,
> in it the grudge of the whole
> generations stirs in its sleep …
> I shall vibrate
> like silver; then everything
> beneath me will live,
> and whatever wanders lost in things
> will strive toward the light
> that from my dancing tone –
> around which the heavens pulse –
> through thin, pining rifts
> into the old
> abysses endlessly
> falls … [27]

It is quite easy to see the Deleuzian universe within the borders of this poem. The room is the territorialized forces of duration in sensation which open up to the chaos, the cosmos depicted by the vastness of the 'darkening land'. The narrator likens himself/herself to a musical instrument expressive of a multiplicity of resonances. In fact, we are taken from the subjective identity of the self, 'I am a string,' to the material object itself, 'things are violin-bodies.' The violin harnesses forces in duration and makes them sensible through musical resonance. By shifting seamlessly from subject to object as a locus for expressions of 'raging resonances,' Rilke portrays a universe unbound by the logic of identity. The musical resonances of the violin vibrate though the subject and object, eliminating both as a source of transcendent signification. That the violin-bodies are full of 'murmuring darkness' (recall the dark precursor from *Difference and Repetition*) – the vast darkness that is harnessed by the vibratory sensation of music – is indicative of the integration of difference in matters of expression.

The narrator's vibration, as an instrument of sense, breathes life into all that exists beneath him/her. The sub-representative, larval selves that synthesize to produce the identity of the self come alive with the repetition of difference in sensation. This vitality is interconnected to 'whatever wanders lost in things', which is also liberated through the non-numeric pulsation of duration in sound. Singularities in molar forms, in stratified 'things', are not locatable. The molecular duration of matter floats in a zone of indiscernibility and can be said to 'wander lost'.[28] The resonance of the violin deterritorializes matter as singularities are released onto abyss of darkness in 'pining rifts'. Vibratory sound creates a broken circle that repeats in waves between subject, object, a-subjective selves and onto the abyss of darkness: chaos. The release of molecular matter through rifts involves a repetition of fragmentation. The rift is a fissure, a crack in identity that conveys a self-differing. The fragmentation exposed by the resonance of the violin is repeated in a plurality of rifts in its opening up onto the cosmos.

Just as we see with Deleuze, Rilke does not paint a stark separation between the stratified forms of things and the inaudible, inexpressible forces of the abyss. Things include that which wanders lost, and the same space that captures durations, the violin, is not disconnected from the murmur of darkness. There remains an ungrounded darkness within the conditions of material expression. And while there is an explicit oneness spanning from the vastness of the dark landscape to the singular vibrations of bodies, this liminal connection consists of fragmentation, or rifts.

The darkness of 'On the Edge of Night' is synonymous with chaos in Deleuze, or a term that Deleuze and Guattari borrow from James Joyce, a chaosmos.[29] Vibrations that territorialize certain forces of chaos – this composed chaos – do not produce constituted individuals but are durational expressions on the plane of composition. The musical vibrations preserve themselves in sensation thus creating a resonance between the actual body of the violin and the murmur of darkness, or Rilke's cosmos. The monument of the work of art cannot compose chaos without the virtual acting as a medium. What one perceives as the timeless nature of the work of art is a complicated product of temporal synthesis.

Through the conditions of subjectivity and objectivity, the artist, the violin-body, employs involuntary memory to produce an aesthetic universe that is entirely impersonal. Like the sonorous vibrations that depart from the narrator and from the object in Rilke, the resonances of art rely upon the virtuality of the pure past.[30] The element of wandering lost within things is analogous to an ontological search in Proust. The term 'lost' implies a desire or search for destination. A mirror of Deleuze's analysis of Proust, resonance in 'On the Edge of Night' is the desired destination of lost time, or in Rilke's case, lost matter. Resonance is a repetition of sensation, and the self-differing of the pure past returns. This return revolves around the forgetting of molar forms and the remembrance of a past that never was, or the non-locatable molecular being of matter.

Actual objects form circuits with virtual images, and this division includes the chronology of the passing present and the ephemeral time of the virtual. The virtual is said to be 'ephemeral' because its duration is shorter than any measurable time from the perspective of the actual. The virtual is not only infinitesimally brief from the vantage point of the actual, but also infinitely long, longer than any measured time. The length of virtual time is attributable to the self-preservation of the pure past as such.[31] It is problematic to talk about the temporality of the virtual in terms of chronological time, as it differs in kind from the measured present. When Deleuze and Guattari state that 'the whole of the refrain [ritornello] is the being of sensation,' they are noting the role of the pure past and involuntary, ontological memory as the ground of art.[32]

The ritornello, the little return in sensation, is not a strict break of the past into the production of the new in the future. While Deleuze, via Klossowski and Nietzsche, stresses the necessity of forgetting for the dramatization of the eternal return, it would be fallacious to claim that the ritornello, as a territorializing function in sensation, performs an absolute break from memory. Without the durational, non-metric conic levels of the pure past Debussy would never have created rhythmic sound blocs. To 'render duration sonorous' does not mean that the musical artist destroys all traces of ontological memory, but, rather, s/he composes the subversive, intensive temporality that reflects aesthetic sensibility. If all of expression were devoid of memory, we would have stockpiles of percepts that have no sense of consistency or condensation. The virtual cone of the pure past provides heterogeneous consistency through the condensation of its virtual levels. Each level of the pure past includes the totality, which is an open totality, constantly integrating the never experienced pure present.

While Deleuze often isolates the three syntheses of time in his analyses, it is important to remember that all three are synthesized intra-temporally, and no temporal synthesis operates independently of the others. In *Proust and Signs* the creative power of memory is emphasized, yet art surpasses the spiritual repetition of the past through the repetition of style.[33] The differential nature of the pure past paves the way for art to repeat itself, emptying past conditions in the moment of sensation. Despite the ritornello's ungrounding of the past in the monument of art, art is never fully beyond the synthesis of the past. The virtual is characterized by durational becoming, wherein the chronological present undergoes a whirring subversion of identity. The virtual is in-itself differential and resistant to the logic of the same, which we see in the temporal split of the quasi-cause in the constitution of the pure past. For this reason, Deleuze himself stresses the inter-syntheses of time in the repetition of art:

> Perhaps the highest object of art is to bring into play simultaneously all these repetitions, with their differences in kind and rhythm, their respective displacements and disguises, their divergences and decentrings; to embed them in one another and to envelop one or the other in illusions the 'effect' of which varies in each case.[34]

Art is generally associated with the third synthesis of time (the future) for Deleuze, and at its best integrates and expresses the repetition of the ground, as well as the repetition of ungrounding. Upon reflection, it is clear why this would be the case, for a repetition of mere ungrounding would lack the potential for resonance with other assemblages, other constructed worlds and concepts. Without any sense of territory at the molecular level, expression would be purely evanescent. Absolute absence of ontological memory would render apprehension and assemblage impossible. Strictly speaking, material expression in sensation requires ontological mapping at the molecular level. This mapping differs from actual spatial coordinates, as it operates at the sub-representative level. The repetition of the differential elements of the pure past in the present of sensation is the meaning of the ritornello.

Deleuze claims in *Difference and Repetition* that the differential elements of the pure past are solely between virtual levels, yet not internal to the levels themselves.[35] The circles of the pure past have not yet been unwound into the straight line of the eternal return, and for this reason there is the risk of the ground of the past falling into a representation of itself in its actualization. The present that evades perception gets swept into the levels of the pure past as it splits off like an ephemeral ghost of the passing present. Dual moments of the present, as perceived and never perceived, contribute to the mirror images of virtual images. The difference in kind between the passing present and the elusive present creates an internal difference within the levels of the pure past in addition to the difference found between the virtual levels. What I am calling the elusive present, a present that never passes through the mechanism of perception, is the 'instant', the aleatory point of the quasi-cause, from *The Logic of Sense*, or what was articulated in Chapter 1 as Deleuze's appropriation of the Moment from *Thus Spoke Zarathustra*. As we recall, Zarathustra declares that there are two opposing lanes of eternity, one running forward, and one running backward, and they come together at a gateway inscribed, 'Moment'. Zarathustra speaks: 'Behold this moment!' I went on. 'From this gateway Moment a long, eternal lane runs *back*: an eternity lies behind us.'[36] This backward moving lane is what most interests Deleuze. In Deleuzian terms, the actual, forward lane and the virtual, backward lane that repeats difference, come together at the gateway of the Moment. The Moment counter-actualizes the forward moving lane, distributing its singularities along the backward moving lane where what returns is not the same. The Moment not only creates chaos out of the two opposing lanes of eternity, as the actual and the virtual, but also connects the lane of eternal return of ontological memory (the forward lane of sensory becoming/ the ritornello) and the lane of the eternal return of ontological forgetting (the backward lane of absolute becoming/the line of Aion). Thus, the Moment of the quasi-cause counter-actualizes line-blocs in sensation and redistributes them in series along the line of Aion in ideation. The Moment splits eternally into the always already and the eternally not yet.

To briefly recapitulate, the pure Moment is not the same as duration, and hence it is not itself the subversion of the chronological present, nor is it the actualized present. The Moment is a ghost of the passing present and *is not*, yet it haunts every present moment that constitutes the pure past. Since blocs of becoming are also mobilized through an encounter of the quasi-cause, simulacra integrate this haunting in a transformation into phantasms on the line of Aion. The elusive other present sparks the unravelling of the circle of the past into the straight line of the future. It functions as a differential operation of zero duration with which each 'present present' engages in the virtual levels of the past as such. The proliferation of the elusive present, differing in kind from duration and from the actual present, injects the levels of the past with difference. As a consequence of the distribution of the elusive present in the pure past, difference is found between levels and within the levels, for identity is fragmented from the former present to its expansion within the context of the pure past. The perverse Moment forces the circles of the past to unfold as a repetition of the future at the same time that it counter-actualizes the present. The Moment extracts the singularities of the passing present and distributes them into the cone of memory, each resonating among all other levels.

To claim that the whole of the ritornello is the being of sensation is the same as saying that the repetition of all de-actualized time is the being of sensation. Sensation houses the expressed syntheses of time in their heterogeneity. The Moment, the elusive present of zero duration, precludes the repetition of the same. Simply because the past is the ground of being does not mean that the repetition of the past produces the same. In Deleuze's framework this is impossible, for the past is not simply a collection of prior presents, but it is ontologically constructed between the cracks of identity. The relationship between the ritornello and ontological memory is unmistakable. This is not the same eternal return from *Difference and Repetition*, nor is it the line of Aion from *The Logic of Sense*. All of the three of the mentioned formulations of the eternal return bear some primordial relation to the in-between. The ritornello is an in-between that corresponds to the differential elements of the pure past. Furthermore, the ritornello is the return that belongs to the plane of sensation, or composition, while the eternal return and the line of Aion belong to the series of events on the plane of immanence. These two planes, while interconnected, correspond to unique temporalities and unique concepts of becoming. Perhaps Ronald Brogue said it best when he distinguished between the artist's plane of composition and the philosopher's plane of immanence: 'Art's "plane of composition", we might say, is one of embodied becoming, philosophy's "plane of immanence" one of disembodied becoming.'[37]

The work of art composes chaotic forces in sensation through the repetitive movement of the ritornello. The embodied becoming that structures the plane of composition is the becoming-mad of *The Logic of Sense*. That is to say, the ritornello is the eternal return reaching into the realm of sensation, thus it carries the ontological memory of qualitative sense, as seen in Proust. Once the eternal return extends into sensation, releasing matter from actuality and structures of sameness, it is no longer a purely 'empty form of time'. As discussed in Chapter 3, the northern line of much of modern art fragments forms, subordinating them to the self-referential a-logical whirls of sense. The northern line is a ritornello.

Subversion of the chronological present and the actual forms contained therein requires an ontological, molecular memory of the arrangements of said forms. The singularities extracted from molar forms and reterritorialized in material expression endure to some extent. The duration of singularities in sensation involves what Bogue calls 'embodied becoming'. It is embodied in the sense that there is a territory, a kind of sensory circle, drawn in space and time, yet still not embodied in terms of corporeal, organic being. A line of the territory, like a bird song, is anomalous and maintains the particles of matter within a zone of indiscernibility, as they wander 'lost in things'.

The milieu and the Ritornello

The ritornello, the Nietzschean eternal return as a little ditty, embodies Nietzsche's notion of action at a distance.[38] In fact, Deleuze describes the refrain's acting at a distance in resonant echoes from *Difference and Repetition* to *A Thousand Plateaus*.[39] The resonant milieus that are composed in sensation do not resemble that which is drawn. For example, a virtual level of the past acts at a distance upon the action produced by its contraction in the present. The virtual levels of the past are milieus that resonate throughout the totality of ontological memory, and this revolving cone's expression in sensation is the ritornello. Bergson, Proust and Nietzsche are grafted together into the ritornello, a molar forgetting, and a molecular reminiscence. Virtual milieus bounce off of one another like waves in the ocean of sensation.

Another perfect example of the ritornello can be found in László Krasznahorkai's *The Melancholy of Resistance* when Mr. Ezster attempts to carve out a territory amid the chaos of the small Hungarian hamlet. By building a living space within his home for the star-gazing Valuska, Eszter creates a becoming in sensation where Valuska's naive reverence of a cosmos in harmony repeats in Eszter's detuning of his piano to reflect the celestial musical temperament that predated Andreas Werckmeister's harmonizing temperament of the equal measure in twelve tonnes. The in-between territory draws a circle within chaos and forms a milieu, a place where Valuska and Eszter can repeat, becoming with disharmony in sensation, released from their respective, prior subjective points of view.

The French *milieu* carries the counterpoints of location and indiscernibility as heterogeneous tendencies within the same word. As in English, *milieu* signifies a setting, a sense of place, yet even stronger are the references to the in-between, of being in the middle, such as *au milieu*. The milieu is not a measured set of spatial coordinates in corporeal being, and it is not the auxiliary space of homogeneous time either. The milieu is a virtual 'location' that defies the quantitative mechanisms of actual measure. Milieus are virtual levels that play off each other in rhythms, rather than metre or melody. Deleuze and Guattari reveal the ontological status of the milieu as in-between and its correlative composition of chaos:

> The notion of the milieu is not unitary: not only does the living thing continually pass from one milieu to another, but the milieus pass into one another; they are essentially communicating. The milieus are open to chaos, which threatens them with exhaustion or intrusion. Rhythm is the milieus' answer to chaos. What chaos and rhythm have in common is the in-between – between two milieus, rhythm-chaos or the chaosmos. ... In this in-between, chaos becomes rhythm, not inexorably, but it has a chance to. Chaos is not the opposite of rhythm, but the milieu of all milieus.[40]

The directional vectors that characterize chaos, effecting resonating milieus, form a rhythm of forces that are expressed in sensation. A great artist is able to express the different levels of vibrating milieus and express them in such a way as to preserve their heterogeneity. Without subjecting rhythms to the homogeneity of representational forms, the artist makes material the differential elements of the virtual past and the elusive present. The perverse Moment pulls the artistic expression out of joint, yet preserves its duration as a perpetual subversion of the actual present; this is the monumental character of the work of art. The ritornello repeats the rhythmic vibrations of chaos, rendering the in-between sensory. This brings us back to Rilke's 'On the Edge of Night' and its treatment of the in-between in resonant echoes from chaos to corporeal being.

The title 'On the Edge of Night' symbolizes the intermezzo of the ritornello. The resonance of music happens between night and day, between the darkness of chaos and the light of constituted individuals. The poem itself takes place in the middle, within the process of expression. The narrator's room is automatically united with vast darkness from the outset as s/he and things serve as mouthpieces for the resonant vibrations of chaos. The cosmic forces within matter yearn to be released through the pulsation of music. Deleuze and Guattari repeat the molecular release of matter onto the cosmic scale expressed in Rilke's poem when they state, 'When forces become necessarily cosmic, material becomes necessarily molecular, with enormous force operating in an infinitesimal space.'[41] This tendency of material expression finds its corollary in Rilke. From the darkness through the vibrating strings of the violin to the release of material forces in pining rifts that find themselves again in the darkness of the abyss, the content of the poem follows the course of Deleuze's continually broken line. Rilke's universe depicts the composition of the forces of chaos in the work of art through his theme of the musicality of the violin, as well as through the boundary drawn by the poem itself. Material forms are released from stratification by the cracks in their identity that reconnect with the milieu of milieus, chaos. The heterogeneous components of the poem are unified without their being reduced to the same. Just as the resonance of milieus communicates difference in the ritornello, the vibrations of 'On the Edge of Night' retain the singularity of that which is repeated, forming a line of individuation that expresses different temporal rhythms.

The ritornello is a variation on Nietzsche's eternal return but extended into the logic of sensation. As we have seen, the ritornello uses resonant milieus to organize space-time in an expression of the new. What is said to be pressed out into sensation are the different repetitions of time. The successful work of art will find a way to preserve the difference between virtual milieus while translating into the logic of the sensible in percepts and affects. The material conditions of an expression may deteriorate or be destroyed, but its material history is independent from its production of blocs of sensation whose singularities are distributed into divergent virtual series at the conceptual level. Points and counterpoints converge and diverge in undulating waves, described by Nietzsche as the will to power, form-fleeing whirlpools of sensation. Like whirlpools with varying durations, there is a fuzzy circle drawn within the chaotic forces creating affects and percepts that render the imperceptible perceptible.

What fundamentally separates the eternal return as the pure and empty form of time from the ritornello – the eternal return in sensation – is the ontological memory of molecular duration. Both formulations of the eternal return require an element of forgetting corresponding to their respective planes. The ritornello's plane is composition, where chaos is composed and organizes itself according to the logic of sensation. Despite being auto-productive and unbound by subjectivity or objectivity, ritornellos retain an ontological memory of the material forms they fracture in a deterritorializing process. The molecular history of matter, which is altogether different from chronological history of actualized presents, is integrated into the network of virtual levels in the pure past, the Bergsonian cone of memory. The singularities of matter in the present are de-actualized by the perverse Moment, the ghost of the actual present at the tip of the cone. Taking a cue from Bergson's *Matter and Memory*, Deleuze's concept of matter involves a temporal circuit of virtual images and actual objects, the latter being inseparable from the former. This close circle creates what Deleuze calls 'a time crystal', which is essentially the Proustian notion of 'a little time in a pure state'.

The time crystal as Ritornello

Ontological memory, as it folds qualitative difference in one moment of sensation in Proust, bears directly upon the notion of the ritornello. The temporal split mentioned earlier in the chapter, where the present is injected with internal difference of the perverse Moment, splits the present into the immediate past and the imminent future. The two sides of this crystal, actual and virtual, are held together by the in-itself of the pure past.[42] The two mirror images that form the time crystal are always open onto the future and do not form closed circuits. As a result, the virtual image is in a perpetual process of de-actualizing the present, and the former present is never absent of the perverse Moment's de-actualization. A former present may at any time have its molecular matter released into new divergent series; both images of the time crystal are thus engaged in an embodied, sensory becoming. Borrowing from Bergson, Deleuze explains the heterogeneous temporality that departs from the time crystal:

> What constitutes the crystal-image is the most fundamental operation of time: since the past is constituted not after the present that it was but at the same time, time has to split itself in two at each moment as present and past, which differ from each other in nature, or, what amounts to the same thing, it has to split the present in two heterogeneous directions, one of which is launched towards the future while the other falls into the past.[43]

The two jets of the present as pure past and former present form a circuit at the intersection of the past and future, the perverse Moment. Hence, the circuit of the present includes the virtual images of the past along with the actual forms of matter, and this is the time crystal. The time crystal, as the instance of the heterogeneous split of the present, is not locatable, and its openness produces a zone of indiscernibility that cannot be pinpointed by the mechanisms of chronological time.

It should not be surprising, then, when Deleuze remarks on the inter-circularity of the circuits throughout the totality of the past. The time crystal responds to its own internal limits, territories drawn through particular milieus, as well as an opening onto other circuits in the universe. The virtual levels of the past are varying degrees of the contracted whole and each level contains the totality in a more or less condensed degree. Different worlds, dreams and memories all depend upon the varying condensation of the temporal circuits that connect the virtual and the actual. The time crystal is itself a small, relative circuit that resonates with other relative, deeper circuits of the pure past.[44] Within the continuum of the actual and the virtual is where dreams, memories and other worlds circulate. There is a precise term that signifies the space between these two extremes: sensation. The communication among resonating time crystals follows the dictates of sensory becoming, where duration subverts the measured present yet is not frozen in the reified forms of the actual.

What can the time crystal tell us about the ritornello? Deleuze responds unequivocally, 'The crystal-image is as much a matter of sound as it is optical, and Félix Guattari was right to define the crystal of time as being a "ritornello" par excellence'.[45] The import of ontological memory for the ritornello is 'the raising or falling back of pasts which are preserved'. The association of the time crystal with the ritornello discloses the concept's affinity with ontological memory. Resonant waves of the pure past are expressed in sensation through the mechanism of the ritornello. The varying milieus or levels of the past which are territorialized as matter are deterritorialized, and the absolute forgetting formulated in Nietzsche's eternal return is assimilated into a Bergsonian-Proustian universe of memory. By developing a theory of what DeLanda has called 'intensive selves', pre-subjective or passive selves, Deleuze has opened the space for the flow of the pure past into the qualitative sensation of the present. Deleuze is not ambivalent about his hybrid construction out of Proust's reminiscence and Nietzsche's eternal return, as ontological memory is able to create difference and is not merely a repetition of the same. He writes, 'The Proustian formula "a little time in its pure state" refers first to the pure past, the in-itself of the past or the erotic syntheses of time, but more profoundly to the pure and empty form of time, the ultimate synthesis, that of the death instinct which leads to the eternity of the return in time.'[46] Time in a pure state is how Deleuze characterizes ontological memory, as well as the time crystal. The virtual-actual circuit of the time crystal, modelled off of Bergson's famous circuit of memory, demonstrates how the pure past interacts with the present of perception. When Deleuze proclaims that the time crystal is a ritornello *par excellence* he is recounting the synthesis of the pure past and the pure difference of the future in one fell swoop. The ritornello is the eternal return in sensation, which expresses the ontological memory of the pure past. Sensation is the non-metric pulsation between the virtual and the actual where becoming is embodied and evinces duration; and as soon as the eternal return enters into the logic of sensation its action is at a distance forming the ritornello.

Initially, it might appear problematic or inconsistent for Deleuze to have such distinct formulations of the eternal return. One form, the ritornello, is embedded in ontological, molecular memory, while the other is the synthesis of the future, the pure and empty form of time. The different temporal frameworks of each of the two forms of the eternal return, the ritornello and the line of Aion, might seem to pose a conceptual roadblock for Deleuze's ontology. How might the same concept be simultaneously tied to duration while also being identified with the duration-less future? The two opposing temporal features of memory and forgetting are different *tendencies* of the same concept. As is the case with becoming, the eternal return is a multiplicity that corresponds to the plane upon which it is operating. The rhizome, the line continually broken in its path from ground to unground, determines the eternal return in Deleuze's ontology.

The concept of the eternal return is a Deleuzian concept through and through. Its consistency is not attributable to a hierarchical distribution of Being but is an anarchic transcendental empiricism. The tripartite features of material: its molecular matter, its particular relationship to forces and its self-referential circuit of consistency do not structure matter according to a transcendental signifier. On the contrary, materiality develops its own tendencies and it is immanent to itself and not to something else. The consistency of a transcendental empiricism does not occur vertically, but transversally. Resonant circuits maintain heterogeneous elements without mixing them together or making them uniform. The eternal return functions in the conceptual manner detailed by Deleuze and Guattari: 'As whole it is absolute, but insofar as it is fragmentary it is relative. It is *infinite through its survey or its speed but finite through its movement that traces the contour of its components.*'[47] The eternal return is the repetition of difference within Deleuze's ontology, and to that extent it is absolute – nothing can escape the centrifugal force of the eternal return. It is also relative in its expression and the effects and affects it produces are fragmented and heterogeneous. Consequentially, the eternal return in sensation operates as a ritornello, while on the plane of immanence it operates as the line of Aion.

Therefore, the eternal return consists of varying temporal rhythms that integrate the logic of materiality (or lack thereof) as a mode of its return. For example, sensation subverts chronological time, causing sensory blocs to relate to difference as absolute alterity. Difference resounds between the levels of the pure past in sensation and eternally returns as otherness. The eternal return in sensation, the ritornello, is not an empty form of time, for it revolutionizes ontological memory by making matter that which is infinitely other. Matter is forced to resist its previous arrangements without losing the cache of molecular memory. The series of events in ideational or absolute becoming are absent of duration and operate according to the dictates of the pure and empty form of time. Aion employs the instant, or the 'perverse Moment', as the inclusive disjunction between the pure past and the future, between the ritornello and the line of Aion.

The paradox of the untimely

As was discussed in Chapter 1, the eternal return referred to as the third synthesis of time in *Difference and Repetition* is referred to as the line of Aion in *The Logic of Sense*. The interchangeability of these two terms is widely recognized in the secondary literature on Deleuze. Keith Ansell-Pearson, a scholar whose knowledge of Bergson has illuminated much of the Bergsonian concepts hiding within the concepts of Deleuze, notes that 'Deleuze refers to the third synthesis of time as the pure and empty form of time, associating it with the elusive time of Aion.'[48] This remark is not in the least controversial, as Deleuze himself used the same expression of 'the pure and empty form of time' to refer to both the future and the line of Aion. The line of Aion is the circle of the second synthesis, the pure past, broken and stretched out. The pure past cannot produce the new without allowing a passage from the present towards the future. When Pearson outlines the 'secret intimacy between the pure past and the future' we notice that the distinction between the two temporal syntheses is not as sharp as would initially appear. The difference within the levels of the pure past is oriented towards the future, which is why Proust's experience of Combray is able to be experienced in its future: the sensation of the tea-soaked madeleine as internalized difference. The present cannot pass without the concurrent constitution of the pure past, as has been discussed countless times in textual attempts to parse out Deleuze's innovative system of temporality, but the pure past cannot be mobilized without the ungrounding machinery of the future.

To complicate matters, Deleuze also reveals that the eternal return is the being of becoming. This proclamation is complex, because Deleuze's ontology does not conform to substance metaphysics where Being reigns supreme. The phrase is an ontological riddle. Being is a loaded concept, and in a sense, we could say that the entirety of Deleuze's oeuvre is an attempt to explicate the proposition that the eternal return is the being of becoming. Throughout Deleuze's works, particularly *Nietzsche and Philosophy*, it is clear that what returns is the act of returning itself. The pure and empty form of time is the being of becoming, fusing temporality and ontology. As he phrases it himself, Deleuze remarks, 'As we have seen, the condition of the action by default does not return; the condition of the agent by default does not return; all that returns, the eternal return, is the *unconditioned* in the product.'[49] It is the selectivity of the eternal return that keeps the first two syntheses from returning, ultimately. The eternal return as the third synthesis shatters the time crystal, purging its content and affirming itself in its return. Nothing that existed in actual form returns in the third synthesis, neither partially nor wholly. All associative chains of memory break, accomplishing what the ritornello was unable to do, namely enact a repetition of pure forgetting.

The line of Aion and the eternal return were shown in Chapter 1 to be different terms for the same temporal process. There is no difference between them, for they are both characterized as the stretched out circle of time, time out of joint, and the pure and empty form of time. Deleuze does not equivocate about the eternal return being the third synthesis of time in *Difference and Repetition*: the eternal return is the future. In *The Logic of Sense* Deleuze again refers to the pure and empty form of time, though this time he uses the figure of Aion to denote the unwound line of time. We could stop there and accept the line of Aion as being another term for the future, but its paradoxical nature requires an examination of the process of the future. Complicating the eternal return's synthesis of the future, Deleuze says, 'Always already passed and eternally yet to come, Aion is the eternal truth of time: *pure empty form of time*, which has freed itself of its present corporeal content and has thereby unwound its own circle, stretching itself out in a straight line.'[50] The consilience of the future as a synthesis and the division of the future and the past by the same mechanism calls for disambiguation. The paradoxical nature of the line of Aion, as that which is always already and eternally yet-to-come, will be analysed from the standpoint of the broken circle, as well as from the standpoint of the Moment. In the process of our analysis, the temporal poles of the line of Aion as past<-->future division, on the one hand, and the eternal return as the synthesis of the future, on the other, will be reconciled.

Differentiation and the moment: 'Once ...'

Time must be understood and lived as out of joint, and seen as a straight line which mercilessly eliminates those who embark upon it, who come upon the scene but repeat once and for all.[51]

Chapter 1 provided a preliminary sketch of the eternal return as it is formulated in *Difference and Repetition* and then repeated as the line of Aion in *The Logic of Sense,* as well as the function of the Moment as the aleatory point that divides the past and the future. The Moment serves as the quasi-causal operator that distributes difference throughout the series of events in static genesis. As will be shown, the line of Aion is Deleuze's perspective of the eternal return from the point of the Moment. The dualist phenomenal properties of light as both wavelength and particle do not amount to an inconsistency in scientific function, and such is the case with the eternal return. The eternal return as the third synthesis is often examined externally in its linearity, the line of Aion, and occasionally it is examined internally as the perverse Moment. The two vantage points combine to form a comprehensive study of the eternal return; a supplement to its development in *Difference and Repetition* as repetition for itself. Deleuze's interpretation of the calculus reinforces the combination of two inverse perspectives in a unified theory of the eternal return. Against Hegel, and with the help of Leibniz, he models the eternal return on the inverse relation of differential and integral calculus. We can map the quasi-causal Moment onto an emphasis on differentials, while the line itself maps onto the integral series of the relation. Understanding from the outset that the dualist nature of the eternal return is only a surface distinction of perspective helps contextualize the following passage. Within the same text, Deleuze identifies the eternal return and the line of Aion on the same terms, and then he goes on to differentiate between them:

> Upon this straight line of Aion, there is also an eternal return, as the most terrible labyrinth of which Borges spoke – one very different from the circular or monocentered return of Chronos: an eternal return which is no longer that of individuals, persons, and worlds, but only of pure events which the instant, displaced over the line, goes on dividing into already past and yet to come.[52]

Deleuze is pinpointing the two different aspects of the eternal return as the proliferation of series: line, as well as the operation of difference: Moment. The line of Aion is defined by the infinite return of the disembodied Moment as an operator of difference. The eternal return upon the line of Aion is not the return of forms, identities or substance. What returns is process, not product. Not even the dreams and memories that characterize the realm of sensation return upon the line of Aion. The eternal return, the 'terrible' Borgesian labyrinth, is the selfsame line of Aion; the catch to this formulation is that neither the line of Aion nor the eternal return assumes an identity.

To get a full grasp of the meaning of the line of Aion as a labyrinth, one must trace Deleuze's re-appropriation of Borges. In *The Non-Philosophy of Gilles Deleuze* Gregg Lambert connects the temporal implications of the straight line of time with reference to Borges, as a corrective to Leibniz. Lambert shows how Borges, closer to the side of Nietzsche than Leibniz in relation to identity, adopts fiction as an affirmation of chaos at the expense of truth.[53] The Leibnizian elaboration of incompossible worlds opens the door for the creative power of the false in Borges. The status of truth has always been made precarious by questions of time, says Deleuze, and Leibniz offers an innovative alternative to the idea of contradiction in relation to time. Consider the following example: there may or may not be an avalanche on the mountain outside my window tomorrow; it is a distinct possibility one way or another. However, no matter what happens tomorrow, one of the previous possibilities will appear to have been an impossibility. If there is an avalanche tomorrow, then the possibility that there would not be an avalanche seems to actually have been impossible. Leibniz's response to the problem of possibility in time is the notion of compossibility. Both of the possibilities of the avalanche happening or not happening are said to be true, but not in the same world; the two exclusionary events are compossible in different worlds but are incompossible in the same one.

It would seem that truth was rescued from the crisis of possibility, but as Deleuze notes, the power of the false is affirmed in the notion of incompossibility. He says, 'For nothing prevents us from affirming that incompossibles belong to the same world, that incompossible worlds belong to the same universe.'[54] This is the critical point where Deleuze's re-appropriation of the eternal return departs from Leibniz's limits of compossibility in favour of Borges's narrative temporality, as seen in 'The Garden of Forking Paths.'[55] In 'The Garden of Forking Paths' a temporal world of infinite forking series is depicted, as conceived by the fictional character, Ts'ui Pên. This universe consists of

> an infinite series of times, in a growing, dizzying net of divergent, convergent and parallel times. This network of times which approached one another, forked, broke off, or were unaware of one another for centuries, embraces *all* possibilities of time. We do not exist in the majority of these times; in some you exist and not I; in other I, and not you; in others, both of us.[56]

As in Borges's garden of forking paths, the incompossibilities of different worlds, contrary to Leibniz's conception, belong to the same universe and are variations of one story. Incompossible presents are traversed while one passes through levels of the past that never were. Deleuze goes on to explain the implications of a universe comprising incompossibilities when he says, 'This is Borges's reply to Leibniz: the straight line as force of time, as labyrinth of time, is also the line which forks and keeps on forking, passing through *incompossible presents*, returning to *not-necessarily true pasts*.'[57] Different identities and lives are affirmed simultaneously by the line of time, and each possibility creates an infinite series of forks to divergent futures. The fictional nature of time is a necessary consequence of a universe of multiplicities devoid of individuality.

The forking of divergent futures described by Borges's labyrinth of time is a perfect depiction of a rhizome. There is no ultimate centre that serves as an organizing principle and no beginning or end of time. The Moment creates a nexus of infinite 'meanwhiles' [*entre-temps*] that are traversed at every step within the labyrinth. Infinite identities are affirmed in one Moment corresponding to the divergent series of incompossible presents. The 'not-necessarily true pasts' are repeated in the differentiation of divergent incompossible presents within the same system and refer to the future's ungrounding of the past. This conception of time as a labyrinth relies upon each incompossible present serving as a fork for future paths where 'all possible outcomes occur'.[58] Everything changes upon the line of time without anything happening.[59]

The proliferation of divergent series upon the line of time necessarily entails a conception of an open moment. The Moment opens onto possible simultaneous futures and recurs upon the line of Aion. Deleuze uses differential calculus for his metaphysical interpretation of the Moment in time. According to Simon Duffy, Deleuze's interpretation of differential calculus as infinitesimal bears directly upon the operation of the Moment. He explains that Deleuze rejects the opposition of differential and integral calculus proposed by Hegel's dialectical logic and opts instead for an infinitesimal interpretation of differential calculus that accounts for integration.[60] The departure from Hegelian logic creates an open proliferation of mathematical series, as opposed to dialectical sublation of difference. Duffy's analysis discloses the function of the Moment as a differential operator in divergent mathematical series. He explains how Deleuze's appropriation of the calculus prefigures the eternal return of the perverse Moment in sub-representational time:

> The differential point of view of the infinitesimal calculus represents not a moment that can simply be sublated and subsumed within the dialectical progression of history, but rather an opening, providing an alternative trajectory for the construction of an alternative history of mathematics; it actually anticipates the return of the infinitesimal in the differential calculus, or non-standard analysis, of contemporary mathematics.[61]

In conjunction with a Spinozist logic of expression as reconciliation for the finite and infinite, for the discontinuous and continuous, Deleuze employs Leibniz's theory of integral calculus to understand differential relations. Integration is not only the summation of differentials, explains Duffy, but also the inverse of the differential relation.[62] The infinitesimal in the differential relation is no doubt a model for the Moment, the incompossible present, on the line of Aion. As the infinitely small quantities in a differential relation approach zero, vanishing, the relationality of the function remains nonetheless intact. The differential dx exists as a vanishing quantity of x, just as dy exists as a vanishing quantity of y, and while approaching 0, they nevertheless exist but are infinitesimal and smaller than any measurable quantity. What is unique in the dy/dx relation is that the terms approach 0 and vanish, yet the relation itself is determinable. The Moment acts as the differential in the equation $dy/dx = 0/0$ when applied to Duffy's analysis of differentials.

> When the differentials are represented as being equal to zero, the relation can no longer be said to exist since the relation between two zeros is zero, that is $0/0 = 0$; there is no relation between two things that do not exist. However, the differentials actually do exist. They exist as vanishing quantities insofar as they continue to vanish as quantities rather than having already vanished as quantities. Therefore, despite the fact that, strictly speaking, they equal zero, they are still not yet, or not equal to, zero.[63]

From Deleuze's infinitesimal view of differential calculus the vanishing quantities are not treated as finite, thus they disappear as determinable terms in their relationality without disappearing completely. The differentials are in a constant process of vanishing, always approaching zero. This mathematical account of vanishing quantity mimics the infinite subdivision of the past and the future from the perspective of the Moment. The Moment is indeterminable as a differential and has no duration; its quantity is intensive. The vanishing process of the differential relation creates a division between always already and not yet. Terms in a function are simultaneously already vanishing while not yet vanished. This division makes the differential, as well as its metaphysical counterpart, the Moment, untimely. The Moment is the differential element in Deleuze's ontology that releases molecular duration from matter and sensation, bringing it into the static genesis of pure events. Deleuze's Moment is the eluded present operating as a quasi-cause at the peak of memory. Being emptied of duration and definable terms, the Moment is time pulled out of joint; it is neither in time, nor eternal.

The untimely, while not situated *in* time, is closely aligned with the future. It is counter to time while acting upon time and the future. The future is not to be conceived as a future 'now', but rather, a disjunctive synthesis. As opposed to thinking of the untimely as non-temporal, it would best be thought of as the truth of temporality. The incompossible presents which fork into divergent futures along the line of Aion are affirmed in a disjunctive synthesis, and the heterogeneity of the labyrinth is preserved. As Deleuze notes, 'The untimely is attained in relation to the most distant past, by the reversal of Platonism; in relation to the present, by the simulacrum conceived as the edge of critical modernity; in relation to the future, it is attained in the phantasm of the eternal return as belief in the future.'[64] As Deleuze relates the untimely to the three syntheses of time, it becomes clear that he is referring to them through the lens of the Moment. First, as the ground of time, the distant past becomes differentiated through the operator of the perverse Moment overturning the logic of the same seen in Platonic reminiscence. Second, we have the foundation of time, the present of habit, which is inverted as the eluded present and is the ephemera of the passing present where the concept of the original is replaced by the concept of simulacrum. Third, the groundlessness of time, the eternal return of the future, and its phantasmal resonance of divergent series, is eternally yet-to-come as a vanishing of terms. The Moment causes the unconditioned to repeat, and as a differential it forces identity out of the concept. Infinite incompossible presents are passed through in order to reactivate the not-necessarily true pasts of the forked series. All series resonate with one another with each repetition of the perverse Moment.

As discussed in Chapter 2, the Moment serves as the gateway between two opposing lanes of time: a chronological conception of the eternal return of the same, premised on what Hegel calls the bad infinite, and the future as an eternal return of difference. The Moment connects the manifest interpretation of the eternal return with the latent interpretation. As it stands in relation to the two lanes of time, the Moment is literally a perpetual point of division between the past and the future. The eternal return of the same is modelled on a notion of the past as recollected former presents in identity, while the eternal return of difference is a disjunctive synthesis of the future. The Moment is also the dividing line between the molecular memory of sensation and the ontological forgetting of the third and final synthesis of time. Klossowski describes the Moment as being ecstatic, it stands outside of time, outside of identity in the concept, and Deleuze picks up on the broken circle implied by this ecstasy. *The Logic of Sense*, perhaps more than any other of his sustained studies of the eternal return, stresses the paradoxical instant, the re-appropriated Nietzschean

Moment. Deleuze fleshes out the manifest and latent levels of the eternal return, reflecting the influence of Klossowski's interpretation upon his own understanding he indicates that the manifest level must be traversed in order for the latent level to operate. The reciprocal relationship between these levels is dropped to a large extent in his collective works with Guattari in favour of the latent level. The feature of Klossowski's re-appropriation of the eternal return that remains intact is the separation of two moments by eternity, or the vicious circle of identity. For Klossowski, this movement requires the coordination of conscious and unconscious willing. Deleuze will want to situate this movement in the contemplation of passive selves, beneath the level of representation. The following account of the movement from one moment to the next along the spiral of the eternal return confirms the forking of incompossible presents in labyrinth of time from Borges. The result is a more comprehensive portrait of the Moment. Klossowksi remarks,

> *Anamnesis* coincides with the revelation of the Return: how could the return not bring back forgetfulness? Not only do I learn that I (Nietzsche) have been brought back to the crucial moment in which the eternity of the circle culminates, the moment in which the truth of its necessary return is revealed to me; but at the same time I learn that I was *other* than I am *now* for having forgotten this truth, and thus that I have become other by learning it. Will I change again, and once more forget that I will necessarily change during an eternity – until I relearn this revelation anew?[65]

In direct contest with the Platonic notion of reminiscence of immutable ideas that presuppose identity, Klossowski introduces the recollection of lost identity through the journey of the eternal return. The Moment in this last passage is a forgetting of incompossible selves but also a recollection of the eternal return as willed. The Moment the eternal return is willed, the self runs through the infinite divergent paths of Borges's labyrinth before the memory of the prior self is effectuated. There is a convergence between the incompossible presents of Borges's corollary to Leibniz and the de-actualized present of Klossowski's eternal return. With a pastiche of Borges, Leibniz, Klossowski and Nietzsche, Deleuze welds a theory of the eternal return from the vantage of the Moment. De-actualizing, an eluded present of incompossibility, the Moment is an untimely division of the always already and not yet. When he speaks of an eternal return upon the line of Aion, Deleuze refers to the paradox of the instant as dividing the syntheses of time without being *in* time. Like the infinitesimal vanishing quantities of differential calculus, the Moment removes determinability from the actual without disturbing the relationality of the initial terms. An infinite series of divergent futures separate one moment from another. The analysis of the eternal return upon the line of Aion presents us with part of the concept of the eternal return from the perspective of the Moment, while its complement rests in the analysis of the broken circle as synthesis. The stretched out line of time is the expanded theory of the eternal return. *Difference and Repetition* provides the most comprehensive treatment of the eternal return as the synthesis of the future. Using Duffy's study of the calculus in Deleuze *we will look at the broken line as the metaphysical equivalent to the sum of differentials in integration and the inverse of the differential relation.* Ultimately, we will discover how to reconcile the intensive features of the eternal return as a division of past and future, as well its features as a synthesis of the future.

Integration and the labyrinth: '... and for All'

Time must be understood and lived as out of joint, and seen as a straight line which mercilessly eliminates those who embark upon it, who come upon the scene but repeat once and for all.[66]

The line of Aion is used to emphasize the infinite division of past and future through the quasi-causal function of the Moment. Aion harkens back to the innocence of becoming from the philosophical fragments of Heraclitus and reiterates the process of absolute becoming which stems from the repetition of untimely moments. Following Bergson, Deleuze repeats that what we have come to understand as the quantifiable present is really the immediate past. The present of perception, no matter how infinitesimally proximate to the initial presentation, is a mental re-presentation. For this reason, the pure present, what we have been referring to as the Moment or paradoxical instant, eludes perception and constitution in static Being. It creates a gap between the future and the past. The Moment makes a ghost of duration and divides the past from the future *in perpetuum*, forcing all three syntheses of time to become according to the logical planes of their operation, whether in sensation or ideational events. An ordinate of the circle, the Moment unwinds the circle of the past as a synthesis of the future. This is the portrait of Deleuze's eternal return that is most prevalent in the secondary literature: the broken circle of time stretched out in a straight line. The third synthesis of time, or the future, finds its most exhaustive exposition in *Difference and Repetition*. It is a re-appropriation of the eternal return as Nietzsche was never able to formulate.

Deleuze argues that the interpretation of Nietzsche's 'heaviest weight' as the eternal return of the same violates the differential currents of his philosophy. Nietzsche was notoriously critical of binary thought, reactivity, static Being, mechanistic causation, as well as identity. To formulate the eternal return in terms of the same or the similar nullifies his theory of competing, sub-representative forces. The third synthesis of time in Deleuze's ontology corresponds to his speculative theory about the third, unwritten enunciation of the eternal return in *Thus Spoke Zarathustra*.[67] Nietzsche's madness and death foreclosed what Deleuze expected to be the final version of the eternal return; a thought of selective being in what was speculated to be the concluding volume of *Thus Spoke Zarathustra*. Nietzsche, a meticulous scholar of ancient Greek thought, would have known of the circular conception of time and would not have found this to be much of a thought experiment, or what Arkady Plotnitsky refers to as Nietzsche's 'seismic idea'.[68] With the exception of Heraclitus, the circle of time was posed antithetically to chaos, Plato being the most ardent proponent of this opposition. Nietzsche, however, combined the notion of return with chaos and becoming. The two instances where the eternal return is presented in *Thus Spoke Zarathustra,* an expanded discussion first appearing in *The Gay Science,* contest the exclusion of becoming from an eternal return. Deleuze mines these two discussions in *Zarathustra* for clues revealing the unspoken truth of the doctrine. In both sections, 'On the Vision and the Riddle' and 'The Convalescent', Zarathustra dismisses the parroted version of the eternal return spoken by the dwarf and the animals, respectively. The dwarf reads the two opposing lanes that meet at the gateway of the Moment as the circularity of time, and Zarathustra upbraids him for his reductionist reading.[69] When the topic of the eternal return is revisited, the animals recite a version of it that ensures the recurrence of reactivity, including the return of the smallest of men. Zarathustra responds to this pronouncement in silence, which Deleuze reads as an implicit rejection of the return of the reactive. The reactive, at the level of ontology, is that which is dependent upon former presents of recollection. That which acts at the surface of static Being is barred from the return in Deleuze's interpretation. The third formulation of the eternal turn in *Thus Spoke Zarathustra,* which Deleuze surmises was planned to be written by Nietzsche before his illness precluded him from doing so, would express the truth of the circle at the end of the straight line of time: the eternal return as affirmation of difference in-itself.

The speculative interpretation of the eternal return as it would be expressed in its third formulation by Zarathustra marks the third synthesis of time for Deleuze. The long lane of time, the circle unwound, is the future. The future is the network of divergent temporal series forked by the Moment. The two aspects of the eternal return – differential Moment and integral synthesis – are indicated in his description of Aion from *The Logic of Sense*: 'But being an empty and unfolded form of time, the Aion subdivides ad infinitum that which haunts it without ever inhabiting it – the Event for all events.'[70] The infinite subdivision refers to the Moment as quasi-causal operator, and the empty and unfolded form of time refers to the synthesis of the future. The synthesis of the future cannot depend upon a cycle drawn by the passing present, or the immediate past, otherwise we make a 'hurdy-gurdy' song out of the eternal return, as Zarathustra retorts to the dwarf. The synthesis of the eternal return is a repetition of the yet-to-come, the future. The future is emptied of content, including all duration, and it is the repetition of the unconditioned. By usurping the ground of the pure past, the third synthesis of time expresses the death of god and man, and appropriately, the destruction of all identity. The self-referential circuit of identity is broken, thereby unwinding the circle. Deleuze explains how the third and final synthesis pulls time out of joint, stretching out the circle and creating the line of Aion. He writes,

> However, the order of time, time as a pure and empty form, has precisely undone that circle. It has undone it in favour of a less simple and much more secret, much more torturous, more nebulous circle, an eternally excentric circle, the decentered circle of difference which is re-formed uniquely in the third time of the series. The 'once and for all' of the order is there only for the 'every time' of the final esoteric circle. The form of time is there only for the revelation of the formless in the eternal return. The extreme formality is there only for an excessive formlessness (Hölderlin's *Unförmliche*). In this manner, the ground has been superseded by a groundlessness, a universal ungrounding which turns upon itself and causes only the yet-to-come to return.[71]

The future is a synthesis of the caesura, that is, the Moment, as it draws difference from the former two passive syntheses and effects absolute change. The aleatory point of the quasi-cause is modelled on the Nietzschean dictum of the eternal return. 'Once [the quasi-causal Moment] and for all [the entire network of disjunctively synthesized paths]' implicates the two points of view taken on by the eternal return of difference. Echoing Klossowski, Deleuze states that the eternal return is the only coherence that remains while all other coherences of self, things and identities, are destroyed in the repetition of the future. Conditions and agents do not return, and nothing that is constructed in light of the passing present returns. What does return is the unconditioned, the pure and empty form of time itself.

It should be noted that the third synthesis, while universally applied to all syntheses and every aspect of the real, is the time of the event in its pure form. Blocs of becoming in sensation are not fully divested of molecular memory, as we see in *A Thousand Plateaus* and *What Is Philosophy?* Instead, the eternal return forms time crystals, ritornellos, in the realm of sensation as a composition of chaos. Deleuze's investigation of the third synthesis of time in *Difference and Repetition* is applied conceptually to ideational events in *The Logic of Sense.* The third synthesis affirms chaos and is the repetition of the empty form of time prior to its territorialization by expression in the ritornello. At the same instant that the unconditioned in the eternal return is territorialized, it deterritorializes everything it chances upon. This is one of the ways in which it effectuates a vicious circle. Deleuze models the vicious circle of time on the affirmation of chaotic forces in Nietzsche, as well as on the notion of the curve in Leibniz. Simon Duffy demonstrated how Deleuze adopts the Leibnizian solution to the problem of the infinite by positing integration as a sum of differential series and inverse to the differential relation.[72] In the previous section we mapped the concept of the Moment onto the relation of the differential, and now we will map the vicious circle onto the integration of differentials as they form a curve.

If the Moment in Deleuze is a metaphysical analogue to the differentiation in Leibniz's infinitesimal calculus, then the broken circle is the metaphysical analogue to integration. As Duffy explains, integration in Leibniz is the sum of differentials and the inverse of the differential relation. Duffy notices that Deleuze is particularly interested in the notion that a differential function derived from a circle does not depend on the relation of the circle itself, but it relies on a tangent. Duffy states, 'A tangent is a line that touches the circle or curve at a point. The gradient of a tangent indicates the rate of change of the curve at that point, that is, that the rate at which the curve changes on the y-axis relative to the x-axis, or the amount of slope of the curve at that point.'[73] Leibniz's use of the tangent to measure the relation of change between the x-axis and the y-axis appeals to Deleuze, not only because it involves the inverse of the differential relation for integration, thus overcoming the opposition between the finite and the infinite, but the relation itself is independent from the terms of the circle of curve: points on a curve are swept away by the tangential line. We saw this tendency before in the differential equation from the standpoint of the infinitesimal, a perpetually vanishing quantity that is indeterminable. The use of a tangent, a *line*, to describe the rate of change of a circle or curve no doubt ramified Deleuze's interpretation of the eternal return as a straight line of time. The truth of the circle is not to be found in the points that compose the circle, but in the sum of differential relations that differ in kind from the terms of the points. As a sum of differential relations, the circle is seen as 'folded forces' in Leibniz's universe.[74] This shift in the seventeenth century from the calculation of finite entities to that of infinitesimal differential relations provides a mathematical complement to Nietzsche's description of nature as qualitative force relations. Deleuze explains that what Nietzsche meant by qualitative relations of force really amounted to intensive relations of quantity.

Mogens Lærke describes how Leibniz's understanding of physical objects is not based on extension or quantity, but on the notion of force and the power exerted by folded forces. The connection between the curve and force reveals the import Leibniz had in Deleuze's understanding of the eternal return as a broken circle of time. Lærke states,

> But how do *folded forces* relate more precisely to actions, that is, to *events?* Deleuze connects these notions as early as *The Logic of Sense:* 'What is an ideal event? It is a singularity – or rather a set of singularities or of singular points characterizing a mathematical curve. ... Singularities are turning points and points of inflexion' (*LS* 52). In Leibniz, the conception of the world as a complex curve is tightly linked to 'the labyrinth of the continuum' he explores through the calculus. The curve of the world cannot be described as a composition of *points (x,y)*, but must be understood as a continuous succession of relations or, as it were, *differential relations (dy/dx)*. Any such differential relation expresses the *curving* itself, that is, the way in which the curve *varies.*[75]

Drawing from *The Logic of Sense*, Lærke relates the event to the sum of singularities, that is, the sum of differential relations which inform the curve, or the circle. The excentric circle of the eternal return reflects the continuous succession or summation of differential relations. The line of Aion, the eternal return outstretched, is understood from the perspective of both the differential and the summation of differentials that shape a mathematical curve. Just as with Leibniz, Deleuze conceives of things as being effects of relations, or ideal events. Disparate elements in the actual are interconnected in the virtual by 'the labyrinth of the continuum'. Deleuze takes this Leibnizian labyrinth and fuses it with the forking paths of Borges where incompossibilities are disjunctively synthesized in the same world. The world is not understood through points in the actual, but through the relation of lines in virtual series. The eternal return is the time of events, and the line of Aion is the Event of all events. The characteristic of the future as the empty form of time integrates Deleuze's appropriation of Leibnizian calculus. The synthesis of difference forms a broken line that changes everything it touches without itself changing. Given terms of a differential relation may change, but the operation of difference remains the same as difference itself. The repetition of the future uses the quasi-causal operator to relate different to different through difference, and its effect upon time is born from the differential's untimeliness.

As Daniel W. Smith argues, Deleuze's most relevant treatments of Leibniz occur in *The Logic of Sense* and *Difference and Repetition*, perhaps having even greater impact on his philosophy than his sustained monograph on Leibniz, *The Fold*.[76] Approached from a decidedly post-Kantian framework, Deleuze's reworking of Leibniz as a philosopher of immanence touches upon the theory of the eternal return as a synthesis of the future. A synthesis of excess, the eternal return can be read, in part, as a synthesis of vanishing qualities, as well as vanishing quantities. We know that Deleuze read qualitative difference through intensive quantitative difference, as he readily admits in *Nietzsche and Philosophy*.[77] The synthesis, or summation of infinitesimals, forms a mathematical curve, or in Deleuze's case an excentric circle. The figure of the eternal return as a broken circle stretched out into a line is a dramatization of the vicious circle in Klossowski, the labyrinth of divergent futures in Borges, the long lanes of time and their corresponding meaning in the unwritten conclusion to *Thus Spoke Zarathustra*, and the inverse relationship between differential and integral relations in Leibniz's calculus.

The synthesis of the eternal return is a complete break from the ties of identity, thus the circuit and the time crystal are decimated. The journey from the moment of willing in Klossowski to the recovered self, the centrifugal force of the eternal return, involves a sudden break, thus unwinding the circle. The circle becomes vicious and eternal but now assumes the figure of the line. Identified more with the differential change measured by the line of the tangent than the ordinary points that are said to compose the circle itself, the eternal return is a summation of divergent series set off by incompossible presents. The figure of the circle is associated with the return of the same, or the recollection of former presents, while the figure of line separates each level of the past, destroying the principle of identity.

Resolution to the paradox

Earlier in the chapter the question was raised as to how we might reconcile the description of the eternal return as being both the synthesis of the future and the infinite subdivision of the past and future. How can the eternal return be both an aleatory point and a broken circle? These two descriptions of the eternal return approach the concept from two different perspectives: the Moment and the synthesis. The Moment is the quasi-causal operator that always separates the passing present from the not yet. Rather than produce discontinuous temporal fragments, the Moment is synthesized as an infinite series of incompossible futures that form a continuous labyrinth. Each divergent path, as we see in Borges, departs from infinite different possible presents that are affirmed simultaneously. These incompossible presents, while being the beginnings of newly forked paths, are always in the middle, *au milieu*. The line of time is a rhizome that causes the divergent paths to resonate in each repetition of the future. The future, then, is not a projection of a former present, but is of a different order altogether. Deleuze's concept of the future is the synthesis of the series that form the open totality of the labyrinth.

With the help of Klossowski, Deleuze begins his elaboration of the third synthesis of time from the speculative standpoint of Nietzsche's unwritten conclusion to *Thus Spoke Zarathustra*. Deducing the meaning of the eternal return from its formulations in *Zarathustra*, as well as from the critical philosophy of Nietzsche, Deleuze offers a portrait of the eternal return that does not lapse into the logic of the same, thus remaining faithful to the remainder of Nietzsche's canon. With ontological ingenuity, Deleuze reveals that the problem with orthodox interpretations of the eternal return is their insistence on what Friedrich Nietzsche, the author, meant in his stated expressions of the doctrine. The more pertinent question is, 'What does Nietzsche's *philosophy* intend by the doctrine of the eternal return?' And clearly, Nietzsche's philosophy does not support an eternal return of the same. Dramatizing the intensive features of Nietzsche's philosophy, such as the untimely, the different, the unequal and the affirmative with the intensive features of Leibniz and Borges enables Deleuze to construct a more Nietzschean reading of the eternal return. We have a new point of view into the temporalizing force of the untimely in becoming.

The untimely Moment is infinitely synthesized into an untimely line that effects change while never changing itself. This conception of the eternal return as the pure and empty form of time takes Leibniz's differential calculus as a metaphysical model for the repetition of difference in the future. The Moment is conceived from the vanishing quantities of differentials in the calculus, while the synthesis of the line is conceived as the integration of differential relations. The differential itself does not express duration, and this contributes to the untimely nature of the future as a synthesis of difference.

Deleuze manages to create a temporal pastiche from the philosophical works of Nietzsche, Klossowski, Borges and Leibniz in his innovative theory of the future. The second half of this chapter has shown the two notions of the eternal return as synthesis and infinitely dividing Moment to flesh out the temporal nuances of Deleuze's concept of the future. The eternal return as examined in *Difference and Repetition*, as well as the line of Aion from *The Logic of Sense*, pertains to the temporality of ideational events. The Moment eternally subdivides the not yet from the already, while the line denoted by the eternal return synthesizes these empty moments into an empty form of time. The terminological use of the line of Aion in *The Logic of Sense* illuminates the role of the Moment in the formation of the line without letting the reader forget that this paradoxical instant forms a serial continuum with other paradoxical instants. By focusing on the perverse Moment as the differential building block for the synthesis of the future, Deleuze gives full meaning to Hamlet's famous line, 'The time is out of joint.'[78]

The fact that Deleuze's philosophy is futural cannot be overstressed. The time of events is the eternal return from the perspective of the Moment and the synthesis of all moments. The future has no content and extends into a long lane where the Moment is repeated eternally. Each moment is separated by an eternity, an infinite series of divergent futures. The Garden of Forking Paths is affirmed with each de-actualization performed by the Moment, creating a seamless continuum of incompossible presents. What Guattari would later name a rhizome is the labyrinth of divergent series in Borges, the straight line of time. The line of Aion only circles back on itself as pure difference, never as a constituted identity. It is a time that floats ungrounded at the plane of immanence, breaking the circuits of memory.

When Deleuze states that the eternal return is the being of becoming and that Aion is the becoming that infinitely subdivides itself into the past and future while eluding the present he is referring to the same process. From *Nietzsche and Philosophy* onward there has been a conceptual dance between the concept of becoming and the concept of temporality. The third synthesis of time vehemently resists the temporal structures of a passing present and is not embedded in time. With the notion of an untimely synthesis, Deleuze manages to bridge the apparent opposition between the non-temporal and the eternal. The future is an eternal return, but not constructed in light of the bad infinite, an infinity of unlimited finite quantities. Instead, Deleuze employs the infinitesimal and its synthesis in the differential relation to redefine our understanding of the future. The future is a synthesis of becoming, absolute becoming. The present is de-actualized and distributed into two jets of time, and this quasi-causal process is the definitive mark of absolute becoming. Absolute becoming is the affirmation of chaos and divergent temporalities without itself being embedded in time: this is the selfsame eternal return of *Difference and Repetition*.

The eternal return participates in the movement of becoming that opened the chapter. It is absolute in its survey and speed, yet it is relative in its contours. To apply this characterization to the two distinct realms of the eternal return, sensation and events, requires a reciprocal characterization of becoming. The eternal return as synthesis and quasi-causal operator remains within the purview of the future only purely in the series of events. As the eternal return traverses sensation, the concept of becoming reflects the logic of sensation. Identity is still thwarted in sensation, but the eternal return takes the form of the whirring ritornello. The ritornello is a line of becoming that still operates according to the differentiation of the Moment, yet it responds to the logic of sensation. The pure past communicates difference through the milieus of sensation, creating a becoming-mad of molecular memory. The singularities extracted from matter wander lost in sensation, forming blocs of becoming that express the variance of duration. What Bogue has called embodied becoming is the sensory becoming described by Deleuze and Guattari in *What Is Philosophy?* Qualitative and intensive, sensation uses expression to territorialize the chaos affirmed in the divergent futures of absolute becoming. The resonance of time crystals through the ritornello reveals the Proustian and Bergsonian components in Deleuze's theory of the eternal return in sensation. The molecular memory exhibited by the sensory becoming of the ritornello is destroyed in the third synthesis of the future, pure forgetting, on the plane of immanence. Together, the ritornello in sensation and the synthesis of differential moments in events form a comprehensive theory of the eternal return in Deleuze. Absolute becoming involves the differential Moment (the pure and empty form of time/ Aion), and sensory becoming involves the integral summation of differentials (molecular memory/ritornello), inverses of one another that correspond to their respective milieus. By remapping the two formulations of the eternal return we have shown their corresponding temporalities and processes of becoming. As Deleuze himself says, 'The Eternal Return is the instant *or* the eternity of becoming eliminating whatever offers resistance.'[79] Time returns eternally *once* as the differential moment *and for all* as the summation of differential moments in integration.

The Becoming of Gilles Deleuze

Deleuze's ontology places primacy on the future, and thus its absolute becoming is an untimely synthesis. The quasi-causal differentiating force of the Moment opens up lines of convergence and divergence. Certain singularities are released from the stratification of the corporeal present and form new convergences, or blocs, with other singularities in sensation, meanwhile they are distributed into divergent futures that resonate in distance. Deleuze's complex system of becoming engages two temporal logics, sensory and absolute, and is synthesized from the virtual to the actual. As the syntheses are disjunctive, the ontological universe of becoming is heterogeneous. Up until this point we have outlined the quasi-causal processes of becoming; examined the concept's temporal logics and lines; and have shown how different concepts are extracted from previous philosophers to create new concepts of time and becoming. Having analysed how the temporal syntheses are involved and expressed, a crystallized portrait of becoming has been brought to the surface. It is now time to fold Deleuze's concept of becoming onto itself. Upon close reflection, it will become evident that Deleuze's philosophical works perform the same processes of becoming he theorizes. Deleuze's concept of becoming operates according to the two temporal logics of becoming: sensory and absolute. The folding of form and content could not have been any other way, because concepts in Deleuze are inexorable from materiality. His writings dramatize the concept of becoming he thematizes in his works, thus making him one of the most innovative philosophers in history. The works themselves exhibit sensory becoming, forming line-blocs and engaging the components of concepts in the madness of molecular memory. This philosophical expression then opens up lines of flight into divergent conceptual futures.

Using *What Is Philosophy?* as the primary reference point for the analysis of becoming as a concept in Deleuze's works, we will map the concept according to the temporal processes developed in previous chapters. As a test case, we will proceed by selecting three key concepts that appeared in previous chapters which are integral to Deleuze's concept of becoming: Duration, the Eternal Return and the Moment. The singularities of these concepts are extracted from their philosophical histories through conceptual re-appropriation. Thus, we will look at how these concepts are released from their previous forms, fused into new blocs of becoming in the expressed works of Deleuze and instantaneously distributed across divergent futures. After observing their singular becomings, the three key temporal concepts will be connected through the figure of the line. The involution of three states of the line reveals a multiplicity of becoming that defeats criticisms of dualist ontology. In a beautiful consistency of form and content, Deleuze's concepts perform the tendencies they simultaneously develop in their singular combination. Staging Duration, the Eternal Return and the Moment in certain arrangements of proximity produce varying affects, percepts and concepts. The result is a vital kaleidoscopic universe of becoming in action, an ontology of pure difference.

Re-appropriation and the concept of becoming: Masks in Deleuze's works

One of the ways that Deleuze uses the two notions of becoming – sensory becoming and absolute becoming – in his works is through the re-appropriation of concepts in the history of philosophy. For Deleuze the task of philosophy is not contemplation or reflection, but is the creation of concepts. Concepts, then, as creative signatures of various philosophers are in a perpetual state of flux and becoming. In the Deleuzean universe this means that the singularities of a given concept are released from the ossified structures in philosophical history, are made radically other through their encounters in sensation on the plane of composition, and are simultaneously distributed into the transcendental field where they relate to other concepts. The survey (*survol*) of concepts directly reflects the processes of becoming investigated in the previous chapters. Deleuze, as the proper name attributed to the individual philosopher, as well as the collective philosopher Deleuze and Guattari, is responsible for the creation of myriad concepts. Given the breadth of concepts created in Deleuze's philosophy, we will look at the invigorated becoming of those key concepts that populate his ontological system. In particular, Duration, the Eternal Return and the Moment will serve as test cases for the process of becoming in Deleuze's ontology, from their ideational distribution to their expressions in sensation. These re-appropriated concepts do not only become ideationally, but also engage with becomings in sensation and thus adopt the distinct logics of these two realms. The lines of sensory and absolute becoming which move from the actual to the virtual and back again will be drawn in the analysis of the three chosen concepts.

Deleuze's philosophical works are unique in that they fold form and content into a multiplicity of ideas and expressions. Few philosophers would be able to lay claim to integrating the content of their treatises into the form of their expression and the development of their philosophy as a whole. Deleuze's philosophy is such an example, as its concepts are released from the chronological history in which they are found in philosophy, simultaneously releasing Deleuze's works from a reading of chronological progression. *A Thousand Plateaus* is the ultimate expression of the collapse of form and content with each chapter connecting to every other chapter through a network of concepts, yet each chapter stands alone and is legible in any order, irrespective of sequence. Accordingly, it is decidedly anti-Deleuzean to analyse the concept of the Eternal Return, for example, as a teleological progression from *Nietzsche and Philosophy* to *What Is Philosophy?*[1] While it is crucial to note the conceptual differences from one work to another, the elaboration of concepts should not be seen as a chronological progression. Deleuze and Guattari refer to the a-historical nature of concepts in light of becoming when they write, 'Philosophy cannot be reduced to its own history, because it continually wrests itself from this history in order to create new concepts that fall back into history but do not come from it.'[2] The becoming of concepts in Deleuze should be evaluated according to the dictates of Deleuze's philosophical system. This is why performing a chronological analysis of Deleuze's writings is ineffectual and why conceptual mapping or periodization, as we see in the works of Anne Sauvagnargues, for example, is methodologically preferable.[3] Rather than look at Deleuze's philosophy as a chronological progression, Sauvagnargues maps his concepts according to his intellectual influences in order to release those concepts from the chronological dates of the writings in which they were written and published.

Unlike Platonic ideas, Deleuze's concepts are mutable and form connective lines across events and sensation. Concepts are infinite in their survey, but they are finite and fragmented in their encounters in Duration. Hence, for Deleuze, concepts are not internally divorced from encounters of materiality. As he explains in 'Letter to Uno: How Félix and I Worked Together',

> Philosophy creates concepts, which are neither generalities nor truths. They are along the lines of the Singular, the Important, the New. *Concepts* are inseparable from *affects*, i.e. from the powerful effects they exert on our life, and *percepts*, i.e. the new ways of seeing or perceiving they provoke in us.[4]

As we see, concepts are not lofty ideas that remain isolated in the realm of the intelligible, but they are intimately involved in expression and perception. The inexorability of concepts and sensation accounts for their relativity, as it is detailed in *What Is Philosophy?*, which can be attributed to their envelopment in the materiality they serve to (de)territorialize. By inscribing creativity within the concept and linking it to the production of the new Deleuze situates it in the differential stream of the future, and thus the untimely field of becoming. As we apply the multiplicity of sensory and absolute becoming and their corresponding temporal rhythms to three of the selected re-appropriated concepts we begin to see their singularity form constellations of thought in Deleuze's works. First, they will be analysed in their singular becoming; then they will be linked together through the figure of the line in order to paint a complete portrait of their becoming as an assemblage. Both sensory becoming and absolute becoming will be ascribed to the concepts analysed, for, Deleuze and Guattari remind us that 'philosophical concepts are also "sensibilia"' and together they create a theory of becoming as a multiplicity.[5] The application of the elaborated theory of becoming(s) to the internal concepts of the theory creates a labyrinth of form and content that is unique to the philosophy of Deleuze. The first re-appropriated concept we examined in Chapter 1 when looking at the development of becoming was Duration, and now we are able to evaluate the concept of Duration as it operates within Deleuze's ontology.

The analysis of a concept is like a stroll through a multi-mirrored universe. The deeper one gets into the intricacies of a concept, the quicker s/he realizes the necessary enlistment of other concepts to understand and fully explicate the initial concept examined. This process of conceptual depth and expansion continues until there is a sense that the system in question can stand alone with reference to its arrangement of intensive features. The open networks of conceptual blocs connect to all other conceptual blocs in rhizomatic lines. Anyone who has attempted to get to the bottom of a certain concept in Deleuze finds roots of other concepts that proliferate like aspen trees. The aspen tree, while perhaps reminiscent of the genealogical model of knowledge criticized by Deleuze, is in fact a de-centred system that spreads like a rhizome. Concepts float freely among ideal events in nomadic distribution, yet they remain susceptible to reification in structures of actuality; the actual being involved in the virtual. Thus the aspen tree best exemplifies the life of the concept, from the actual genealogical effect of the trunk, leaves and branches, to its rhizomatic root structure which is without beginning or end. As a symbol for the production of representation out of the sub-representative, the aspen exemplifies the process of involution in Deleuze's ontology. From molar forms to the network of molecular becomings, Deleuze's ontology rests on the re-appropriation of Bergson's *durée*, or Duration.

The becoming of duration

What we have been calling molecular memory is a re-appropriation of the concept of Duration as it is displaced in Deleuze's system of becoming. A true philosophical collagist, Deleuze takes a particular concept and then introduces other influences to create a new concept. Bergson's influence is felt throughout Deleuze's philosophy. Bergson's concept of Duration, as an unfolding continuous heterogeneous multiplicity that subverts chronological time, is integral to Deleuze's theory of becoming, which we analysed in Chapter 1. Before having written a complex theory of becomings which we see in *A Thousand Plateaus,* for example, Deleuze plunged concepts located in the works of previous philosophers in the processes of becoming he would later formulate. This phenomenon does not amount to an anachronism, but the counter-effectuation of concepts within the course of his thought. Deleuze was notorious for performing heterodox readings of previous philosophers and artists, especially in his various monographs, where he breathed life into their rigidified concepts. Largely overlooking *Time and Free Will* as the key text that investigates the concept of Duration in Bergson, Deleuze instead focuses on *Matter and Memory.* The decision to orient Duration around the process of self-differing in the constitution of the pure past already begins to release the concept from Bergson's grip. *Time and Free Will* outlines the fundamental characteristics of Duration – its qualitative properties and interpenetrating states of consciousness in a continuous, heterogeneous multiplicity – a theory of temporality that reads more like the synthesis of sensations in the present and less like temporal rhythms of memory. In *Time and Free Will* Duration is distinguished from successive, linear time of extension, and Bergson had not yet integrated the concept into a larger commentary on voluntary and involuntary memory, or the past. However, *Matter and Memory* struck Deleuze, arguably, more than any other work by Bergson, as we read in his monograph on the philosopher, *Bergsonism.* Here we see the concept of Duration de-actualized from the writings of Bergson in a particular trajectory that slowly tranforms Duration into the self-differing becoming of memory.

Taking Duration further ontologically than Bergson himself was willing to do until late in his career, Deleuze imbues Duration with an impersonal flux that does not emerge from transcendental unity of a subject. Duration is not relegated to the psychological or the subjective but ontological. Duration, for Deleuze, also does not immediately concern the present. The present is spoken of as either a contemplation of habit; a first synthesis and foundation of time; the immediate past; the infinite contraction of the past; or the eluded present as the paradoxical instant. Duration is not the time of the actual, nor is it untimely, but it constitutes the non-metric pulsed time of various spatiotemporal rhythms. Since we cannot encounter Duration for Bergson save for throwing ourselves within its streams in acts of intuition, Deleuze moves to Proust for a sensible rendering of the non-metric temporality. The virtual levels of the past and its constitutive layers of varying Duration are folded into one sensation of internalized difference. The reading of Duration through the lens of creative reminiscence in Proust disengages the concept from the trappings of individuation. Defined often within the same work as a chronological subversion as well as the bifurcation of time into two diverse streams, Deleuze maintains a tension in the concept of Duration that creates a temporal 'pathology'.[6] Duration is that which differs from itself while subverting the actual present by way of ontological memory traces. The 'pathology of Duration' sounds eerily close to the becoming-mad that is perversely connected to measured time, and this temporal madness is a clue to Deleuze's re-appropriation of Bergsonian Duration. Duration is re-appropriated in terms of becoming-mad at the same moment it undergoes a becoming-mad as a concept.

Becoming-mad, or embodied becoming, subverts the chronological present by means of a differential past that disconnects materiality from identity. As we have demonstrated, the result is absolute otherness in sensation. Materiality is dislocated from identity structures as the molecular ordinates of sense take on the self-differing of Duration. The virtual image remains connected to the actual image despite bearing no resemblance to it. Ontological memory and the differential levels of the past upon which it draws unhinge the chronological present from itself. As singularities are redistributed into new blocs of becoming, materiality is swept under by self-relation as other. Meanwhile, the concept of Duration is expressed in Deleuze's creative philosophical works as a differential self-relation. The features of a continuous, heterogeneous multiplicity that subverts the present of perception through spatiotemporal rhythms are extracted from Bergson's Duration. Consequently, Duration is dislodged from Bergson's philosophy and made radically other while retaining the molecular memory of the concept.

In Deleuze's re-appropriation of Duration consciousness is replaced by the concept of singularities, and intuition is abandoned as a methodology. What is unique about the pathology of Duration is its referential break from fixed time. The Hatter and the Hare from Lewis Carroll's *Alice's Adventures in Wonderland* are the literary expressions for the madness of Duration. There is a restless tension of self-differing and divergent forking of time. Teatime serves as a symbolic present that is outside chronological time where the characters participate in an endless game of otherness, since they are always either too early or too late, switching places indefinitely. They are never on time.[7] Their madness expresses the broken loop of identity in the constitution of the pure past. Duration is inseparable from materiality, yet it is dissimulated from the fixed measure of the actual present. Is becoming-mad not the very process of becoming-other of the concept of Duration in Deleuze's works?

Duration is masked in many of Deleuze's works as expressed sensory blocs that shape the contours of what is expressed in his writing, and thus what is perceivable empirically. At the level of sensation Duration is the concept that in its otherness 'caught in a matter of expression'. The concept of Duration appears in Deleuze's works as that which it never was and that which it will be. Never is Duration a replication of its expression in Bergson's works, and its shaping of Deleuze's philosophical writing style effects a restless otherness. This is evidenced in his collective works with Guattari, in the counter-chronological elaboration of concepts and a self-differing in texts which appeals to a philosophical past that never was and has not yet arrived. Duration is a telescoping of divergent times in sensation and is known by other aliases.

The re-appropriated concept of Duration helps Deleuze create a universe of sensation in his philosophy. Like Nietzsche, Deleuze could be misread as producing an inconsistent philosophical system, where concepts take on different processes in different texts, and on occasion even within the same text. Such a criticism would miss the point of his ontology of difference and the tensions held by the temporal splitting of Duration. To truly evaluate Deleuze on his own terms, one must look at his writings as a defiance of resemblance, opposition, analogy and identity. His re-appropriation of Duration in various texts, appearing under the guises of 'ontological memory', 'becoming-mad', 'sensory becoming' and 'blocs of becoming', expresses the relativity of the concept. It is relative in its fragmentary forms in sensation, while it is absolute in its distribution across series. The multiple masks of Duration allow different sensory blocs to be created and expressed in the writing. The trick, however, is to locate the re-appropriated concepts in his writings and map the different features that are created through their relationality with other concepts. If we recognize that a particular concept is repeated within the text, enduring and becoming other, his ontology surfaces more clearly.

By venturing through the qualitative sensation of Proust, and the singularities of Leibniz, Bergsonian Duration becomes that which it is not while remaining what it is. The convergence of heterogeneity, continuity and multiplicity in the concept of Duration endures across different texts, creating a dialogue between Bergson and other thinkers through the philosophy of Deleuze. He states that it is not two different points that are of interest but what happens between them. As he forces different philosophers to confront one another in a conceptual dramatization, said concepts exhibit new tendencies and are pushed to their limits in thought and sensation.

Duration is able to become what it is through its encounters with the concept of singularity in Leibniz and the concept of ontological memory in Proust. It is released from the processes of consciousness, put into the virtuality of the pure past while it envelops diverse times in a singular sensation. The collaborative writings of Deleuze and Guattari push their separate individualities to the level of the impersonal assemblage. As one becomes the other *ad infinitum*, we are able to see Duration not only thematized but also dramatized in their works. The tensions expressed by Duration are upheld in Deleuze and Guattari's writing process. Deleuze claims neither of them came to understand the concepts they created in exactly the same way, and this demonstrates the implicit difference within the concepts expressed. The subjective intentions and connections to the individual authors are irrelevant, and the concepts they create live autonomously through their writings. Bergson's intention for Duration is not what is at stake but the question is what the concept is able to do and how it might create different percepts and affects. Through his re-appropriation in terms of the madness of the temporal split in sensation we are able to see how each text creates a singular universe through its relation of concepts. The different constellations of thought that endure as an ontological past which repeats difference is encountered through the sensory becoming of Deleuze's writings. His works form a continuous multiplicity where Duration is folded into other concepts in unique ways.

For example, *A Thousand Plateaus* consists of chapters that were intended to be read in any order, defying the succession of time in the actual. The mechanics of reading, turning pages, feeling the weight of the book in measured, homogeneous time functions as the anchor in the actual engagement with the text, but the text itself initiates sensory blocs that unhinge chronological time. In the same sense that forms are subordinated to the abstract northern line in

Pollock's drip paintings, the written word is subordinated to the re-appropriated versions of Duration and their corresponding assemblages. None of Deleuze's works can be designated as being a beginning or endpoint, and each work has its own temporal speed. *Bergsonism* explores the implications of difference and the past, for instance, while *The Time-Image* explores the Duration of images in film. Becoming-mad in *The Logic of Sense* applies the pathology of Duration to signs, and *A Thousand Plateaus* discusses the ability of music to take the imperceptible forces of Duration and make them perceptible. These are just some examples of the ways Duration is made radically other in separate texts. Putting different concepts and conditions in the face of Duration produces different tendencies and singular concepts that sprout off of one another. This does not mean that there is an *a priori* truth to Duration, but rather, new tendencies are created as Duration becomes what it is through differentiation.

Duration is released from its relationship to the particular concepts posed in Bergson's works through its positioning in respect to alternative concepts. The multiplicity of Duration is an effect of the resonance between its various re-appropriations. We witness the resonance of the circuit of the time crystal with the difference between the levels of the pure past in the passive synthesis of involuntary memory. As new conceptual tendencies are created in the various re-appropriations of Duration new alliances and heterogeneous series are proliferated on the plane of immanence. Just as Proust showed tendencies of Duration that Bergson never dramatized, Deleuze reconfigures the concept with aspects that became possible through different conceptual and artistic encounters. What appears on the surface as an evolution of a concept across thinkers is an implication, or folding, of tendencies that de-actualize previous constructions through a process of involution.

The creative act of Deleuze's written – where 'written' refers to an expanded Derridian understanding of the text – philosophy removes Duration from the conditions of subjective consciousness in Bergson and from the qualitative sensation of Proust. Consequently, it becomes swept away in diverse conceptual relations and its thematized heterogeneity is mirrored in its distribution among ideal events. It is through its articulation as a splitting of the pure past and the future that Duration is distributed into divergent futures that fork infinitely off of one another.

What we realize is that neither the re-appropriated concepts of Duration nor the infinite divergent series through which it is distributed is originary; both are created simultaneously. The moment in time that the concept of Duration is created is always too early and too late. It is not a historical product but resonates throughout history, seeming at once necessary and contingent. The historical trajectory of Duration reveals the manifest content of the concept and the latent content in a combination that creates new resonances across times in simultaneous, disjunctive synthesis. Deleuze's affinity for the elaboration of temporal differentiation in *Matter and Memory* forges a trajectory of Duration that relates to molecular memory. His writings reflect the heterogeneity he extracts from Duration. The concept operates in his work as a multiplicity whose identity is developed by becoming other. As it is posited in different conceptual relations, Duration refers back to a past it never was and a future it has not produced. Unleashed in different temporal rhythms expressed as radically other, while continuing to be what it is, Duration forms a qualitative universe in Deleuze's vast and varied writings that is then distributed into divergent series, vibrating between sensory and absolute becoming. One of the confrontations posed to Duration is that of the Eternal Return, and their proximity produces a series of temporal rhythms that affect the tendencies of both concepts.

The becoming of the eternal return

What, if some day or night a demon were to steal after you into your loneliest loneliness and say to you:

> This life as you now live it and have lived it, you will have to live once more and innumerable times more; and there will be nothing new in it, but every pain and every joy and every thought and sigh and everything unutterably small or great in your life will have to return to you, all in the same succession and sequence – even this spider and this moonlight between the trees, and even this moment and I myself. The eternal hourglass of existence is turned upside down again and again, and you with it, speck of dust![8]

This opening to the aphorism entitled 'The Greatest Weight' from Nietzsche's *The Gay Science* presents his first formulation of the Eternal Return. The overwhelming majority of Nietzsche scholars interpret the Eternal Return as a repetition of the same, including that which is not only active but also reactive.[9] Even in Robin Small's contemporary analysis of Nietzsche's Eternal Return Deleuze's interpretation of the doctrine as the return of difference is conspicuously absent from consideration.[10] Robin Small reads time as the interpretation to the fact of becoming; a perspective that Deleuze would patently reject. Ascribing interpretation to time is one alternative to the conventional reading of 'The

Greatest Weight' where an atomistic conception of matter is implied, and Small's account of the Eternal Return is a subtle rejection of Deleuze's ontological reading of time, which sees time not relegated to the activity of consciousness but to an a-subjective synthesis. An atomistic reading relies upon a linear conception of time in the guise of circularity, as it is a function of succession. Isolated from the rest of Nietzsche's works, an interpretation of the Eternal Return as a circular effect of succession is not unfathomable, as Nietzsche himself used those terms to describe the return. There is a historical precedent for this interpretation, it turns out, and Heinrich Heine's formulation of the eternal recurrence is often assigned to Nietzsche's version of the concept.

Walter Kaufmann reveals that one of the books in Nietzsche's catalogued library was a text written by Heinrich Heine which addresses the eternal recurrence of material forms in infinite time. Heine, whose poetic mastery of the German language was revered by Nietzsche, pinned the cyclical nature of time on the confluence of infinite time and finite matter.[11] Nietzsche's affinity for the German poet is a reason to believe that his version of eternal recurrence held import for Nietzsche's development of the concept in his own philosophy. Traditionally, the reading of Nietzsche's Eternal Return through the writings of Heine reiterates the repetition of the same and an atomistic conception of matter. How could a philosopher so critical of metaphysical constructs, such as the self, causality and substance, advocate an Eternal Return of the same?[12] This is where Deleuze steps in.

The initial description of the Eternal Return in Nietzsche's *The Gay Science* prefigures its further elaboration in *Thus Spoke Zarathustra*. Deleuze's speculative reading of the third, unwritten description of the Eternal Return in *Zarathustra* is also informed by the entirety of Nietzsche's works. Time and time again Nietzsche undermines the universal 'truth' of metaphysical concepts, and he finds faith in cause and effect particularly abhorrent. It is the inadequacy of consciousness to apprehend the pure flux of nature that, like in Bergson, leads to a model of change premised on immobile snapshots strung together as an afterthought. And despite his relentless critiques of the apologetics of causality, Nietzsche is assumed by most of the secondary literature to have literally stated the Eternal Return in his writings. Thus he is claimed to have countenanced a cosmological principle that accepts mechanistic causality and the coherence of the self. Rightly so, Deleuze is doubtful of the surface reading of the Eternal Return as it is constructed in *The Gay Science*. The surface reading is the gateway to a deeper reading of the doctrine that affirms Nietzsche's metaphysical critiques and insight into the becoming of forces which restlessly fluctuate in the will to power. Choosing to utilize a systemic analysis of Nietzsche's works as a support, rather than the literal, face value readings of a few passages, Deleuze restates the doctrine of the Eternal Return as Nietzsche never had. Extending enormous charity to Nietzsche's intentions for the Eternal Return, Deleuze rescues the philosopher from a theory that would unwittingly support the very conceptual operations he criticized in all of his works.

The account of the Eternal Return as a repetition of the same is de-actualized in Deleuze's interpretation. Orthodox Nietzsche scholars often reject Deleuze's interpretation of the Eternal Return as the repetition of difference on the grounds that it is not what Nietzsche explicitly stated, and that Nietzsche's writings clearly indicate a repetition of the same. Is this not an outmoded methodology of reading? Instead of employing a correspondence theory of truth to explicate the doctrine, Deleuze uses the theory of sub-representative forces of becoming that permeates Nietzsche's own works in order to dynamize the concept of the Eternal Return. Deleuze's reading, then, upholds the Nietzschean appeal to synthesis and a concomitance of impermanent, contingent forces in one will to power. The conventional reading of the Eternal Return entails discrete combinations pulled from implicated forces and strewn together through mechanistic cause and effect. Nietzsche, a metonym for the author's collective works and ideas, denounces a reading of the Eternal Return through categories of substance metaphysics. To separate the temporality of the Eternal Return from becoming as an interpretation, as we see in Robin Small's text, still implies a model of individuation that is founded on a theory of self prior to the death of god. Who is doing the interpreting? We have not veered far enough off the course of subjectivity if we align time with interpretation. Small's reference to Klossowski's poststructuralist reading rather than to Deleuze's indicates a discomfort with fully wresting the time of the Eternal Return from consciousness. If Deleuze's version of the Eternal Return shows us anything, it is that Deleuze is even more Nietzschean than Nietzsche himself.

Just as we saw with his revolution of the concept of Duration, Deleuze manages to de-actualize the Eternal Return from petrified structures of identity. To ask whether Nietzsche, the man, intended the Eternal Return to repeat difference or identity is to pose the wrong question. A better problematic would examine the way the doctrine is integrated into the critiques posed by his philosophy and how it reinforces the conceptual relations within his corpus. From his early work on Nietzsche in 1963, *Nietzsche and Philosophy*, Deleuze alters the course of Nietzschean scholarship by taking seriously the two intensive features of the Eternal Return: chaos and cycling. The becoming of repetition pulls time out of the hands of an individuated subject and inscribes it into the wheel of time itself. The otherness effected by the Eternal Return does not depend upon a willing subject, as claimed by Klossowski, but is an affirmation of chaos at the pre-individual level. The Eternal Return is investigated through its relation to a new set of concepts, pushing its conceptual tendencies across events and sensory blocs. Depending on which set of concepts the Eternal Return is faced with, different tendencies are drawn out. As has been discussed in previous chapters, the problematics posed by *Difference and Repetition* and, say, *A Thousand Plateaus* produce divergent paths for the concept of the Eternal Return. An attempt to understand temporality as passive syntheses reveals the futurity of the Eternal Return. Examining how the Eternal Return behaves in sensation gives rise to the concept of the ritornello. The ritornello's territorialization of chaos through composition is evidenced in Deleuze's writings.

The proximity of the Eternal Return and Duration in the realm of sensation engenders a radical becoming-other of Nietzsche's doctrine. The determinability often implied in the conventional readings of the Eternal Return of the same is de-actualized in a universe where time is disconnected from fixed chronology. The ritornello is a kind of Bergson–Proust–Nietzsche hybrid where intensive relations between enveloped sensations across time resonate. It is through the ritornello that we begin to understand the tensions of the Eternal Return. The repetition of different contracted layers of the ontological past marks Deleuze's writings. When reading his works there is sense of conceptual déjà vu, and the previous chapters have worked to expose these resonances and folds. A skilled artist will succeed in expressing the different durational rhythms in sensation by constructing a ritornello, and this is what Deleuze's writings accomplish.

Keith Ansell-Pearson reads the Eternal Return in *Nietzsche and Philosophy* as an early attempt to answer the question of the passage of time, thus reading the doctrine through the second synthesis of time.[13] However, the question of time passing does not relegate the Eternal Return to the second synthesis, but shifts focus to the differential function of the Moment. The present cannot pass without the coexistence of the past, true, but it cannot pass either without the restlessness of the future, and the Moment is the division of these two temporal streams. It is important to resist the temptation to read Deleuze's concepts through chronological history, as Pearson has done in this instance. The fact that the Eternal Return is not formulated exclusively or predominantly in *Nietzsche and Philosophy* as a synthesis does not mean that this is proof of an early stage of Deleuze's theory of time. On the contrary, the Eternal Return develops alternative intensive features when confronted with the intensive features of the Moment.

Deleuze uses the tangent of selective ontology or the return of affirmation, to describe the becoming of the Eternal Return. A gradient that demonstrates the relation between affirmation and becoming is one that expresses the Eternal Return in terms of the Moment. Deleuze supports this reading when he says, 'Returning is everything but everything affirmed in a single *moment*.'[14] What is described as an aleatory moment in *The Logic of Sense* is the differential operator of becoming. If the Eternal Return is described as a synthesis of the future or an untimely moment we know that the absolute heterogeneity of ideal events is at stake. Deleuze's language turns towards the otherness of self-differing when the Eternal Return is re-appropriated in the logic of sensation. Each of these becomings of the Eternal Return – absolute and sensory – folds into the other in an act of textual resonance.

Each book where the Eternal Return is stretched to its limits serves as a forking path that diverges from the others. The selective ontology of *Nietzsche and Philosophy*; the synthesis of the future in *Difference and Repetition*; the ritornello in *A Thousand Plateaus* and the perverse Moment in *The Logic of Sense* all form divergent paths in possible futures which are synthesized disjunctively. That is to say, all of Deleuze's vast evaluations and applications of the Eternal Return fork off other conceptual relations in a labyrinth. *Nietzsche and Philosophy* is not the beginning of a theory of the Eternal Return of difference, nor is *A Thousand Plateaus* its purposive endpoint. The Eternal Return is staged in accordance with different problems and different sets of concepts, thus leading to the proliferation of divergent series. All of Deleuze's texts find the Eternal Return already in the middle, the in-between of singular concepts and blocs of becoming. He takes cues from the cross-fertilization of the Eternal Return and the time of sensation, Duration, to invent the concept of the ritornello with Guattari. The Eternal Return is pushed into the incompossible presents of Borges as it displays infinite speed across divergent events.

Deleuze's re-appropriations of the Eternal Return create a mirrored effect between the concept itself and its written expression. Each work repeats the Eternal Return in difference as its contours reflect various conceptual arrangements. Absolute becoming, the perverse Moment, the synthesis of the future and the ritornello resonate in a nexus of ontological forgetting–remembering. Not only do the fragmented expressions of the Eternal Return vibrate throughout Deleuze's writings, but the works themselves stage a repetition of becoming in sense and events. The antiquated reading of the Eternal Return of the same is liberated from Nietzsche and it is reanimated in expressed otherness of Deleuze's writings. The broken identity of the Eternal Return encounters concepts of Duration, affirmation, heterogeneity and other conceptual lines forging infinite divergent paths that form a temporal labyrinth of incompossible presents. New conceptual tendencies emerge from the Eternal Return in its staged confrontations of various problematics and combinations of concepts. De-actualized from the restrictive framework of consciousness and identity, the Eternal Return fuses the untimely Moment with the synthesis of the future. As such, the de-centred expressions of the Eternal Return are distributed along the straight line of Aion in absolute becoming. Labyrinthine in its construction, the body of Deleuze's works read as a multiplicity of divergent lines that outline the Eternal Return. The collection of writings successfully expresses the temporal rhythms of repetition, from the virtuality of sensation to the absolute heterogeneous becoming of the line of Aion in immanence.

The becoming of the moment

Integral to Deleuze's theory of temporality and the Eternal Return is the concept of the Moment. The Moment is often considered a qualitative inversion of the quantified present. For his theory of time and becoming, Deleuze seizes upon the gateway of the Moment in *Thus Spoke Zarathustra*, the division between the opposing lanes of the past and the future. The Moment's ability to form continuity between the past and future flowing together is adopted in Deleuze's appropriation of the concept. An inversion of the extensive, quantifiable present, the Moment operates according to a corresponding inversion of causality. As opposed to the mechanistic causality of a perceived present, the Moment is counter-causal. Deleuze cleverly draws a line from the Nietzschean Moment to his critique of mechanistic causality. Nietzsche's criticism of the interjection of causal processes in the apprehension of time corresponds to the Bergsonian critique of the intellect's freezing of flux in order to reconstitute change. The Moment is more of a poetic device in Nietzsche than an element of a thematized temporal theory. Deleuze takes the confluence of the past and future at the gateway of the Moment to articulate an alternative account of causality which supports Nietzsche's criticisms. Therefore, the Moment must not resemble the measured present in any sense. Being fully extricated from incorporation, the Moment is a temporal concept that is not in time. The Moment is an answer to the question pertaining to the relation of the Eternal Return and becoming. If the Eternal Return of the same is vehemently rejected, then the question is how can becoming be said to cohere with the act of returning. The Moment is elaborated along the lines of the repetition of difference. In addition to the study of becoming in *Nietzsche and Philosophy*, the Moment is addressed extensively in *The Logic of Sense* and *Difference and Repetition*. The line of Aion that is populated with ideal events differentiates the Moment throughout these key texts.

Taking Nietzsche's denunciation of causal processes in the nature of time and becoming to its ultimate conclusion, Deleuze de-actualizes the Moment from all associations with chronological time. Instead, the Moment becomes the counter-causal connection between the two opposed lanes of eternity. The embodied becoming of the pure past and the incorporeal becoming of the future are bridged by the Moment. Re-appropriated through the Nietzschean notion of the untimely, the Moment avoids incorporation and becomes a differential relation between the past and the future. Deleuze creates a new constellation of concepts in *The Logic of Sense*, in particular, which produces new tendencies for the Moment, moving beyond the qualitative into the operation of pure difference. In *Zarathustra* the qualitative, poetic symbol of the Moment is the point of convergence–divergence for the forces of time. Nietzsche muses about the complex of temporal forces at the gateway of the returning Moment: 'Must not this gateway too have been here before? And are not all things knotted together so firmly that this moment draws after it *all* that is to come? Therefore – itself too?'[15] The diverse streams of the past and the future flow together and eternally repeat. Strikingly, individuated forms are not the only 'objects' subjected to the force of repetition, but the conditions for return and time also return. That is to say, the gateway, as the condition for the temporal encounter, does not remain outside of time. Agents, conditions and time itself are immersed in a repetition without beginning or end. Deleuze extracts the Moment's tendency to deconstruct the opposition between the particular and the universal from *Zarathustra* when creating a synthesizing system of time and becoming.

Nietzsche's late notebooks hint at the synthetic power of the Moment as it appeared in 'On the Vision and the Riddle'. Unlike the addition of homogeneous units of measured time that combine to produce a whole, such as the addition of twenty-four successive hours in one day, the Moment contains the whole of time in Nietzsche. The Moment serves as a microcosm of the infinity of time resulting in a collapse of particular and universal. To this end, Nietzsche says, 'At a particular moment of force, an absolute conditionality of the redistribution of all its forces is given: it cannot stand still.'[16] This passage elucidates the synthetic character of the Moment which Deleuze expands into his own temporal syntheses. The Moment's enveloping of temporal forces indicates a repetition of the affirmative, or becoming. We know that in *Nietzsche and Philosophy* Deleuze describes reactivity as the separation of a force from what it can do. The Moment does not suffer from separation of capacity, and its power lies in the ability to cause all that steps through its gateway to return. The only condition that is attributed to the Moment is the redistribution of the synthesis of the past and future. What constitute 'all its forces given' are the two lanes of eternity which are conceived in terms of synthesis.

Focusing on the synthesis of temporal forces at the gateway of the Moment, Deleuze uses Nietzsche to show that becoming absolutely revolts against identity. It is his theory of forces as a heterogeneous monism that enables Deleuze to connect the differential Moment to the notion of synthesis.[17] According to Nietzsche's notebook from the summer of 1885, restlessness derived from synthesized redistribution of force conditions the Moment.[18] As Deleuze reads this redistribution, conditionality itself does not survive the restlessness of the Moment. *Nietzsche and Philosophy* provides a clear picture of the relationship between synthesis and pure difference. 'According to Nietzsche the Eternal Return is in no sense a thought of the identical but rather a thought of synthesis, a thought of the absolutely different which calls for a new principle outside science.'[19] Synthesis is another expression for relationality and it accounts for the maintaining of heterogeneity by way of continuity. Deleuze reads the synthesis of forces in Nietzsche as a description of quantitative and not qualitative difference. When Nietzsche critiques the becoming-equal of scientific measure he is nonetheless stressing quantitative difference, says Deleuze. Situating the Moment in a relationship of intensive quantities removes the concept from an exclusively qualitative reading, as well as from a reading that apprehends the Moment as a strictly poetic device. First extracting the Moment from *Zarathustra*, then placing it in proximity to Leibnizian calculus and Borgesian fiction produces new conceptual components that inform Deleuze's works.

Deleuze so skilfully synthesizes concepts from different philosophers that it is imaginable to see his ontological system as re-appropriation of either one of Leibniz, Nietzsche, Spinoza or, say, Bergson taken to the limit. For example, certain scholars see Deleuze as a unique expression of Leibniz through and through, yet it is equally conceivable to interpret his philosophy as a purely immanent systemetization of Nietzsche, Bergson or Spinoza, among others. The convincing set of masks Deleuze dons in all of his writings is a testament to his integration of differential synthesis as described in *Nietzsche and Philosophy*. Daniel W. Smith argues, for example, that Deleuze's use of synthesis is an immanent reworking of Leibniz's metaphysics. Leibniz's concepts of singularity, differential relations, virtual modality and their corresponding syntheses help

Deleuze create his system of ontological difference, claims Smith.[20] From Smith's prompting we are able to read the singular concepts in Deleuze's works through concepts developed by Leibniz. What is remarkable is that we can read those same Deleuzian concepts through the network of concepts created by Nietzsche, Bergson and so on. Rather than read Deleuze as an immanent systematizing of Leibniz, one could do as Keith Ansell-Pearson has done and read much of Deleuze's ontology as a revolutionary assimilation of Bergson's metaphysics, drawing from the concepts of virtuality, memory and Duration in order to deduce a principle of difference. Furthermore, we have just witnessed how tracing Deleuze's re-appropriation of the Moment from *Zarathustra* leads to an arrangement of conceptual components staged by Nietzsche, such as synthesis, force and repetition. All of these conceptual components demonstrate how Deleuze's systematizing of Nietzsche enabled him to deduce his concept of difference.

Did Deleuze lament, 'Two roads diverged in a yellow wood/ And sorry I could not travel both?'[21] No, on the contrary, he rejects the either/or framing of problems that result from individuated forms of being. He certainly took the road less travelled by, and this is accomplished through an affirmation of both/ and in disjunctive synthesis – a refusal of binary conditions – and *that* made all the difference. Choose all the roads, roads that have not yet been formed, roads that exist but have not yet been rendered perceptible and choose them all simultaneously. This is how Deleuze approaches the virtual roads between artists, philosophers, scientists and mathematicians. There is a conceptual pastiche unique to Deleuze's philosophy that includes a re-appropriation of different ideas in a multitude of historical contexts.

Concepts in Deleuze are pieces of mirrored glass in a vital, philosophical kaleidoscope. The patterns of one viewing reveal the colours of a Leibnizian universe, another viewing reflects the patterned colours of a Nietzschean universe and the same goes for myriad philosophers that influenced Deleuze. With becoming's shake of the hand, or shift in angle, the same concepts may distribute light that echoes the worlds of Proust, Scotus, Maimon or Riemann taken to the differential limit.[22] These concepts not only converge across philosophers, creating new universes in thought, but they also diverge to reflect the separate conceptual lines of particular thinkers, effecting communication at a distance. The ultimate artist-philosopher, Deleuze is more Bergsonian than Bergson, more Leibnizian than Leibniz, more Proustian than Proust. Deleuze transforms each philosopher of interest into a mirror, constructing a maze of absolute and relative reflections in a universe of refracted light. It is the re-appropriated Moment that serves as the point of convergence in sensation, the point of divergence in immanence, allowing for the interplay of concepts across philosophical worlds.

As it is extracted from 'The Vision and the Riddle', the Moment is developed in accordance with Leibniz's vanishing quantities in the differential relation and in accordance with Borges's labyrinth of incompossible presents. Deleuze reminds the reader that the becoming of the Eternal Return is not a circular movement of the same, and he adopts the lanes of eternity in *Zarathustra*. The line of Aion refers eternally to the repetition of the Moment and the gateway of time. Under any one of its aliases, such as the paradoxical instant, or the quasi-cause, the perverse Moment repeatedly bifurcates the present. Since it is not embedded in time, the Moment escapes Duration and is a non-present present. Operating like a ghostly machine, the paradoxical instant is what Nietzsche calls a particular moment of force, and therefore, it redistributes all its forces of time without the aid of subjective agency. Unlike Nietzsche, however, the perverse Moment is not said to change in time, and instead it conditions change without changing. At this point, Deleuze uses Leibniz's notions of singularities and differential relations to create a theory of quasi-causality.

By figuring Leibniz's concept of singularity into the re-appropriation of the Moment, the final break is made between the Eternal Return and subjectivity. Singular points mark the differential change of a curve in mathematics and are distinct from the ordinary points that compose the curve itself. The theory of singularities sidesteps determinations according to categories of the particular and the universal. As opposed to a hierarchical genus-species, universal-particular production of change, singularities converge and diverge in assemblages without intermixing. Daniel W. Smith explains the significance of the singular in mathematics and how Deleuze's ontology takes advantage of this unconventional notion. He says,

> In logic, the notion of the 'singular' has long been understood in relation to the 'universal'. In mathematics, however, the singular is related to a very different set of notions: the singular is distinguished from or opposed to the regular: the singular is what escapes the regularity of the rule. More importantly, mathematics distinguishes between points that are singular or remarkable, and those that are ordinary.[23]

Leibniz's singular point is not an individuated element, and as Arkady Plotnitsky explains when explicating Riemann's use of the point in his theory of multiplicity, it is an expression of change in a differential relation.[24] Plotnitsky traces the term 'point' in Riemannian space to theory of continuous multiplicity that serves as a conglomerate of local spaces, as opposed to the spatial model of discrete multiplicities and their corresponding 'elements'. The system of points in Riemann's theory of continuous multiplicity passes through Bergson and converges with Leibniz's notion of singularity as read by Deleuze. Singularities, Smith explains, form the conceptual bridge between the law of continuity and the principle of indiscernibles.[25] It is important for Deleuze to maintain internal difference in the concept, and not just qualitatively as we see with Bergson, but also quantitatively. The theory of singular points relates difference without reducing it to a transcendental signifier. According to Leibniz's principle of indiscernibles each thing contains a different concept, yet the law of continuity states that everything relates by way of infinitesimal, vanishing differences. This means that things become independently of their terms and through their relationality alone. To ensure that this relationality is not distorted by mechanisms of identity, Deleuze connects Riemannian points in continuous multiplicities with the singular points of Leibniz; the effect of which is a de-deification of the classical philosopher, turning him instead into a philosopher of pure heterogeneity and *dis*harmony.

In many ways, the theory of singularities and its appropriation through Riemannian space provides Deleuze with the necessary tools to develop Nietzsche's Moment. The rejection of homogeneous quantification does not necessitate an interpretation of forces through qualitative becoming. Singularities, as opposed to regular points, dovetail with the idea that only the most extreme forms return eternally. Excess survives the Eternal Return at the expense of the ordinary, and the singular point is a mark of the extraordinary. Deleuze contrasts the bare repetition of the same with the clothed repetition of the Eternal Return. He reveals the blending of Nietzsche and Leibniz in his conception of differential time:

> One of these repetitions is of the same, having no difference but that which is subtracted or drawn off; the other is of the Different, and includes difference. One has fixed terms and places; the other essentially includes displacement and disguise. One is negative and by default; the other is positive and by excess. One is of elements, extrinsic parts, cases and times; the other is of variable internal totalities, degrees and levels. One involves succession in fact, the other coexistence in principle. One is static; the other dynamic. One is extensive, the other intensive. One is ordinary; the other distinctive and involving singularities.[26]

This passage outlines the features of the Eternal Return and its masked repetition of difference. Displacement and disguise are contrasted with discrete space, as well as fixed terms. We are reminded of the infinitesimal, vanishing quantities that correspond to the elimination of fixed terms in the differential relation. The denunciation of fixed place in the repetition of difference recalls the continuous multiplicity of the Riemannian manifold. Meanwhile, the variable totalities and levels refer to the virtual pure past in Bergson/Proust and the coexistence of temporal syntheses. Excess is underscored in the affirmative selection of difference and it is aligned with the notion of singularity. Extreme forms return, and the differential limit in Leibniz is connected to the selective ontology of the active in Nietzsche. Deleuze remarks, 'Only the extreme forms return – those which, large or small, are deployed within the limit and extend to the limit of their power, transforming themselves and changing one into the other.'[27] It is clear from this passage that Deleuze conceives of the extreme, or the excessive, with an eye towards Leibniz's differential calculus. The language of approaching limits and inverse relations refers to the infinitesimal, vanishing quantities that were ignored in finite interpretations of the calculus. These unassignable quantities approach 0 eternally, a simultaneous splitting of the always already and the eternally not yet, which Deleuze describes perspicuously in his lectures in the 1980s on Leibniz at the University of Vincennes, at St. Denis.[28] The excessive is that which escapes the terms of a function and is pushed to the limit. That unassignable excess is what repeats eternally while it creates paradoxical time. The integration of excess is synthesized in an inverse operation of differential relations. The synthesis performed in integration is mapped onto the totality of forces that Nietzsche says are redistributed in a particular moment of force. Integration is the synthesis of divergent series, while differentiation is the quasi-causal operator of the Moment.

The Moment connects actual forms to virtual fields. Forging a synthesis that is not founded on a transcendental subject, the Moment extracts singularities from molar objects and distributes them into two simultaneous molecular streams of the past and the future. What is excessive in the actual indicates a singularity that is dislodged from other ordinary elements. The Moment eludes the present of individuation and repeatedly pulls time out of joint. Without being embedded in time, the Moment both synthesizes and differentiates the excessive. Distributing singularities that either converge with other singularities or diverge into separate series create an instantaneous temporality of pure events. The Moment, being untimely and a quasi-causal operator, instantaneously affirms all the divergent series of incompossible presents, once and for all. The entirety of Deleuze's philosophical works forms a labyrinth of incompossible presents and forking paths. The kaleidoscope effect of his work reflects the divergent and convergent possibilities at once. A particular concept, such as the Moment, can be read as a point of convergence across diverse philosophers, mathematicians and artists, such as Leibniz, Borges, Riemann, Bergson and Nietzsche; and it can also be read as a reflection of each philosopher's thought taken independently to the limit, proliferating new divergent series. The extreme forms of thinkers taken into consideration by Deleuze are repeated in his texts. What is excessive of each philosophical concept is synthesized in convergent and divergent ways by a redistribution of singularities. Certain singularities run into other singularities submerging a concept in becoming. The entanglement of forces of time is extracted from Nietzsche's Moment, interpreted through the intensive quantification of differential calculus in Leibniz, and distributed in networks that affirm the power of the false in Borges's labyrinth. This is an example of conceptual components condensing as they release the Moment from the gateway of *Zarathustra,* distributing the re-appropriated concept into de-actualized streams of the past and future.

Conceptual lines and the defeat of dualist ontology

The perverse Moment connects the three key re-appropriated concepts examined in this chapter by redistributing them along the line of Aion. Deleuze deliberately chooses the line to express a theory of eternity that opposes the cyclical time in Plato. As the line which the past and future unfold simultaneously, Deleuze inverts the criticism that circular time is never divorced from a more fundamental linear, chronometric, successive concept of time. This was the problem with the conventional interpretation of the Eternal Return in terms of the same; it implied a circularity of successive, linear, homogeneous time. Employing the differentiation of the Moment in the production of time Deleuze shows that truly linear time does not require a homogeneous sum of particular measurements of time. The line is instead a broken circle that expels all identity in the concept. And while the line of Aion produces segmented lines that break into individuated forms, it does not itself fall back into homogeneous linear forms.

There is nothing simple about the line in Deleuze; it is at once complex and involved. The straight line of Aion is the pure and empty form of time that proceeds as a labyrinth of untimely presents. The difference between the Moment and the line is *synthesis*. While the Moment is the quasi-causal differentiator of the present, the line upon which it repeats is the synthesis of repeated difference. Of course, the synthesis of the line is an elaborate series of divergence and convergence in absolute becoming – pure events as the synthesis of the future. The line-blocs in sensation orient differential series in such a way as to encourage various singularities to fall into one another, a process that accounts for the convergence of molecular becoming. Deleuze constructs a logic of becoming through his redefinition of the line. All of the conceptual components that arise from re-appropriations of Duration, the Eternal Return and the Moment involve and fold together in a line of becoming. Mapping the three aforementioned concepts also exposes the continuously broken line of becoming constituted by Deleuze's works. We will illustrate how Duration, the Eternal Return and the Moment each change in kind alone the broken line of Deleuze's concept of becoming. From singular events to actual forms, the process of individuation causes the line in Deleuze to constantly change in kind. Depending on which temporal processes are at work, the line emphasizes either: disjunctive synthesis (line of Aion), dissolution of form (abstract line), madness in sensation (northern line), co-presence (line-bloc) or escape from determination (line of flight). All of these listed tendencies respond to continuity in the line of becoming, but they also reflect different relationships to time.

We have chosen to focus on three particular re-appropriated concepts that inform Deleuze's theory of becoming to show how Deleuze performs this theory in his published works. There are points of condensation between Duration, the Eternal Return and the Moment that cause their assemblage to become at the same time that they each become as singular concepts. We have shown how each singular concept evinces becoming in Deleuze's writings as constantly re-appropriated concepts, and now we will investigate their becoming as a conceptual conglomerate.[29] We will witness the becoming of concepts in process.

Pre-individual singularities of each concept are extracted from the philosophical works in which they appear – in this case, the works of Bergson and Nietzsche – and these singularities are blocked together in sensation, then they are differentiated across virtual series. The conceptual tendencies that Deleuze extracted from other philosophers, which were shown above, emerged through the concepts' combined consideration in his writings. Heterogeneity, multiplicity, continuity, ontological memory and incessant otherness were some of the tendencies extracted from Bergson's concept of Duration, for instance. Forgetting, repetition, synthesis and futurity are important features that Deleuze extracts from the Eternal Return. Within the re-appropriation of Nietzsche's

Moment, intensive quantity, difference, paradox and distribution are stressed. By extracting these singular tendencies, Deleuze is able to paint a singular concept of becoming that integrates the chosen conglomeration of components. All of these selected tendencies fold into one another in new ways that indicate incompossible paths in their previous philosophical incarnations.

Reminiscent of the line-bloc formed between the wasp and the orchid, the line-bloc formed by Duration, the Eternal Return and the Moment does not share the same philosophical genealogy. Different philosophers are used to draw out new tendencies in each concept. We can indubitably say that Nietzsche did not theorize the Moment through Leibnizian calculus, Bergson did not develop Duration through Proustian sensation, and Nietzsche did not use the self-differing of Duration to create his doctrine of the Eternal Return. However, Deleuze masks himself as several philosophers to explore the limits of a concept. If Duration, the Eternal Return and the Moment are singular points, then the line-bloc sweeps them away from their fixed relation within the history of philosophy. Each exhibits tendencies that involve in an endless game of becoming-other.

When blocked with the molecular memory of Duration, the Eternal Return creates a whirring expression of self-referential madness in sensation: the ritornello. Duration remains tied to molecular memory in sensation which produces an otherness that is dynamic, like the Hatter and the Hare who trade places with one another without stopping. The time crystal of the ritornello is not yet shattered in sensation and involves a circuit between the virtual image and the actual object related through difference. A virtual image does not resemble its actual object; however, molecular memory remains in the relation of condensed singularities. Since the concept of the Eternal Return is in a perpetual play of becoming, it cannot operate in the same way independently of the material it is repeating. That is why Duration is used to explicate the Eternal Return in sensation. Duration, as Deleuze has appropriated it from Bergson, is embodied becoming with temporal components that are related to the notion of the pure past. Levels of the pure past are interrelated through difference and communicate through resonance. Difference is still affirmed by the Eternal Return, but now the affirmation takes its cue from the logic of sensation. Folding the components of Duration into the components of the Eternal Return draws a line in the map of becoming which accounts for the logic of sensation.

Deleuze keeps his word about concepts not reflecting general truths but the singularity of the material they envelop. When it comes to expression in sensation Duration is a becoming-eternal-return and the Eternal Return is a becoming-

Duration. The line-bloc of the two concepts thus proliferates in sensation as the ritornello. Resonating tendencies of ritornellos create the conditions for different worlds, concepts and for their corresponding singularities to converge in new affects and percepts. As such, the combination of components in the Eternal Return and Duration outline a logic of sensation that accounts for the relationship between the actual and the virtual. Singularities are extracted according to their molecular memory, although released from the molar structure of actual objects. Those singularities form a virtual-actual circuit that resonates across levels of the pure past. Resonance is a differential relation through synthesis, and the line-bloc of Duration and the Eternal Return produces a heterogeneous, continuous, differential synthesis through molecular memory. The co-presence of Duration and the Eternal Return in Deleuze's writings animates a tendency of becoming that expresses the northern line of art. That is to say that all forms in the actual are subjected to the becoming-mad of identity through difference. Different temporal rhythms refer to the never experienced pure past of memory in qualitative encounters, like we read of Combray and the tea-soaked madeleine. A formal forgetting envelops ontological memory, hence pulling materiality outside itself. It would be mistaken to see the line-bloc of Duration and the Eternal Return within Deleuze's works as instituting homogeneity in sensation.

It is the case that all expressions in sensation communicate in resonating levels of molecular memory, but there is no limit to the ways in which materiality is expressed. The line-bloc formed by the co-presence of Duration and the Eternal Return folds in on itself in sensation. The condensed tendencies of heterogeneity, continuity, repetition, difference and ontological memory create the conditions for the construction of the ritornello by composing a territory within Deleuze's concept of difference. Put simply, *creating the concept of the ritornello is only made possible by composing a ritornello in sensation*. In a move that pulls concepts out of chronological history, Deleuze takes the points of Duration in Bergson, and the Eternal Return in Nietzsche and draws a nebulous contour around them which makes their location indeterminable. Their singularities are unleashed from the conceptual combinations of previous texts and diverted into new combinations; these combinations use distance to resonate the differential return of sensation. The line-bloc of Duration and the Eternal Return illuminates how sensory becoming produces a schizophrenic disordering of the fixed in matter.

In *What Is Philosophy?* a concept is defined as a combination of a finite number of heterogeneous components that are inseparable from one another.[30] A component refers to the Leibnizian singularity, or what Deleuze calls an intensive ordinate. These singularities are variations in the concept and should not be understood in terms of extension or comprehension. Singular components, like the concepts they assemble, are always in process. This means that the singular points that are extracted from the concepts of Duration, the Eternal Return and the Moment are co-present in the concept of becoming. How the concept of becoming varies depends on the plane upon which it is unfolded and the particular problem to which it is responding. Components are thus oriented in various ways depending on relative conditions and this allows them to remain distinct while becoming indiscernible. By creating communicative lines among components a concept encourages a becoming-other. We can see this conceptual interchange between the singular components of Duration, the Eternal Return and the Moment. An indiscernibility arises in the conceptual neighbourhoods of the components. As Deleuze and Guattari explain, 'There is an area *ab* that belongs to both *a* and *b*, where *a* and *b* 'become' indiscernible. These zones, thresholds, or becomings, this inseparability, define the internal consistency of the concept.'[31] Another term for the shared area of conceptual components is the line-bloc. A concept is a finite series of line-blocs that allow components to relate in new ways, thereby developing new aspects of any given concept. The ritornello is a shared area between the components of Duration and the Eternal Return, and certain singularities of these two concepts are released and combined in this new conglomerate. Since a concept is always in process, the relation of components is ever changing. To state it more concretely, posing a particular problem or forming a resonant bridge to another concept may involve subtracting, adding or reordering singularities. Developing the concept of becoming according to the plane of immanence, rather than sensation, involves the displacement of singularities of ontological memory in favour of the singularities of the ontologically forgetful future, for instance. The result is a conceptual reordering whose logic is that of the abstract line.

Redon's description of the abstract line in chiaroscuro is adopted in Deleuze's philosophy to show how the contemplation of the future dissolves forms. Against notions of linear, teleological progression, the line operates through involution. Components are folded together in complexes that undo actual forms and subject singularities to a radical forgetting. The dissolution of forms that releases singularities into diverse streams or abstract lines is a function of the future. Pre-individual, larval selves contemplate a groundless future which dislodges forms from the actual present. Contemplation in this restrictive sense is a synthesis of eluded presents that are integrated in the Eternal Return of the future.

We notice right away that the rising groundlessness enacted by the abstract line puts components of the Moment and the Eternal Return into proximity. The tension between the differentiating Moment and the synthesizing repetition of the Eternal Return is reflected in the logic of the abstract line. Where we previously saw singularities of Duration, Eternal Return and memory combined in the concept of the ritornello, the abstract line is a temporal contemplation that expels memory. Pure heterogenesis connects conceptual components by the contemplated groundlessness of the abstract line. As they block off a shared area, the Eternal Return and the Moment exchange singularities. They simultaneously integrate and split the excessive within the actual present, and this reveals the future to be an instantaneous temporality. The perverse Moment pushes fixed points in the actual to differential limits by redistributing their singularities into divergent lines of incompossible worlds. Dissimulated and diverted, forms are abstracted by the repetition of the future. At every moment that a form is de-actualized, the entire open series of divergent worlds is instantaneously synthesized.

Deleuze offers a glimpse into the instantaneous time of absolute becoming in his preface to the American edition of *Nietzsche and Philosophy*. He writes, 'The Eternal Return is the instant or the eternity of becoming eliminating whatever offers resistance.'[32] The elimination of anything – and any thing – that offers resistance corresponds to the transmutation of represented form into an abstract line. Without the restriction of a time that endures, the future dislocates singularities from embodied structures and instantaneously distributes them into divergent lines. All of the ideational events in absolute becoming are interconnected through relations of distance, thus the entire network resonates at every moment, at every paradoxical instant.

This gives a new meaning to Nietzsche's 'once and for all'. At the level of sensation, specifically in Deleuze's writings, the Moment is co-present with the Eternal Return, and their components pass back and forth across an abstract line. It is fair to say, then, that the absolute becoming of instantaneous time is inexorably tied to the sensory becoming of molecular memory. Otherwise, we would have a strict dualism where effectuated causality of the actual remained disconnected from the instantaneity of events. The logic of sensation and its embodied mad becoming provides an intermediary between the two. By temporally dynamizing Bergson's qualitative revision of the Riemannian continuous multiplicity along the abstract lines of the future, Deleuze accounts for heterogenetic change. An abstract line is a dissimulating connection between singularities as they are embedded in actual forms and the virtuality of events. Sensation disorganizes the temporal fixity of actual forms and is subject to perpetual division, which cannot be accomplished without changing that which is divided in kind. Therefore, an actual form undergoes a process of dissimilarity changing in nature at each moment of division. Whereas the efficient causation of states of affairs can be divided *ad infinitum* without changing in kind, the quasi-causal operator of the Moment evokes change in kind with each division.

The Moment is the point of connection between the actual and the virtual. It extracts singularities from actual forms, creates blocs of becoming in sensation and distributes them into divergent series through absolute becoming. A bridge is thus formed between the line of flight, or pure differential distribution, and the segmented linearity of actual forms. Deleuze and Guattari assign three fundamental lines between the actual and the virtual, and the intermediary line of sensation keeps the other two lines from forming two separate ontologies. 'In short, *there is a line of flight, which is already complex since it has singularities; and there is a customary or molar line with segments; and between the two (?), there is a molecular line with quanta that cause it to tip to one side or the other.*'[33] From the contemplation of the future as it cracks the corporeal present into the pure past and the future to the homogeneous causal lines in the actual we find the disruptive molecular line of sensation. What Deleuze and Guattari describe as a 'supple segmentarity' is a loosening of singularities that work either to causally create new individuated forms or to quasi-causally escape form in lines of flight. The line of flight is deemed the most primary of all the three lines (line of flight, molar line and molecular line), for it is a radical deterritorialization that sets heterogenesis in motion, but the assignation of three lines that differ in kind speaks volumes about the tripartite nature of Deleuze's ontology. Each of the lines responds to a separate onto-temporality. Customary segmented lines correspond to successive, linear time of the corporeal present; molecular lines correspond to the sensory becomings of molecular memory and lines of flight correspond to the absolute becoming of the future. By introducing a third term between absolute becoming and static Being Deleuze outlines an ontological system that would best be characterized as a heterogeneous monism.

Against the quick and easy criticism that Deleuze's ontology lapses into a dualism of parallel lines, such as that launched by Žižek, François Zourabichvili accounts for the nuances of the line.[34] He explains that Deleuze's philosophy is not a simple expression of fixed forms versus a world of becoming. All constituted forms are an effect of lines that change state from the virtual to the actual, the line being a sign that envelops time and is the basis for a semiotics of duration. There are also different variations of lines, and all forms are differenciated according to any number of lines that are immanent to themselves. Zourabichvili's analysis of lines helps demystify the previously antithetical realms of becoming and being. Matter, he says, moves transversally throughout the three primary lines (segmentary lines in Being, the line of Aion and the ambiguous, plastic line of molecular memory), two of which pertain to becoming. Matter does not move horizontally without an engagement with its molecular disorientation and eventual differentiation along the line of Aion. As Zourabichvili says, 'Thus, there isn't a world of fixed forms and a world of becoming, but different states of the line, different types of lines, whose involution constitutes a *map* amenable to life.'[35] The three re-appropriated concepts considered: Duration, the Eternal Return and the Moment create a temporal map through the lines of becoming.

The components of these three concepts combine to form the concept of becoming in Deleuze, which is, of course, a multiplicity, or rhizome. These components are not terms but pure relations that are faster or slower according to the temporal frameworks they work to define. As singularities, they reach infinite speed as lines of flight that crack identities open, drawing an abstract line through actual forms. Individuated forms are rendered ambiguous while their singularities relentlessly engage in games of sensory becoming. This is a stage in the line where fragmentation defines the dynamisms of materiality. Flashing durations collide in the formation of new conditions of experience, in affects and percepts.

Taking a cue from Spinoza, Deleuze removes sensation from the effectuated temporality of the actual and instead articulates lines of change through relational blockages. Deleuze and Guattari state, 'What is called "perception" is no longer a state of affairs but a state of the body as induced by another body, and "affection" is the passage of this state to another state as increase or decrease of potential-power through the action of other bodies.'[36] We see that affects and percepts are not matters of fact in actual experience but are a-subjective conditions of experience. Their logic is that of molecular line where the pathology of Duration maps ambiguous territories in sensation. These molecular lines are expressed as northern lines which resonate across molecular becomings. The embodied components of Duration bring out different affective expressions in the Eternal Return. Embodied becomings disorient matter through the differential force of the quasi-cause, and this Moment effects dynamic genesis in sensation, static genesis across events. Matter and memory are hence fully connected through differential, broken lines. Customary lines are broken by abstraction, disoriented in molecular lines of memory and distributed into divergent, fleeing lines of the future in Aion. In their essay, 'Rhizome,' Deleuze and Guattari explain how all of the diverse temporal lines of the rhizome defeat dualistic readings of their ontology. They say,

> A rhizome may be broken, shattered at a given spot, but it will start up again on one of its old lines, or on new lines. You can never get rid of ants because they form an animal rhizome that can rebound time and again after most of it has been destroyed. Every rhizome contains lines of segmentarity according to which it is stratified, territorialized, organized, signified, attributed, etc., as well as lines of deterritorialization down which it constantly flees. There is a rupture in the rhizome whenever segmentary lines explode into a line of flight, but the line of flight is part of the rhizome. These lines always tie back to one another. That is why one can never posit a dualism or a dichotomy, even in the rudimentary form of the good and the bad. You may make a rupture, draw a line of flight, yet there is still a danger that you will reencounter organizations that restratify everything, formations that restore power to a signifier, attributions that reconstitute a subject.[37]

Never is it the case that lines of flight remain permanently disconnected from lines of segmentarity, and vice versa. For this reason the ontological system of Deleuze resists the binary logic of becoming versus Being. An elaborate network of intensive virtual resonances entangle with extensive productions in actual forms. The instantaneous time of the quasi-cause (the Moment) repeats eternally (Eternal Return), expressing itself through molecular lines of memory (Duration), echoing through individuated structures in the corporeal present. Depending upon which rung of the temporal ladder matter is caught, it will take on the temporal logic of the untimely quasi-cause; the disjunctively synthesized future; the contemplated habit of the sub-representational present; the resonant levels of the pure past; or the efficient causation of the perceived present. What Deleuze and Guattari have defined as absolute becoming is the pure distribution of singularities in divergent lines of the future. Completely devoid of memory – whether molar or molecular – the future repeats the untimely, dividing moment in an Eternal Return. We know, however, that this is only part of the story. As Deleuze and Guattari explain, the theory of multiplicity requires that there be at least two types of multiplicities for the concept to work. They state, 'This is not because dualism is better than unity but because the multiplicity is precisely what happens between the two.'[38] Without the nebulous clouds of sensory becoming, the line between present and future would remain unarticulated. Line-blocs reveal the logic of sensation to resonate worlds through the differential rhythms of the pure past. Re-appropriating concepts from diverse philosophers releases concepts from their individuated histories, Deleuze plunges concepts into a sea of becoming. Deleuze's ontology fuses becoming with temporality: the one relentlessly becoming the other. With absolute becoming, sensory becoming and the illusory effectuated Being, Deleuze's ontology is tripartite, and is not a dualism of Being and Event, as Žižek claims. All three realms are intertwined: the incorporeal line of Aion in the virtual, along with the intermediary nebulae of sensory becoming, and the segmentary, individuated lines of the actual.

This book opened with the question 'What is becoming?' and we were able to trace Deleuze's conceptual history into the heart of his ontological system. Through his innovative re-appropriations of concepts in Bergson and Nietzsche we began to map the complex network of temporal lines from the actual to the virtual. Creating a pastiche of concepts cut from additional thinkers, such as Leibniz, Borges, Riemann and Spinoza, allowed Deleuze to develop new conceptual tendencies in the components that inform his concept of becoming. Along the way we discovered that there are two fundamental concepts of becoming in Deleuze's ontology: sensory becoming and absolute becoming. By dramatizing the intensive features of the concepts of becoming, we were able to map the corresponding temporal logics they involve. Any ambiguity arising within Deleuze's terminological variance in relation to his concept of becoming has been resolved; as a result, this study may be used for conceptual precision in the literature which aims to employ Deleuze's concept of becoming. The point of divergence between absolute becoming and sensory becoming was shown to be the temporal logics which they unfolded. Bergsonian Duration was made radically other by displacing itself within the currents of Proustian reminiscence, one of the lanes of time in *Thus Spoke Zarathustra*, and Riemannian multiplicity. Still self-differing between the resonant layers of the pure past, the quasi-cause of the eluded present formed a chasm between the past and the future.

Taken as the Moment of a particular force, the quasi-cause was shown to de-actualize the present in two simultaneous streams along the line of Aion. The line of Aion, however, characterizes both the Eternal Return of difference as a synthesis and absolute becoming of the perverse Moment. Investigated according to an integration of infinitesimal difference, the Eternal Return synthesizes singularities in divergent futures. Like Borges's labyrinth, the future is the unconditioned repetition of incompossible presents which have been de-actualized. Every form that coincides with the Moment becomes mad through a bifurcation of past and future, and extracted singularities may or may not converge with other, new singularities in sensation forming new worlds destined to become enveloped in other worlds. Nothing stays still for long, and the restless system of becoming infinitely divides individuals in a game of chance. Deleuze's divergent concept of becoming portrays a heterogeneous universe of immanent temporal syntheses and conceptual innovation: a nomadology. Using his philosophical works to dramatize the differential logic he thematizes, Deleuze creates a multi-mirrored universe where form and content infinitely refract in a vital kaleidoscope of becoming.

Notes

Introduction

1 In order to think pure becoming, or pure difference, the concept must be rescued from the distorting mechanisms of representation. 'To rescue difference from its maledictory state seems, therefore, to be the project of the philosophy of difference. Cannot difference become a harmonious organism and relate determination to other determinations within a form – that is to say, within the coherent medium of an organic representation? There are four principal aspects to "reason" in so far as it is the medium of representation: identity, in the form of the *undetermined* concept; analogy, in the relation between ultimate *determinable* concepts; opposition, in the relation between *determinations* within concepts; resemblance, in the *determined* object of the concept itself. These forms are like the four heads or the four shackles of mediation. Difference is "mediated" to the extent that it is subjected to the fourfold root of identity, opposition, analogy and resemblance.' Deleuze, *Difference and Repetition*, 37–8.

2 The famous parable of the death of God appears in §125 of *The Gay Science* and prefigures its eventual elaboration in *Thus Spoke Zarathustra*. Friedrich Nietzsche, *The Gay Science*, trans. Walter Kaufmann (New York: Vintage Press, 1974), 181–2.

3 Michel Foucault, *The Order of Things* (New York: Random House, Inc., 1970), 342.

4 See Deleuze's preface to the English edition of *Nietzsche and Philosophy*. Gilles Deleuze, *Nietzsche and Philosophy*, trans. Hugh Tomlinson (New York: Columbia University Press, 1983), xi.

5 For a comprehensive, perspicuous account of Deleuze's three syntheses of time, see: James Williams, *Gilles Deleuze's Philosophy of Time* (Edinburgh: Edinburgh University Press, 2011).

6 Gilles Deleuze and Félix Guattari, *A Thousand Plateaus*, trans. Brian Massumi (London: Continuum Press, 2004), 336.

7 Deleuze, *Difference and Repetition*, xx.

8 Jorge Luis Borges's short story, 'The Garden of Forking Paths', helps Deleuze connect Nietzsche's power of the false with Leibniz's notion of incompossibility in a construction of a temporal theory of becoming, which will be discussed in Chapter 4.

9 Gilles Deleuze and Félix Guattari, *What Is Philosophy?*, trans. Hugh Tomlinson and Graham Burchell (New York: Columbia University Press, 1994), 126.

10 The axiomatic analysis of philosophy and science in Deleuze and Guattari has influenced new scientific and mathematical theories which implement intensive features and virtual processes. In particular, see the works of Manuel DeLanda and Arkady Plotnitsky.

11 Deleuze and Guattari, *What Is Philosophy?*, 42.

12 Deleuze, *Nietzsche and Philosophy*, 40.

13 Deleuze, *Difference and Repetition*, xvii.

14 Deleuze and Guattari, *What Is Philosophy?*, 21.

15 For a detailed analysis of the concept as a complex conglomerate of components see Arkady Plotnitsky's essay, 'Bernhard Riemann', Arkady Plotnitsky, 'Bernhard Riemann', in *Deleuze's Philosophical Lineage* (Edinburgh: Edinburgh University Press, 2009), 190–208.

16. It should be noted that Deleuze's revolutionary re-interpretations of temporality also include a conception of time from the vantage point of the untimely, influenced by Nietzsche.

17 Even though 'a' becoming refers to a single becoming, it logically implies a plurality of different becomings. While *A Thousand Plateaus* is the most obvious text wherein the concept of becoming is spoken as a plurality (e.g. becomings, or a becoming), however, we see this pluralizing tendency in his earlier works, as well, such as *Nietzsche and Philosophy* and *Bergsonism*.

18 In the singular form, becoming is never an exemplar but a univocal, unconditioned unfolding to which everything is subordinated, including becomings (plural). Expressions of absolute becoming can be found across Deleuze's philosophical trajectory, often intermingled or conflated with the relative plurality of becomings. The terminological variance signifying two distinct concepts of becoming produces conceptual obfuscation in Deleuze, which we aim to clarify in the course of this book.

19 These two terms are drawn from Deleuze and Guattari's description of two concepts of becoming in *What Is Philosophy?* We have chosen not to adopt one of the original term, 'conceptual becoming', since it leads to confusion. Conceptual becoming in Deleuze and Guattari is absolute, infinite and unconditioned; sensory becoming is relative, finite and conditioned. And while conceptual becoming is absolute and unconditioned, *concepts* in Deleuze are both absolute in their survey and relative in their contours. However, there is nothing relative or conditioned in what they call conceptual becoming. Therefore, 'absolute becoming' has been substituted to avoid confusion. 'Sensory becoming' does not lead to the same sort of confusion, so it has remained unchanged. Together they account for the two sides of a concept: absolute and relative; unconditioned and conditioned; infinite and finite. Paul Patton and John Protevi also make this distinction between the absolute, unconditioned features of conceptual becoming, versus the conditioned features of sensory becoming. Paul Patton and John Protevi, *Between Deleuze and Derrida* (London: Continuum, 2003), 22. The original passage where Deleuze

and Guattari distinguish between two concepts of becoming appears in *What Is Philosophy?* They say, 'Sensory becoming is the action by which something or someone is ceaselessly becoming-other (while continuing to be what they are), sunflower or Ahab, whereas conceptual becoming is the action by which the common event itself eludes what it is. Conceptual becoming is heterogeneity grasped in an absolute form; sensory becoming is otherness caught in a matter of expression.' Deleuze and Guattari, *What Is Philosophy?*, 117.

20 The term multiplicity is taken from Bernhard Riemann via Bergson, particularly as Deleuze appropriates the notion from *Time and Free Will*.

21 We will respond to the accusation of dualist ontology launched by a leading representative of the criticism: Slavoj Žižek.

22 'It would not be an exaggeration to say that almost all of Deleuze's fundamental metaphysical concepts (difference, singularity, multiplicity, virtuality) are derived from this Leibnizian matrix.' Daniel W Smith, 'G. W. F. Leibniz', in *Deleuze's Philosophical Lineage* (Edinburgh: Edinburgh University Press, 2009), 63 In many ways, the success of *Deleuze's Philosophical Lineage* rests in its ability to portray simultaneous philosophical worlds in Deleuze's thought.

23 Pearson's book, *Philosophy and the Adventure of the Virtual*, investigates the architecture of Deleuze's thought as a sustained encounter with Bergson. Keith Ansell-Pearson, *Philosophy and the Adventure of the Virtual: Bergson and the Time of Life* (New York: Routledge, 2002).

24 A notable instance where Deleuze's understanding of Nietzsche is argued to evidence a grafting of Bergsonism appears in Giovanna Borradori's scholarship. Giovanna Borradori, 'On the Presence of Bergson in Deleuze's Nietzsche', *Philosophy Today* 43 (1999), 140–6.

25 Simondon, Maimon and Scotus all come to mind, for instance, as pivotal figures in the development of Deleuze's philosophical project. Nonetheless, this study argues that these thinkers are secondary to Deleuze's re-appropriation of the temporal concepts that inform his theory of becoming.

26 Gilles Deleuze, *Desert Islands and Other Texts 1953-1974*, ed. David Lapoujade, trans. Michael Taormina (Los Angeles: Semiotext(e), 2004), 94.

27 Ibid.

28 Deleuze adopts Bergson's view that posing a problem is a creative act that conditions and produces its solution. Deleuze, *Bergsonism*, 15–16.

Chapter 1

1 One of the more compelling studies of Deleuze's concept of becoming can be found in Craig Lundy's *History and Becoming: Deleuze's Philosophy of Creativity.* In this impressive work, Lundy outlines three modes of becoming in Deleuze, constructed

through a reading of *The Logic of Sense*. Lundy is immediately faced with a problem when accounting for successive, incremental changes in history. The becoming of incorporeal events is instantaneous and infinitely distributive, while, on the other hand, the becoming of depths plunges all forms into dynamic chaos. For this reason Lundy posits a third mode of becoming, 'developmental becoming'. He writes, 'Unlike surface becomings [the becoming of events], developmental becomings involve an incomplete process, something not yet fully achieved; they are always at some stage of undress, in the process of becoming-other'. Craig Lundy, *History and Becoming: Deleuze's Philosophy of Creativity* (Edinburgh: Edinburgh University Press, 2012), 48. The intuition that another mode of becoming is called for to account for the dynamism between ideality and the state of affairs is on track, but the intrusion of sensory becoming in the actual, which Lundy has convoluted by mixing elements of Aion (the innocent boy child of Heraclitus, marked by ontological forgetting in Nietzsche) with the schizophrenic becoming of the body without organs in sensory becoming. Chapter 2 provides further elaboration of the temporal processes of Aion and Chronos in *The Logic of Sense*.

2   The critique of Deleuze as a philosopher of the One, witnessed most infamously in the works of Alain Badiou and Slavoj Žižek, is founded on the privileging of incorporeal becoming of the Event, theorized most extensively by Deleuze in *The Logic of Sense*. This specific critique subordinates the dynamic becoming of sensation in the selfsame text to the logic of the Event, presenting a false image of incompatible dualism. For a comprehensive look at Badiou's reading of the Deleuzian Event, see: Jon Roffe, 'The Event in Deleuze', in *Badiou's Deleuze* (Montreal: McGill-Queen's University Press, 2012), 104–28.

Conversely, there is inconsistency among Deleuze scholars with respect to the concept of becoming, many of whom employ the dynamic becoming of sensation from *A Thousand Plateaus* at the expense of static genesis in absolute becoming. This is particularly visible in postcolonial and feminist scholarship, which makes use of Deleuze and Guattari's notion of 'becoming-woman'. The aspects of becoming most coloured by Bergsonism, exemplified by 'sensory becoming' in *What Is Philosophy?* or 'becomings' in *A Thousand Plateaus* heavily populate the secondary literature. Compare, for instance, Rosi Braidotti's underlining of 'rememoration' in her materialist reading of becoming to Deleuze and Guattari's description of sensory becoming, fn. 19 of the Introduction. Rosi Braidotti, 'Meta(l)morphoses', *Culture, Theory & Society* 14, no. 2 (1997): 67–80.

3   Just as Žižek treats Badiou's (per)version of the Deleuzian Event as a ready-made artefact of his concept of becoming, a tendency in Deleuzian scholarship has emerged where the same passage in Chapter 10 of *A Thousand Plateaus* is used in countless articles and books as a cutout for Deleuze's concept of becoming. The passage in question reads: 'Becoming is to emit particles that take on certain

relations of movement and rest because they enter a particular zone of proximity. Or, it is to emit particles that enter that zone because they take on those relations'. This is not to say that the uses of the aforementioned passage are necessarily erroneous, but one must be careful not to neglect the temporal interstices of both modes of becoming, to be developed in this and subsequent chapters, when deploying the concept of becoming. Deleuze and Guattari, *A Thousand Plateaus*, 301.

4   This refers to the reinterpretation of the history of philosophy as an effect of immanent causality, as opposed to an accumulation of chronological events in successive, linear time. The most notable exposition of the becoming of concepts in the history of philosophy is *What Is Philosophy?* For an expanded analysis of Deleuze's (and Guattari's) notion of history, see Jay Lampert's *Deleuze and Guattari's Philosophy of History*. Jay Lampert, *Deleuze and Guattari's Philosophy of History* (London: Continuum Press, 2006).

5   'Becoming (singular)' is meant to denote numerical singularity evidenced in language, as the process of becoming is one of infinite, continuous, virtual intensities. Likewise, 'becomings (plural)' involve a separate conglomerate of finite, continuous sensible processes within the fold of absolute becoming.

6   Gilles Deleuze, *Bergsonism*, trans. Hugh Tomlinson and Barbara Habberjam (New York: Zone Books, 1991), 37.

7   Henri Bergson, *Creative Evolution*, trans. Arthur Mitchell (Mineola: Dover Publications, 1998), 304.

8   Points of becoming are actually lines contesting the punctual notion of time and space, as we will see Chapter 3.

9   Deleuze and Guattari, *A Thousand Plateaus*, 303. Sensory becoming involves a molecular composition that defies the effectuated causality of representation. Molecular becoming is connected to the 'pathology of duration', whereby the relationship established between two things encourages the exchange of their intensive features, or their molecules. 'Yes, all becomings are molecular: the animal, flower, or stone one becomes are molecular collectivities, haecceities, not molar subjects, objects, or form that we know from the outside and recognize from experience, through science, or by habit.'

10   Elizabeth Grosz distinguishes between the active transformation of becoming versus the persistence and preservation of Duration, which also participates in transformation. Elizabeth Grosz, 'Thinking the New,' in *Becomings*, ed. Elizabeth Grosz (Ithaca: Cornell University Press, 1999), 15–28.

11   Cliff Stagoll, 'Becoming,' in *The Deleuze Dictionary* (Edinburgh: Edinburgh University Press, 2005), 21–2.

12   Henri Bergson, *The Creative Mind: An Introduction to Metaphysics*, trans. Mabelle L Andison (New York: First Carol Publishing Group, 1992), 142. Deleuze borrows this temporalization of the features of continuous multiplicity from Bergson.

Becoming unfolds as a multiplicity, for Deleuze and Guattari state, 'Becoming and multiplicity are the same thing. A multiplicity is defined not by its elements, nor by a center of unification or comprehension. It is defined by the number of dimensions it has; it is not divisible, it cannot lose or gain a dimension *without changing its nature.*' Deleuze and Guattari, *A Thousand Plateaus*, 275.

13 Deleuze and Guattari, *A Thousand Plateaus*, 327.

14 From 'The Drunken Boat' Arthur Rimbaud, *Arthur Rimbaud: Complete Works*, trans. Paul Schmidt (New York: Harper and Rowe, 1967).

15 Bergson, *The Creative Mind: An Introduction to Metaphysics*, 147.

16 Pearson, *Philosophy and the Adventure of the Virtual: Bergson and the Time of Life*, 72.

17 Williams, *Gilles Deleuze's Philosophy of Time*, 67.

18 Deleuze, *Bergsonism*, 51. Deleuze's concept of sensory becoming carries over what he interprets as the identification of duration and memory in Bergson. 'Duration is essentially memory, consciousness and freedom. It is consciousness and freedom because it is primarily memory. Now, Bergson always presents this identity of memory and duration in two ways: "the conservation *and* preservation of the past in the present".' Deleuze's re-appropriation of duration extricates the role of consciousness by using Leibniz's notion of singularities in order to conceive of becoming as an impersonal, pre-subjective process, but the role of duration in his concept of becoming is unmistakable.

19 'This (non)-being is the differential element in which affirmation, as multiple affirmation, finds the principle of its genesis ... beyond contradiction, difference – beyond *non*-being, (non)-being; beyond the negative, problems and questions.' Deleuze, *Difference and Repetition*, 77.

20 For Bergson, the intellect functions like a cinematograph, where single, motionless snapshots are strung along in succession to create the perception of movement. This movement, or change, is subordinated to the immobilizing perception of static forms of being. Bergson, *Creative Evolution*, 306.

21 Deleuze, *Bergsonism*, 44.

22 Bergson, *Creative Evolution*, 314.

23 Ibid., 315.

24 Deleuze, *Bergsonism*, 45–6.

25 The description of becoming as an empty form of time is prevalent in *The Logic of Sense*, yet it appears in other texts, as well, including *Difference and Repetition* and *A Thousand Plateaus*.

26 Martin Heidegger, *Being and Time*, trans. John Macquarrie and Edward Robinson (New York: Harper and Row, 1962), 1. Our study is indebted to the fundamental ontology of Heidegger, whose investigation into the meaning of Being and its distinction from beings informs our distinction between Deleuzian becoming and becomings.

27 One is able to witness this tendency in much of the feminist literature on Deleuze, which leans towards theories of embodiment. For instance, Rosi Braidotti explains, 'In my reading, the process of becoming is like the patient task of approximating, through a series of adaptations, the raw simplicity of the forces that shape one's embodied intensity or existential temperature. Becoming is a process of approaching what we are, that is to say reducing oneself to the naked bone of one's speed of rememoration one's capacity for perception, one's empathy for and impact on others' (Braidotti, 'Meta(l)morphoses', 68–9). The emphasis on spatiotemporal dynamisms and use of 'rememoration' invokes the molecular memory of Bergsonian duration, specifically sensory becoming as it is unfurled in *A Thousand Plateaus*.

28 Deleuze and Guattari, *A Thousand Plateaus*, 322.

29 Gaston Bachelard, *Dialectic of Duration*, trans. Mary McAllister Jones (Manchester: Clinamen Press , 2000).

30 Grosz, 'Thinking the New', 19.

31 Absolute becoming does not endure, for example, only those becomings in sensibility do so.

32 François Dosse, *Gilles Deleuze and Félix Guattari: Intersecting Lives*, trans. Deborah Glassman (New York: Columbia University Press, 2010), 406–7.

33 Anne Sauvagnargues, *Artmachines: Deleuze, Guattari, Simondon*, trans. Suzanne Verderber with Eugene W. Holland (Edinburgh: Edinburgh University Press, 2016), 97.

34 Bergson, *Creative Evolution*, 11.

35 Ibid., 248.

36 For an expanded analysis of Deleuze's systematization of Nietzsche's philosophy see: Samantha Bankston, 'To Have Done with the Judgment of "Reason": Deleuze's Aesthetic Ontology', in *Deleuze and the Passions* (New York: Punctum Press, 2016), 41–57.

37 Daniel W Smith, 'The Conditions of the New', *Deleuze Studies* (2007): 1–21.

38 In *Bergsonism* Deleuze explains that matter is 'the most expanded (*détendu*) degree of duration'. Deleuze, *Bergsonism*, 93.

39 Singularities are the intensive features, or components, of a concept. The notion of singularity is taken from Leibniz in order to construct an immanent universe of pre-individual singularities. As Daniel W. Smith explains, 'The theory of singularities also provides Deleuze with a model of individuation or determination: one can say of any determination in general (any "thing") that it is *a combination of the singular and ordinary*, that is, it is a "multiplicity" constituted by its singular and ordinary points. Just as mathematical curves are determined by their points of inflection (extrema, minima, maxima, etc.), so physical states of affairs can be said to be determined by singularities that mark a change of phase (boiling points,

points of condensation, fusion, coagulation, crystallization, etc.).' Smith, 'G. W. F. Leibniz,' 61.

40 Henri Bergson, *Time and Free Will: An Essay on the Immediate Data of Consciousness*, trans. F. L. Pogson (New York: Dover Publications, Inc., 2001), 110.

41. Elizabeth Grosz, 'Bergson, Deleuze and the Becoming of Unbecoming', *Parallax*, XI (2005): 4–13.

42 DeLanda, *Intensive Science and Virtual Philosophy*, 128.

43 Deleuze and Guattari, *A Thousand Plateaus*, 324.

44 Deleuze, *Bergsonism*, 52.

45 Ontological memory is not organized by a transcendental subject, but is interconnected through the durational paths of immanent life.

46 Ibid., 55.

47 'Memories of a Moviegoer', 'Memories of a naturalist', 'Memories of a Bergsonian', 'Memories of a Sorcerer, I, II, and III', 'Memories of a Theologian', 'Memories of a Spinozist I and II', 'Memories of a Haecceity', 'Memories of a Plan(e) Maker', 'Memories of a Molecule', 'Memories of the Secret', 'Memories and Becomings, Points, and Blocks'. Deleuze and Guattari, *A Thousand Plateaus*.

48 Ibid., 324.

49 This is a clear example of Deleuze and Guattari's conflation of the two concepts of becoming.

50 Deleuze and Guattari, *A Thousand Plateaus*, 324.

51 Gilles Deleuze, *Proust and Signs*, trans. Richard Howard (Minneapolis: University of Minnesota Press, 2000), 111.

52 For example, two competing conceptions of Deleuzian becoming are located in the works of Elizabeth Grosz and Manuel DeLanda. DeLanda often talks of pure becoming, which is strictly opposed to duration, and Grosz intimately connects becoming and duration without making a distinction between sensory and absolute becoming, a distinction which cannot be relegated to numerical difference. The most successful distinction between absolute becoming and sensory becoming appears in *Between Deleuze and Derrida*, by Paul Patton and John Protevi. They separate the conditioned forms of sensory becoming from the unconditioned form of absolute becoming. They write, 'Deleuze and Guattari's concept of becoming, which in its pure form amounts to something very similar to what Derrida calls iteration, also involves a distinction between conditioned forms of becoming and an absolute or pure form.' Patton and Protevi, *Between Deleuze and Derrida*, 22.

53 Deleuze, *Two Regimes of Madness*, 207.

54 Ibid.

55 Deleuze, *Nietzsche and Philosophy*, 22.

56 Deleuze, *Difference and Repetition*, 183.

57 We should note that this self-referencing does not appeal to a transcendental self, but to the larval, pre-individualities of elements in relation.

58 Gilles Deleuze, *Pure Immanence: Essays on a Life*, trans. Anne Boyman (New York: Zone Books, 2005), 85.

59 Deleuze, *Nietzsche and Philosophy*, 156.

60 Deleuze, *Two Regimes of Madness*, 206.

61 Deleuze, *Nietzsche and Philosophy*, 48.

62 Deleuze, *Difference and Repetition*, 299.

63 Deleuze, *Two Regimes of Madness*, 206–07.

64 Deleuze, *Difference and Repetition*, 299.

65 Daniel W Smith, 'The Concept of the Simulacrum: Deleuze and the Overturning of Platonism', *Continental Philosophy Review* 38 (2006): 89–123.

66 Gilles Deleuze, 'Active and Reactive', in *The New Nietzsche*, ed. David B Allison (Cambridge: The MIT Press, 1985), 80–106.

67 Friedrich Nietzsche, *Writings from the Late Notebooks*, ed. Rudiger Bittner, trans. Kate Sturge (Cambridge: Cambridge University Press, 2003), 38.

68 Deleuze eventually fades the language of simulacra out of his writings and chooses new concepts to describe the proliferation of multiplicities in becoming. In 'Letter-Preface to Jean-Clet Martin', Deleuze explains some of the changes to his terminological register. He says, '"Rhizome" is the best term to designate multiplicities. On the other hand, it seems to me that I have totally abandoned the notion of simulacrum, which is all but worthless. *A Thousand Plateaus* is the book dedicated to multiplicities for themselves (becomings, lines, etc.)'. Deleuze, *Two Regimes of Madness*, 366.

69 The following passage on Klossowski demonstrates the confluence of the will to power and the eternal return as effectively undoing the opposition between the one and the many. The connection to willing and becoming-other reappears in Deleuze's ontology as the relationship between the manifest levels of the eternal return in willing and the latent levels of the return in pre-subjective chaos. 'It is in this sense that Mr. Klossowski wanted to show us a world of intense fluctuations in the will to power, where identities are lost, and where each one cannot want itself without wanting all the other possibilities, without becoming innumerable "others", without apprehending itself as a fortuitous moment, whose very chance implies the necessity of the whole series.' Deleuze, *Desert Islands and Other Texts 1953-1974*, 122.

70 Ibid., 123.

71 Williams, *Gilles Deleuze's Philosophy of Time*, 184.

72 Pierre Klossowski, 'Nietzsche's Experience of the Eternal Return', in *The New Nietzsche*, ed. David B Allison (Cambridge, MA: The MIT Press, 1985), 107–20.

73 'Nietzsche's treatment of this problem is formulated as the relation of "in one moment" to "in every moment." This does *not* coincide with the relation of one moment to the continuous flux of time, for the phrase "in every moment," which occurs frequently and in the most decisive passages, has nothing to do with the whole of time conceived as continuous flow or even extension (duration). It has a disparate, discrete character.' As Stambaugh equates duration with extension, it becomes evident that she is not addressing the qualitative heterogeneity of Bergsonian duration, but rather, a notion of duration premised on substantiality and not relationality. Joan Stambaugh, *Nietzsche's Thought of Eternal Return* (Baltimore: The John Hopkins University Press, 1972), 7.

74 Ontic 'now' points are factical considerations of time that attribute extensive, homogeneous measurement to time. The ontic formulation of time is opposed to the ontological, ecstatic time from which it derives in *Being and Time*. Heidegger, *Being and Time*, 32.

75 In *The Gay Science* for example, Nietzsche critiques mechanistic causality by stating, 'Cause and Effect: such a duality probably never exists; in truth we are confronted by a continuum out of which we isolate a couple of pieces, just as we perceive motion only as isolated points and then infer it without ever actually seeing it.' Nietzsche, *The Gay Science*, 173. Notice this is the *exact* same critique offered by Henri Bergson in *Creative Evolution*.

76 Using Nietzsche's emphasis on forgetfulness in the eternal return causes a stark division between Deleuze's concept of becoming and the one offered by Hegel. Through the ontological work of forgetting, contradiction is eliminated from an immanent concept of becoming.

77 Deleuze, *Difference and Repetition*, 55.

78 By 'forms' we mean blocs of becoming in sensation which produce new affects and percepts.

79 Klossowski, 'Nietzsche's Experience of the Eternal Return,' 109.

80 We see clear evidence of this in 'Of the Vision and the Riddle' in *Thus Spoke Zarathustra,* where the thought of the eternal return results in a forgetting of circumstances and the act of willing. Shortly upon seeing the gateway of the Moment where the lanes of eternity meet in an eternal return, Zarathustra loses the footing of his identity and asks, 'Where was the dwarf now gone? And the gateway? And the spider? And all the whispering? Was I dreaming, then? Was I waking up?' Nietzsche, *Thus Spoke Zarathustra*, 159.

81 Deleuze, *Difference and Repetition*, 297.

82 Ibid., 7.

83 Nietzsche, *Writings from the Late Notebooks*, 55. We must recall that for Nietzsche, as well as Deleuze, thoughts are actions, and they are creative.

84 Deleuze, *Nietzsche and Philosophy*, 71.

85 In *Nietzsche and Philosophy* Deleuze initially uses Aion to refer to time, and in *Difference and Repetition* he employs Aion as another expression for the eternal return. In *The Logic of Sense* the exchangeability of the eternal return and becoming is complete. He writes, 'They [events] are not living presents, but infinitives: the unlimited Aion, the becoming which divides itself infinitely into past and future and always eludes the present.' Deleuze, *The Logic of Sense*, 5. However, in *Nietzsche and Philosophy* there is one mention of Aion: 'In this game of becoming, the being of becoming, the being of becoming also plays the game with itself; the *aeon* (time), says Heraclitus, is a child who plays, plays at draughts (*Diels* 53). The being of becoming, the eternal return, is the second moment of the game, but also the third term, identical to the two moments and valid for the whole.' Deleuze, *Nietzsche and Philosophy*, 23.

86 Friedrich Nietzsche, *The Pre-Platonic Philosophers*, trans. Greg Whitlock (Urbana and Chicago: University of Illinois Press, 2001), 70.

87 Deleuze, *Difference and Repetition*, 355.

88 Ibid., 149. In *Difference and Repetition* Deleuze describes the third synthesis of time (the future, or the eternal return) as the pure empty form of time. 'The Proustian formula "a little time in its pure state" refers first to the pure past, the in-itself of the past or the erotic synthesis of time, but more profoundly to *the pure and empty form of time*, the ultimate synthesis, that of the death instinct which leads to the eternity of the return in time.' This description is then repeated in the definition of Aion in *The Logic of Sense*. The identification of both the eternal return and Aion as the pure and empty form of time makes sense, as they are different terms for the process of absolute becoming.

89 Ibid., 369.

90 Deleuze, *Desert Islands and Other Texts 1953-1974*, 124.

91 Deleuze, *The Logic of Sense*, 165.

92 Deleuze and Guattari, *A Thousand Plateaus*, 290.

93 James Williams offers a clear explanation of the evaded present of Aion as it relates to the undoing of the lived present in Chronos. 'The present is never separate from all other processes of pure becoming, nor before or after them. Instead, the present as an actual living present is undone in its expression of pure becoming, because each contraction of the past and of the future on to that living present is undone through the wider determination of all the pure ways of becoming.' Williams, *Gilles Deleuze's Philosophy of Time*, 140.

94 Deleuze, *The Logic of Sense*, 168.

95 Ibid., 165.

96 Williams, *Gilles Deleuze's Philosophy of Time*, 154.

97 Ibid.

98 Deleuze, *Desert Islands and Other Texts 1953-1974*, 124.

99 Deleuze and Guattari, *A Thousand Plateaus*, 336.

100 Nietzsche, *The Will to Power*, 550.

Chapter 2

1   Nietzsche, *The Gay Science*, 172. In this sense, Deleuze's innovative counter-effectuating causality can be seen as a tribute to Nietzsche. Deleuze reconstructs causality to correct the criticisms launched by Nietzsche. The imagistic construction of causality, and its elimination of difference and becoming, is absorbed into an anti-causal causality in Deleuze. Nietzsche ruthlessly critiqued the retroactive projection of cause and effect into the flux of nature. We see this salient criticism often in his works, particularly in *The Gay Science*. 'We have uncovered a manifold one-after-another where the naïve man and inquirer of older cultures only saw two separate things "Cause" and "effect" is what one says; but we have merely perfected the image of becoming without reaching beyond the image or behind it.'

2   Deleuze, *The Logic of Sense*, 164.

3   'The eternal return is neither qualitative nor extensive but intensive, purely intensive.' Deleuze, *Difference and Repetition*, 303.

4   Steven Shaviro, 'Novelty and Double Causality,' in *Deleuze, Guattari and the Production of the New*, ed. Simon O'Sullivan and Stephen Zepke (London: Continuum Books, 2008), 206–16.

5   Ibid., 214.

6   Ibid., 215.

7   Alfred North Whitehead, *Modes of Thought* (New York: Simon and Schuster, 1968), 150.

8   Immanuel Kant, *Critique of Judgment* (New York: Hafner Press, 1951), 219.

9   Deleuze, *The Logic of Sense*, 21.

10 DeLanda, *Intensive Science and Virtual Philosophy*, 162.

11 Daniel W Smith, 'The Doctrine of Univocity,' in *Deleuze and Religion* (London: Routledge, 2001), 167–83.

12 Deleuze, *The Logic of Sense*, 62.

13 Smith, 'The Doctrine of Univocity,' 174.

14 Deleuze, *The Logic of Sense*, 95.

15 DeLanda, *Intensive Science and Virtual Philosophy*, 124–5.

16 Slavoj Žižek, *Organs without Bodies* (New York: Routledge, 2004), 27.

17 Ibid., 28.

18 Ibid., 27. 'This is also why Lacan appreciated so much *The Logic of Sense*: Is the Deleuzian quasi cause not the exact equivalent of Lacan's *objet petit a*, this pure, immaterial, spectral entity that serves as the object-cause of desire?'

19 Samantha Bankston, 'Difference, Repetition, and the N[on(e)-All]: The Parallactic Mirror of Žižek and Deleuze,' *International Journal of Žižek Studies,* eds Paul A. Taylor and David J. Gunkel 9, no. 2 (2015).

20 Daniel W Smith, 'From the Surface to the Depths,' in *Gilles Deleuze: The Intensive Reduction*, ed. Constantin V Boundas (London: Continuum Press, 2009), 89.

21 The similarity between Deleuze and Žižek was already pointed out years prior by Daniel W Smith in 'The Inverse Side of Structure: Žižek on Deleuze and Lacan,' in *Essays on Deleuze*, 312–24. Smith claims that Lacan finally got the Deleuze he always wanted in Žižek.

22 He is referring specifically to page 164 in *The Logic of Sense*. Slavoj Žižek, *Less Than Nothing: Hegel and the Shadow of Dialectical Materialism* (London: Verso, 2012), 64.

23 It should be noted that the elevation of the Event as a central component of Deleuze's philosophy distorts the rest of the philosopher's ontology. It is the work of his opponents, most notably, Badiou and Žižek, who have exaggerated the meaning of the Event, which is most prominent in *The Logic of Sense*, and plays a less significant role in the remainder of his œuvre.

24 Žižek readily admits that his reading of Deleuze is heavily influenced by Alain Badiou.

25 Žižek, *Organs without Bodies*, 28.

26 No genetic analysis of the wasp will reveal the orchid in its lineage, and yet they form a symbiotic relationship that is based on their capacities, as opposed to their genetic coding.

27 Deleuze, *The Logic of Sense*, 55.

28 Cliff Stagoll, 'Event,' in *The Deleuze Dictionary*, ed. Adrian Parr (New York: Columbia University Press, 2005), 87–8.

29 Deleuze, *The Logic of Sense*, 56.

30 Lampert, *Deleuze and Guattari's Philosophy of History*, 102.

31 Ibid., 104.

32 Roffe, *Badiou's Deleuze*, 16.

33 Deleuze, *Bergsonism*, 118. The pathology of duration is its splitting of the present into two simultaneous streams of the past and future.

34 Deleuze, *The Logic of Sense*, 79.

35 Ibid., 222.

36 Ibid., 221.

37 Deleuze and Guattari, *A Thousand Plateaus*, 290.

38 Ibid., 300.

39 Ibid., 301.

40 Deleuze, *The Logic of Sense*, 153.

41 The surface is referred to more readily in later works as the plane of immanence.

42 Deleuze and Guattari, *What Is Philosophy?*, 96. Deleuze and Guattari discuss the error evoked in posing the 'why now' question. The question involves an imposition of representational thought on the untimely nature of becoming.

43 Ibid.

44 Lampert, *Deleuze and Guattari's Philosophy of History*, 147.

45 Deleuze, *Pure Immanence: Essays on a Life*, 27.

46 Deleuze, *The Logic of Sense*, 56.

47 Roffe, *Badiou's Deleuze*, 114.

48 The infinite others we become in the sensory encounter of the eternal return is recalled in a moment of forgetting. '*Anamnesis* coincides with the revelation of the Return: how could the return not bring back forgetfulness? Not only do I learn that I (Nietzsche) have been brought to the crucial moment in which the eternity of the circle culminates, the truth in which the truth of its necessary return is revealed to me; but at the same time I learn that I was *other* than I am *now* for having forgotten this truth, and thus that I have becoming another by learning it.' Pierre Klossowski, *Nietzsche and the Vicious Circle*, trans. Daniel W Smith (New York: Continuum, 2005), 57.

49 Deleuze, *The Logic of Sense*, 113.

50 Ibid., 172.

51 Ibid., 174.

52 Ibid., 264.

53 Lampert, *Deleuze and Guattari's Philosophy of History*, 106.

54 Ibid. The argument for the measureless depth of bodies in succession appears in section 6a of the text, not section 4a, which is a mislabelling.

55 Ibid., 37.

56 Deleuze, *Bergsonism*, 58.

57 Deleuze, *The Logic of Sense*, 124.

58 Ibid., 125.

59 Nietzsche, *Thus Spoke Zarathustra*, 158.

60 Nietzsche, *The Gay Science*, 273.

61 Friedrich Nietzsche, *On the Genealogy of Morals*, trans. Walter Kaufmann and R. J. Hollingdale (New York: Random House, Inc., 1967), 113.

62 For an expanded discussion on how our hubris regarding causality connects to the new image of thought in Deleuze, see: Paolo A. Bolaños, *On Affirmation and Becoming: A Deleuzian Introduction to Nietzsche's Ethics and Ontology* (London: Cambridge Scholars Publishing, 2014), 56.

63 Deleuze, *The Logic of Sense*, 168. Deleuze goes on to say, 'It is not the present of subversion [becoming-mad of duration] or actualization [measured time], but that of the counter-actualization, which keeps the former from overturning the latter, and the latter from being confused with the former, and which comes to duplicate the lining *(redoubler la doublure)*.' The counter-actualizing quasi-cause (i.e. the Moment) keeps the becoming-mad of duration from overturning the actual present like the inverted world of Hegel. The quasi-cause is the operating function that allows all forms to be absorbed in becoming without falling into an undifferentiated chaos.

64 An expanded analysis of the Moment, or the quasi-cause, will be dramatized through Leibniz's infinitesimal, differential calculus and Borges's labyrinth of forking paths in Chapter 4.

65 DeLanda, *Intensive Science and Virtual Philosophy*, 127–8.

66 Deleuze, *The Logic of Sense*, 63.

67 Jacques Derrida, *Spurs: Nietzsche's Styles*, trans. Barbara Harlow (Chicago: University of Chicago Press, 1978).

68 Another reading of immanent causation can be found through the lens of the will to power, as we see in 'Will to Power as Alternative to Causality' in *The Journal of Speculative Philosophy*, by Joshua Rayman. He situates the immanent Events of Nietzsche's eternal return in the sub-representational will: 'Because it denies the temporal and spatial externality of origins and products of events, this notion of will to power as an immanent source of movement, a *physis*, replaces causal thinking without sustaining its logic. And will to power is immanent not only within each isolated case of action but also in its ever-presence, which enables it to overcome the metaphysical separation implicit in causal notions' 364.

Chapter 3

1 'For Nietzsche, becoming is a fact, whereas time is an interpretation' Robin Small, *Time and Becoming in Nietzsche's Thought* (London: Continuum Press, 2010), 34.

2 Deleuze, *Desert Islands*, 142, bold in original.

3 'Time' denotes Deleuze's sub-representational notion of time, not the chronometric time of the clock.

4 Gilles Deleuze, *Francis Bacon: the logic of sensation*, trans. Daniel W Smith (Minneapolis: University of Minnesota Press, 2003), 105.

5 Deleuze, *Difference and Repetition*, 276.

6 Ibid., 114.

7 Odilon Redon, *A Soi-Même: Journal, 1867-1915* (Paris: Fleury, 1922), 26. Deleuze footnotes Redon's journal when presenting the idea of the abstract line acting upon the soul as the ground rises up in autonomous existence. 'No plastic form will be found in my works, I mean any form perceived objectively, for itself, according to the laws of light and shadow, through the conventional means of relief. … All of my art is confined solely to the resources of *chiaroscuro,* and also owes much to the effects of the abstract line, that agent from a profound source, acting directly upon the spirit.'

8 Deleuze, *Difference and Repetition*, 346.

9 Redon, *A Soi-Même: Journal, 1867-1915*, 27.

10 Ibid., 26. See Note 7.

11   Deleuze, *Difference and Repetition*, 37.

12   Ibid., 95.

13   Deleuze, *Difference and Repetition*, 100. 'There is a self wherever a furtive contemplation has been established, whenever a contracting machine capable of drawing a difference from repetition functions somewhere. The self does not undergo modifications, it is itself a modification – this term designating precisely the difference drawn. Finally, one is what one *has*: here being is formed or the passive self *is*, by having.'

14   Bergson, *Mind-Energy*, 16–17.

15   Bergson, *Mind-Energy*.

16   Deleuze and Guattari, *What Is Philosophy?*, 169.

17   Deleuze, *Difference and Repetition*, 371.

18   Deleuze and Guattari, *What Is Philosophy?*, 182.

19   Ibid., 177.

20   Deleuze, *Francis Bacon: The Logic of Sensation*, 105.

21   Ronald Bogue, *Deleuze on Music, Painting, and the Arts* (New York: Routledge, 2003), 149.

22   Wilhelm Worringer, *Form in Gothic*, trans. Herbert Read (New York: Schocken Books, 1957), 56–7.

23   Deleuze, *Difference and Repetition*, 373.

24   Ibid., 373.

25   Mihály Vig's piece, 'Circle Dance I,' composed for Bela Tarr's film, *Damnation*, is an intoxicatingly beautiful expression of the northern line in sound.

26   Odilon Redon, 'Below, I Saw the Vaporous Outline of a Human Form,' 1896. Lithograph on China paper, 45 × 31.8 cm. Metropolitan Museum of Art, New York.

27   Redon, *A Soi-Même: Journal, 1867-1915*.

28   Bogue, *Deleuze on Music, Painting, and the Arts*, 151.

29   Stephen Zepke, *Art as Abstract Machine: Ontology and Aesthetics in Deleuze and Guattari* (New York: Routledge, 2005), 132.

30   For a discussion of the different haptic qualities of colourism in art see Ronald Bogue's *Deleuze on Music, Painting, and the Arts*. Bogue, *Deleuze on Music, Painting, and the Arts*.

31   Deleuze and Guattari, *What Is Philosophy?*, 182.

32   Deleuze, *Difference and Repetition*, 113.

33   The original French '*bloc*' conveys the meanings of both 'block' and 'bloc' in English. The French term is preferable, as it conveys a sense of resistance (e.g. blocking something out), integration (e.g. Soviet bloc), and components (e.g. building blocks) at the same time. For this reason we have chosen to retain the original French term.

34   We are considering the new lines of becoming in *A Thousand Plateaus*, not the sedimentary lines they resist in the actual.

35 Bergson, *Creative Evolution*, 309.

36 Deleuze and Guattari, *A Thousand Plateaus*, 322.

37 Ibid., 324.

38 Ibid., 323–4.

39 Deleuze, *Francis Bacon: The Logic of Sensation*, 85.

40 Deleuze and Guattari, *A Thousand Plateaus*, 290.

41 Anne Sauvagnargues, 'Deleuze. De l'animal à l'art,' in *La philosophie de Deleuze* (Paris: Presses Universitaires de France, 2004), 194.

42 Deleuze and Guattari, *A Thousand Plateaus*, 289.

43 Sauvagnargues, 'Deleuze. De l'animal à l'art,' 194 (translation mine).

44 Ibid., 193.

45 Deleuze and Guattari, *A Thousand Plateaus*, 288.

46 Ibid., 263.

47 In her autobiography, *Living My Life*, Goldman recounts a story from her youth when she was chastised for aligning herself with revolution and simultaneously exhibiting joy and 'frivolity' at dances. She responded by saying that if the revolution meant denying vitality and joy, she did not wish to participate. Emma Goldman, *Living My Life* (New York: Knopf, 1934), 56.

48 Jacques Derrida, *Points.Interviews, 1974-1994*, ed. Elizabeth Weber, trans. Peggy Kamuf (Stanford: Stanford University Press, 1995), 93.

49 Deleuze and Guattari, *A Thousand Plateaus*, 305.

50 Ibid., 306.

51 The co-presence of these two temporal orders forms diagonal music that is neither limited to the horizontality of melody, nor the verticality of rhythm, as is described in Deleuze's essay, 'Occupy without Counting: Boulez, Proust and Time.' He states, 'The blocks of duration therefore follow a striated space-time where they trace their diagonals according to the speed of their pulsations and the variation of their measures. However, a *smooth* or non-pulsed space-time detaches itself in turn from the striated one. It only refers to chronometry in a global way: the cuts are indeterminate, of an irrational type, and the measures are replaced by distances and proximities that cannot be broken down and that express the density or rareness of what appears there (statistical distribution of events).' Deleuze, *Two Regimes of Madness*, 294.

52 Klossowski, *Nietzsche and the Vicious Circle*.

53 Ibid., 165.

54 'Pierre Klossowski has clearly noted this point in the articles referred to above: taken in its strict sense, eternal return means that each thing exists only in returning, copy of an infinity of copies which allows neither original nor origin to subsist. That is why the eternal return is called "parodic": it qualifies as simulacrum that which it causes to be (and to return). When eternal return is the power of (formless) Being, the simulacrum is the true character of form – the "being" – of that which is. When the identity of things dissolves, being escapes to attain

univocity, and begins to revolve around the different'. Deleuze, *Difference and Repetition*, 80.

55 Ian James, 'Pierre Klossowski', in *Deleuze's Philosophical Lineage* (Edinburgh: Edinburgh University Press, 2009), 339–56.

56 Ibid.

57 Deleuze, *Two Regimes of Madness*, 380.

58 Deleuze and Guattari, *A Thousand Plateaus*, 9.

59 Deleuze and Guattari explicate Kafka's repetition of blocks as a literary bloc that underscores both contiguity and distance. We may take this analysis as the model of expression for the abstract line in sensation. Kafka's blocks are said to be form segments that are discontinuous and at a distance from one another, yet 'since they persist, it is the blocks themselves that have to change their form [becoming-mad], at the very least by moving from one point of view to another. And, in fact, if it is true that each block-segment has an opening or a door onto the line of the hallway [Aion] – one that is usually quite far from the door or the opening of the following block – it is also true that all the blocks have back doors that are contiguous.' Gilles Deleuze and Félix Guattari, *Kafka: Toward a Minor Literature*, trans. Terry Cochran (Minneapolis: Minneapolis University Press, 1986), 73.

60 Jerry Saltz, 'The Tempest: One of the Greatest Acts of Aesthetic Desperation in all of Art', *Village Voice*, 12 September 2006.

61 Deleuze, *Two Regimes of Madness*, 178.

62 Saltz, 'The Tempest: One of the Greatest Acts of Aesthetic Desperation in all of Art'.

63 Ibid.

64 Deleuze, *Francis Bacon: The Logic of Sensation*, 105.

Chapter 4

1 Sauvagnargues, *Artmachines*, 127.

2 Deleuze and Guattari, *What Is Philosophy?*, 20–1.

3 Ibid.

4 Ibid.

5 Deleuze and Guattari, *A Thousand Plateaus*, 366.

6 Deleuze can be said to align with Nietzsche in this respect. The eternal nature of the concept in substance metaphysics is to be denied. Does this mean that the concept is in time? Not chronological time, but the concept is primordially temporal (untimely). Nietzsche's critique of the immutable essence is adopted by Deleuze's understanding of concepts, which are *constructed*, not found or discovered *a priori*. Nietzsche notes, '"Timeless" to be rejected. At a particular moment of a force, an absolute conditionality of the redistribution of all its forces

is given: it cannot stand still. "Change" is part of the essence, and therefore so is temporality – which, however, just amounts to one more conceptual positing of the necessity of change.' Nietzsche, *Writings from the Late Notebooks*, 21.

7   When elaborating the eternal return of difference in *Difference and Repetition,* Deleuze remarks, 'Time must be understood and lived as out of joint, and seen as a straight line which mercilessly eliminates those who embark upon it, who come upon the scene but repeat once and for all.' We repeat eternally once and for all.

8   Deleuze and Guattari, *What Is Philosophy?*, 184.

9   Deleuze and Guattari, *A Thousand Plateaus*, 378.

10 Ibid., 343.

11 Deleuze and Guattari, *What Is Philosophy?*, 185.

12 Nietzsche, *The Will to Power*.

13 Giovanna Borradori, 'On the Presence of Bergson in Deleuze's Nietzsche', *Philosophy Today* 43 (1999): 140–6.

14 'In *Nietzsche and Philosophy* Deleuze is reading eternal return through a Bergsonian lens in as much as the focus is on the problem of time's passage. A distinctly Nietzschean problematic is added, however, and this revolves around the determination of a becoming-active of forces.' Pearson, *Philosophy and the Adventure of the Virtual: Bergson and the Time of Life*, 201.

15 Deleuze and Guattari, *A Thousand Plateaus*, 378.

16 Nietzsche, *The Gay Science*, 143. A musician-philosopher is able to give voice to the mute forces of becoming. Nietzsche says, 'Here is a musician who, more than any other musician, is a master at discovering the tones out of the realm of suffering, depressed, tormented souls and at giving speech to even dumb animals. Nobody equals him in the colors of the late fall, the indescribable moving happiness of the last, very last, very briefest enjoyment; he finds sounds for those secret and uncanny midnights of the soul in which cause and effect appear to be unhinged and any moment something can come into being out of "nothing".

17 Marcel Proust, *Swann's Way*, trans. Lydia Davis (New York: Penguin Books, 2002), 44.

18 Deleuze, *Bergsonism*, 88.

19 Deleuze and Guattari, *What Is Philosophy?*, 184.

20 Deleuze and Guattari, *A Thousand Plateaus*, 379.

21 'And involuntary memory retains its two powers: the difference in the past moment, the repetition in the present one.' Deleuze, *Proust and Signs*, 61.

22 Ibid., 111.

23 Ibid., 60.

24 William Blake, 'Auguries of Innocence', in *The Complete Poetry and Prose of William Blake*, ed. David V Erdman (New York: Anchor Books, 1988), 490–3.

25 Bogue, *Deleuze on Music, Painting, and the Arts*, 165.

26 Notice the similarity between Bachelard's interpretation of the house of one's childhood and Deleuze's account of Proustian reminiscence. Bachelard states, 'Indeed, at times dreams go back so far into an undefined, dateless past that clear memories of our childhood home appear to be detached from us. Such dreams unsettle our daydreaming and we reach a point where we begin to doubt that we ever lived where we lived. Our past is elsewhere, and both time and place are impregnated with a sense of unreality'. Gaston Bachelard, *The Poetics of Space*, trans. Maria Jolas (Boston: Beacon Press, 1969), 57–8.

27 Rainer Maria Rilke, *The Book of Images*, trans. Edward Snow (New York: North Point Press, 1991), 87.

28 The interjection of cosmic forces within constituted identities, or molar forms, is described by both Deleuze and Rilke. The presence of that which is wandering lost in things is explained by Deleuze and Guattari as the preservation of forces between forms in the work of art. 'But equally, the most baleful forces themselves are what produces zones of indiscernibility in the broken tones of a face, slapping, scratching, and melting it in every way, and these zones of indiscernibility reveal the forces lurking in the area of plain, uniform color (Bacon).' Deleuze and Guattari, *What Is Philosophy?*, 182. Beneath the uniform, static surface of colour is a restless virtuality of forces that are not locatable within the concrete forms of identity. The 'things' of Rilke's poem also form a virtual circuit that mingles with actuality, and these forms cannot escape from the subverting work of difference.

29 'Art is not chaos but a composition of chaos that yields the vision or sensation, so that it constitutes, as Joyce says, a chaosmos, a composed chaos – neither foreseen nor preconceived. … Art struggles with chaos but it does so in order to render it sensory, even through the most charming character, the most enchanting landscape (Watteau).' Ibid., 204–5.

30 The impersonal signs of art and their emergence from the subjective and objective conditions of searching are discussed at length in relation to Proust's writings. 'In the course of the Search, if the resonance-as-ecstasy appears as the ultimate goal of life, it is difficult to see what art can add to it, and the narrator suffers the greatest doubts about art. Then later on the resonance appears as the producer of a certain effect, but under given natural conditions, objective and subjective, and by means of the unconscious machine of involuntary memory. But at the end, we see that what art is capable of adding to nature: it produces resonances themselves, because *style* sets up a resonance between any two objects and from them extracts a "precious image", *substituting for the determined conditions of an unconscious natural product the free conditions of an artistic production*' (III, 878, 889). Deleuze, *Proust and Signs*, 155. Just as the narrator of 'On the Edge of Night' is the point of departure for the musical resonance of the darkness of night, the situatedness of subject and object is superseded by artistic expression.

31 Deleuze, *Dialogues II*, 114.

32 Deleuze and Guattari, *What Is Philosophy?*, 184.

33 'To Occupy without Counting: Boulez, Proust and Time' reveals that Deleuze's reading of duration in Bergson is fundamentally linked to memory, and his reading of memory in Proust is fundamentally linked to forgetting. Since both thinkers are indelibly intertwined for Deleuze, we begin to understand the inherent tension between memory and forgetting in his concept of becoming. Deleuze, *Two Regimes of Madness*, 296.

34 Deleuze, *Difference and Repetition*, 365.

35 'The second repetition still participates in all the ambiguities of memory and ground. It includes difference, but includes it only *between* the degrees or levels. As we saw, it appears first in the form of circles of the past coexistent in themselves; then in the form of a circle of coexistence of the past and the present; and finally in the form of a circle of all the presents which pass and which coexist in the relation to the object=x.' Ibid., 364.

36 Nietzsche, *Thus Spoke Zarathustra*, 178.

37 Bogue, *Deleuze on Music, Painting, and the Arts*, 177.

38 Nietzsche posits 'action at a distance' against mechanistic causal processes. The result is a theory of causal processes that maintain the heterogeneity of its components that may exert influence across domains. '"Action at a distance" cannot be eliminated: *something draws something else closer, something feels drawn*. This is the fundamental fact: compared to this, the mechanistic notion of pressing and pushing is merely a hypothesis based on *sight* and *touch*, even if it does indeed serve us as a regulative hypothesis for the world of sight!' Nietzsche, *Writings from the Late Notebooks*, 15.

39 Deleuze, *Difference and Repetition*, 105.

40 Deleuze and Guattari, *A Thousand Plateaus*, 345.

41 Ibid., 378.

42 'The crystal always lives at the limit, it is itself the "vanishing limit between the immediate past which is already no longer and the immediate future which is not yet … mobile mirror which endlessly reflects perception in recollection".' Deleuze, *Cinema 2: The Time-Image*, 81.

43 Ibid.

44 Ibid.

45 Ibid., 92.

46 Deleuze, *Difference and Repetition*, 149.

47 Deleuze and Guattari, *What Is Philosophy?*, 21.

48 Pearson, *Philosophy and the Adventure of the Virtual: Bergson and the Time of Life*, 197.

49 Deleuze, *Difference and Repetition*, 370.

50 Deleuze, *The Logic of Sense*, 165.

51 Deleuze, *Difference and Repetition*, 371.

52 Ibid., 176.

53 Lambert, *The Non-Philosophy of Gilles Deleuze*, 90.

54 Deleuze, *Cinema 2: The Time-Image*, 131.

55 Jorge Luis Borges, *Labyrinths, Selected Stories and Other Writings* (New York: New Directions Books, 1962), 27.

56 Ibid., 28.

57 Deleuze, *Cinema 2: The Time-Image*, 131.

58 Borges, *Labyrinths, Selected Stories and Other Writings*, 27.

59 See Deleuze and Guattari on virtual change among events: 'Each component of the event is *actualized or effectuated* in an instant, and the event in the time that passes between these instants; but nothing happens with *the virtuality* that has only meanwhiles as components and an event as composite becoming. Nothing happens there, but everything becomes, so that the event has the privilege of beginning again when time is past. Nothing happens, and yet everything changes, because becoming continues to pass through its components again and to restore the event that is actualized elsewhere, at a different moment. When time passes and takes the instant away, there is always a meanwhile [entre-temps] to restore the event.' Deleuze and Guattari, *What Is Philosophy?*, 158.

60 Simon Duffy, 'The Logic of Expression in Deleuze's Expressionism and Philosophy: Spinoza: A Strategy of Engagement', *International Journal of Philosophical Studies* 12 (2004): 47–60.

61 Ibid., 54–5.

62 Ibid., 52.

63 Ibid., 51–2.

64 Deleuze, *The Logic of Sense*, 265.

65 Klossowski, *Nietzsche and the Vicious Circle*, 45.

66 Deleuze, *Difference and Repetition*, 371.

67 An expanded discussion of his speculative reading of the eternal return appears in the American preface to *Nietzsche and Philosophy*: 'In two passages of *Zarathustra*, Nietzsche explicitly denies that the Eternal Return is a circle that brings back the Same. The Eternal Return is strictly the opposite, since it is inseparable from a selection, a twofold selection. First, it is the selection of will or thought (Nietzsche's ethics): to will only those things whose eternal return we also will (to eliminate all half-willing, what we will when we say "just this once, only once"). Second, it is the selection of Being (Nietzsche's ontology): what returns, or is apt to return, is only that which *becomes* in the fullest sense of the word. Only action and affirmation return: Being belongs to becoming and only to becoming. Whatever is opposed to becoming – the Same or the Identical – is not, rigorously speaking.' Deleuze, *Two Regimes of Madness*, 206.

68 Arkady Plotnitsky, 'Zarathustra's Ladders: Hebraism, Hellenism, and Practical Philosophy in Nietzsche', *Poetics Today* 19 (1998): 209.

69 Nietzsche, *Thus Spoke Zarathustra*, 158.

70 Deleuze, *The Logic of Sense*, 64.

71 Deleuze, *Difference and Repetition*, 114.

72 Duffy, 'The Logic of Expression in Deleuze's Expressionism and Philosophy: Spinoza: A Strategy of Engagement'.

73 Ibid., 52.

74 Mogens Laerke, 'Four Things Deleuze Learned from Leibniz', in *Deleuze and The Fold: A Critical Reader*, ed. Sjoerd van Tuinen and Niamh McDonnell (London: Palgrave Macmillan, 2010), 28.

75 Ibid.

76 Daniel W. Smith, 'Genesis and Difference', in *Deleuze and The Fold: A Critical Reader*, ed. Sjoerd van Tuinen and Niamh McDonnell (London: Palgrave Macmillan, 2010), 139.

77 Deleuze, *Nietzsche and Philosophy*, 40. 'Quality is nothing but difference in quantity and corresponds to it each time forces enter into relation.'

78 Deleuze, *Difference and Repetition*, 111.

79 Deleuze, *Two Regimes of Madness*, 207 (italics mine).

Chapter 5

1 For a comprehensive critique of chronological history see Jay Lampert's chapter 'Dates and Destiny: The Problem of Historical Chronology' from *Deleuze and Guattari's Philosophy of History*. Lampert, *Deleuze and Guattari's Philosophy of History*.

2 Deleuze and Guattari, *What Is Philosophy?*, 96.

3 See *Deleuze and Art* for what is one of the most thorough explications of Deleuze's terms as they engage with the particular ideas of specific disciplines in points in history. Sauvagnargues, *Deleuze and Art*.

4 Deleuze, *Two Regimes of Madness*, 238.

5 Deleuze and Guattari, *What Is Philosophy?*, 5.

6 Deleuze, *Two Regimes of Madness*, 342.

7 Deleuze, *The Logic of Sense*, 76.

8 Nietzsche, *The Gay Science*, 273.

9 See, for example, *Nietzsche's Philosophy of the Eternal Recurrence of the Same*. Karl Löwith, *Nietzsche's Philosophy of the Eternal Recurrence of the Same*, trans. J Harvey Lomax (Berkeley: University of California Press, 1997).

10 Small, *Time and Becoming in Nietzsche's Thought*.

11   The following passage of Heine's is cited in *Nietzsche: Philosopher, Psychologist,*
     Antichrist: 'For time is infinite, but the things in time, the concrete bodies, are
     finite. They may indeed disperse into the smallest particles; but these particles, the
     atoms, have their determinate numbers, and the numbers of the configurations
     which, all of themselves, are formed out of them is also determinate. Now, however
     long a time may pass, according to the eternal laws governing the combinations of
     this eternal play of repetition, all configurations which have previously existed on
     this earth must yet meet, attract, repulse, kiss, and corrupt each other again.' Walter
     A Kaufmann, *Nietzsche: Philosopher, Psychologist, Antichrist* (Princeton: Princeton
     University Press, 1974), 318.

12   A poignant critique of transcendental concepts and binary logic can be found in
     §111 from *The Gay Science*.

13   Pearson, *Philosophy and the Adventure of the Virtual: Bergson and the Time of Life*.

14   Deleuze, *Nietzsche and Philosophy*, 67 (italics mine).

15   Nietzsche, *Thus Spoke Zarathustra*, 158.

16   Nietzsche, *Writings from the Late Notebooks*, 21.

17   Ibid., 45. We know that Nietzsche considered the isolation of forces an illusion
     enacted by the Understanding. 'Thinking itself is an action like this, which *takes*
     apart what is really one. Everywhere, even in thinking, is the *illusion* that there are
     multiplicities whose contents can be counted.' Of course, Nietzsche is referring to
     discrete multiplicities that amount to homogeneous measure.

18   Ibid., 21.

19   Deleuze, *Nietzsche and Philosophy*, 43.

20   Smith, 'G. W. F. Leibniz,' 63.

21   Robert Frost, *The Poetry of Robert Frost: The Collective Poems, Complete and*
     Unabridged (New York: Henry Holt and Company, Inc., 1969), 105.

22   Deleuze's skilful re-appropriation of concepts can be found in *Deleuze's*
     Philosophical Lineage. Each chapter of this text discusses how a particular
     philosopher informs Deleuze's thought.

23   Smith, 'G. W. F. Leibniz,' 60–1.

24   Plotnitsky, 'Bernhard Riemann,' 198.

25   Smith, 'G. W. F. Leibniz,' 60.

26   Deleuze, *Difference and Repetition*, 358–9.

27   Ibid., 51.

28   Gilles Deleuze, 'Sur Leibniz' www.webdeleuze.com/php/sommaire.html

29   This notion of a conglomerate is adopted from Arkady Plotnitsky's explication
     of the conceptual architecture of Deleuze and Guattari. Plotnitsky, "Bernhard
     Riemann".

30   Deleuze and Guattari, *What Is Philosophy?*, 21.

31   Ibid., 20.

32 Deleuze, *Two Regimes of Madness*, 207.

33 Deleuze and Guattari, *A Thousand Plateaus*, 225.

34 Zourabichvili, *Le Vocabulaire de Deleuze*, 45.

35 Ibid. Translation is mine.

36 Deleuze and Guattari, *What Is Philosophy?*, 154.

37 Deleuze and Guattari, *A Thousand Plateaus*, 10.

38 Deleuze and Guattari, *What Is Philosophy?*, 152.

Bibliography

Artaud, Antonin. *Antonin Artaud, Selected Writings*. Edited by Susan Sontag. Translated by Helen Weaver. Berkeley: University of California Press, 1973.

Bachelard, Gaston. *The Poetics of Space*. Translated by Maria Jolas. Boston: Beacon Press, 1969.

Bachelard, Gaston. *Dialectic of Duration*. Translated by Mary McAllister Jones. Manchester: Clinamen Press, 2000.

Badiou, Alain. *The Clamor of Being: Deleuze and Consequences*. Translated by Louise Burchill. Minneapolis: University of Minnesota Press, 1999.

Bankston, Samantha. 'Difference, Repetition, and the N[on(e)-All]: the Parallactic Mirror of Žižek and Deleuze', *International Journal of Žižek Studies* 9, no. 2 (2015).

Bankston, Samantha. 'To Have Done with the Judgment of "Reason": Deleuze's Aesthetic Ontology', in *Deleuze and the Passions*, edited by Ceciel Meiborg and Sjoerd van Tuinen, 41–59. Earth: Punctum Books, 2016.

Bergson, Henri. *Creative Evolution*. Translated by Arthur Mitchell. Mineola: Dover Publications, 1998.

Bergson, Henri. *Matter and Memory*. Translated by Nancy Margaret Paul and William Scott Palmer. New York: Zone Books, 1991.

Bergson, Henri. *Mind-Energy*. Translated by H. Wildon Carr. New York: Palgrave Macmillan, 2007.

Bergson, Henri. *The Creative Mind: An Introduction to Metaphysics*. Translated by Mabelle L. Andison. New York: First Carol Publishing Group, 1992.

Bergson, Henri. *Time and Free Will: An Essay on the Immediate Data of Consciousness*. Translated by Frank Lubecki Pogson. New York: Dover Publications, Inc., 2001.

Blake, William. 'Auguries of Innocence', in *The Complete Poetry and Prose of William Blake*, edited by David V. Erdman, 490–93. New York: Anchor Books, 1988.

Bogue, Ronald. *Deleuze on Music, Painting, and the Arts*. New York: Routledge, 2003.

Bolaños, Paolo A. *On Affirmation and Becoming: A Deleuzian Introduction to Nietzsche's Ethics and Ontology*. London: Cambridge Scholars Publishing, 2014.

Borges, Jorge Luis. *Labyrinths, Selected Stories and Other Writings*. New York: New Directions Books, 1962.

Borradori, Giovanna. 'On the Presence of Bergson in Deleuze's Nietzsche'. *Philosophy Today* 43 (1999): 140–6.

Braidotti, Rosi. 'Meta(l)morphoses'. *Theory, Culture & Society* 14, no. 2 (1997): 67–80.

Colebrook, Claire. 'From Radical Representations to Corporeal Becomings: The Feminist Philosophy of Lloyd, Grosz, and Gatens'. *Hypatia* 15, no. 2 (2000): 76–93.

Crockett, Clayton. *Deleuze beyond Badiou: Ontology, Multiplicity, and Event.* New York: Columbia University Press, 2013.

DeLanda, Manuel. *Intensive Science and Virtual Philosophy.* New York: Continuum Press, 2002.

Deleuze, Gilles. 'Active and Reactive'. In *The New Nietzsche*, edited by David B. Allison, 80–106. Cambridge, MA: The MIT Press, 1985.

Deleuze, Gilles. *Bergsonism.* Translated by Hugh Tomlinson and Barbara Habberjam. New York: Zone Books, 1991.

Deleuze, Gilles. 'Bergson's Conception of Difference'. In *The New Bergson*, edited by John Mullarkey, 47–8. Translated by Melissa McMahon. Manchester: Manchester University Press, 1999.

Deleuze, Gilles. *Cinema 2: The Time-Image.* Translated by Hugh Tomlinson and Robert Galeta. Minneapolis: University of Minnesota Press, 2003.

Deleuze, Gilles. *Desert Islands and Other Texts 1953–1974.* Edited by David Lapoujade. Translated by Michael Taormina. Los Angeles: Semiotext(e), 2004.

Deleuze, Gilles. *Dialogues II.* Translated by Hugh Tomlinson, Barbara Habberjam and Eliot Ross Albert. New York: Continuum, 2002.

Deleuze, Gilles. *Difference and Repetition.* Translated by Paul Patton. New York: Continuum Press, 2004.

Deleuze, Gilles. *Francis Bacon: the logic of sensation.* Translated by Daniel W. Smith. Minneapolis: University of Minnesota Press, 2003.

Deleuze, Gilles. *Nietzsche and Philosophy.* Translated by Hugh Tomlinson. New York: Columbia University Press, 1983.

Deleuze, Gilles. *Proust and Signs.* Translated by Richard Howard. Minneapolis: University of Minnesota Press, 2000.

Deleuze, Gilles. *Pure Immanence: Essays on a Life.* Translated by Anne Boyman. New York: Zone Books, 2005.

Deleuze, Gilles. *Sur Leibniz.* www.webdeleuze.com/php/sommaire.html.

Deleuze, Gilles. *The Logic of Sense.* Edited by Constantin V. Boundas. Translated by Mark Lester and Charles Stivale. New York: Columbia University Press, 1990.

Deleuze, Gilles. *Two Regimes of Madness.* Edited by David Lapoujade. New York: Semiotext(e), 2006.

Deleuze, Gilles, and Félix Guattari. *A Thousand Plateaus.* Translated by Brian Massumi. London: Continuum Press, 2004.

Deleuze, Gilles, and Félix Guattari. *Kafka: Toward a Minor Literature.* Translated by Terry Cochran. Minneapolis: Minneapolis University Press, 1986.

Deleuze, Gilles, and Félix Guattari. *What Is Philosophy?* Translated by Hugh Tomlinson and Graham Burchell. New York: Columbia University Press, 1994.

Derrida, Jacques. *Acts of Literature.* Edited by David Attridge. New York: Routledge, 1992.

Derrida, Jacques. *Margins of Philosophy.* Edited by Alan Bass. Chicago: University of Chicago Press, 1982.

Derrida, Jacques. *Points ... Interviews, 1974-1994.* Edited by Elizabeth Weber. Translated by Peggy Kamuf. Stanford: Stanford University Press, 1995.

Derrida, Jacques. *Specters of Marx.* Translated by Peggy Kamuf. New York: Routledge, 1994.

Derrida, Jacques. *Spurs: Nietzsche's Styles.* Translated by Barbara Harlow. Chicago: University of Chicago Press, 1978.

Dosse, François. *Gilles Deleuze and Félix Guattari: Intersecting Lives.* Translated by Deborah Glassman. New York: Columbia University Press, 2011.

Duffy, Simon. 'The Logic of Expression in Deleuze's Expressionism and Philosophy: Spinoza: A Strategy of Engagement'. *International Journal of Philosophical Studies* 12, no. 1 (March 2004): 47–60.

Durie, Robin. 'Splitting Time: Bergson's Philosophical Legacy'. *Philosophy Today* 44, no. 2 (2000): 152–68.

Faulkner, Keith W. *The Force of Time.* Lanham: University Press of America, 2008.

Feder, Ellen K., and Emily Zakin. 'Flirting with the Truth'. in *Derrida and Feminism,* edited by Ellen K. Feder, Emily Zakin and Mary C. Rawlinson. New York: Routledge, 1997.

Fitzgerald F. Scott. *Tender is the Night.* New York: Scribner, 1933.

Foucault, Michel. *The Order of Things.* New York: Random House, Inc., 1970.

Frost, Robert. *The Poetry of Robert Frost: The Collective Poems, Complete and Unabridged.* New York: Henry Holt and Company, Inc., 1969.

Goldman, Emma. *Living My Life.* New York: Knopf, 1934.

Grosz, Elizabeth. 'Bergson, Deleuze and the Becoming of Unbecoming'. *Parallax* XI, no. 2 (2005): 4–13.

Grosz, Elizabeth. *Chaos, Territory, Art.* New York: Columbia University Press, 2008.

Grosz, Elizabeth. 'Thinking the New', in *Becomings,* edited by Elizabeth Grosz, 15–28. Ithaca: Cornell University Press, 1999.

Heidegger, Martin. *Being and Time.* Translated by John Macquarrie and Edward Robinson. New York: Harper and Row, 1962.

Invisible Committee, The. *The Coming Insurrection.* Los Angeles: Semiotext(e), 2009.

James, Ian. 'Pierre Klossowski', in *Deleuze's Philosophical Lineage,* edited by Graham Jones and Jon Roffe, 339–56. Edinburgh: Edinburgh University Press, 2009.

Kant, Immanuel. *Critique of Judgment.* New York: Hafner Press, 1951.

Kaufmann, Walter. *Nietzsche: Philosopher, Psychologist, Antichrist.* Princeton: Princeton University Press, 1974.

Klossowski, Pierre. *Nietzsche and the Vicious Circle.* Translated by Daniel W. Smith. New York: Continuum Press, 2005.

Klossowski, Pierre. 'Nietzsche's Experience of the Eternal Return', in *The New Nietzsche,* edited by David B. Allison, 107–20. Cambridge, MA: The MIT Press, 1985.

Laerke, Mogens. 'Four Things Deleuze Learned from Leibniz'. in *Deleuze and The Fold: A Critical Reader,* edited by Sjoerd van Tuinen and Niamh McDonnell, 25–46. London: Palgrave Macmillan, 2010.

Lambert, Gregg. *The Non-Philosophy of Gilles Deleuze*. London : Continuum Press, 2002.

Lampert, Jay. *Deleuze and Guattari's Philosophy of History*. London: Continuum Press, 2006.

Lawlor, Leonard. 'Follow the Rats: Becoming-Animal in Deleuze and Guattari'. *SubStance* 37, no. 3 (2008): 169–87.

Leigh, James A. 'Deleuze, Nietzsche and the Eternal Return'. *Philosophy Today* 22, no. 3 (Fall 1978): 206–23.

Loeb, Paul S. 'The Thought-Drama of Eternal Recurrence'. *Journal of Nietzsche Studies* 34 (Autumn 2007): 79–95.

Löwith, Karl. *Nietzsche's Philosophy of the Eternal Recurrence of the Same*. Translated by J. Harvey Lomax. Berkeley: University of California Press, 1997.

Lundy, Craig. *History and Becoming: Deleuze's Philosophy of Creativity*. Edinburgh: Edinburgh University Press, 2012.

Marcuse, Herbert. *The Aesthetic Dimension*. Boston: Beacon Press, 1978.

Martin, Jean-Clet. *La philosophie de Gilles Deleuze*. Paris: Editions Payots & Rivages, 1993.

Massumi, Brian. *A Shock to Thought*. Edited by Brian Massumi. New York: Routledge, 2002.

Nancy, Jean-Luc. 'Elliptical Sense', in *Derrida: A Critical Reader*, edited by David Wood. London: Wiley-Blackwell, 1992.

Nietzsche, Friedrich. *The Gay Science*. Translated by Walter Kaufmann. New York: Random House, 1974.

Nietzsche, Friedrich. *The Nietzsche Reader*. Edited by Ansell-Pearson. Malden: Blackwell Publishing, 2006.

Nietzsche, Friedrich. *The Pre-Platonic Philosophers*. Translated by Greg Whitlock. Urbana and Chicago: University of Illinois Press, 2001.

Nietzsche, Friedrich. *The Will to Power*. Translated by Walter Kaufmann. New York: Random House, 1967.

Nietzsche, Friedrich. *Thus Spoke Zarathustra*. Edited and translated by Walter Kaufmann. New York: Viking Penguin Inc., 1966.

Nietzsche, Friedrich. 'Truth and Lie in an Extra-Moral Sense', in *The Portable Nietzsche*, edited and translated by Walter Kaufmann. New York: Penguin Books, 1977.

Nietzsche, Friedrich. *Writings from the Late Notebooks*. Edited by Rudiger Bittner. Translated by Kate Sturge. Cambridge: Cambridge University Press, 2003.

O'Sullivan, Simon. *Art Encounters Deleuze and Guattari: Thought Beyond Representation*. New York: Palgrave Macmillan, 2008.

Patton, Paul. *Deleuze and the Political*. New York: Routledge, 2000.

Patton, Paul, and John Protevi. *Between Deleuze and Derrida*. London: Continuum Press, 2003.

Pearson, Keith Ansell. 'Bergson and Creative Evolution/Involution', in *The New Bergsonism*, edited by John Mullarkey, 146–67. Manchester: Manchester University Press, 1999.

Pearson, Keith Ansell *Philosophy and the Adventure of the Virtual: Bergson and the Time of Life*. New York: Routledge, 2002.

Plath, Sylvia. *The Unabridged Journals of Sylvia Plath*. New York: Anchor Books, 2000.

Plotnitsky, Arkady. 'Bernard Riemann', in *Deleuze's Philosophical Lineage*, edited by Graham Jones and Jon Roffe, 190–208. Edinburgh: Edinburgh University Press, 2009.

Plotnitsky, Arkady. 'Zarathustra's Ladders: Hebraism, Hellenism, and Practical Philosophy in Nietzsche'. *Poetics Today* 19, no. 2 (1998): 199–219.

Pollock, Jackson. *Full Fathom Five*, 1947. Oil on canvas with nails, tacks, buttons, key, coins, cigarettes, matches, etc., 50 7/8 × 30 1/8 cm. Museum of Modern Art, New York.

Proust, Marcel. *Swann's Way*. Translated by Lydia Davis. New York: Penguin Books, 2002.

Rayman, Joshua. 'Will to Power as Alternative to Causality'. *The Journal of Speculative Philosophy* 30, no. 3 (2016): 361–72.

Redon, Odilon. *A Soi-Même: Journal, 1867–1915*. Paris: Fleury, 1922.

Redon, Odilon. *Below, I Saw the Vaporous Outline of a Human Form*, 1896. Lithograph on China paper, 252 × 180 mm. Metropolitan Museum of Art, New York.

Redon, Odilon. *Ophelia, c. 1900–1905*. Pastel on paper mounted on board, 50.5 × 67.3 cm. The Woodner Collection.

Rilke, Rainer Maria. *The Book of Images*. Translated by Edward Snow. New York: North Point Press, 1991.

Rimbaud, Arthur. *Arthur Rimbaud: Complete Works*. Translated by Paul Schmidt. New York: Harper and Rowe, 1967.

Roffe, Jon. *Badiou's Deleuze*. Montreal: McGill-Queen's University Press, 2012.

Saltz, Jerry. 'The Tempest: One of the Greatest Acts of Aesthetic Desperation in all of Art'. *Village Voice*, 12 September 2006.

Sauvagnarges, Anne. *Artmachines : Deleuze, Guattari, Simondon*. Translated by Suzanne Verderber and Eugene W. Holland. Edinburgh : Edinburgh University Press, 2016.

Sauvagnarges, Anne. *Deleuze and Art*. Translated by Samantha Bankston. London: Bloomsbury Publications/Continuum, 2013.

Sauvagnarges, Anne. 'Deleuze. De l'animal à l'art'. in *La philosophie de Deleuze*, by François Zourabichvili, Anne Sauvagnargues and Paola Marrati. Paris: Presses Universitaires de France, 2004.

Shaviro, Steven. 'Novelty and Double Causality', in *Deleuze, Guattari and the Production of the New*, edited by Simon O'Sullivan and Stephen Zepke, 206–16. London: Continuum Books, 2008.

Small, Robin. 'Nietzsche, Spir, and Time'. *Journal of the History of Philosophy* 32 (January 1994): 85–102.

Small, Robin. *Time and Becoming in Nietzsche's Thought*. London: Continuum Press, 2010.

Smith, Daniel W. 'From the Surface to the Depths', in *Gilles Deleuze: The Intensive Reduction*, edited by Constantin V. Boundas, 82–97. London: Continuum Press, 2009.

Smith, Daniel W. 'The Concept of the Simulacrum: Deleuze and the Overturning of Platonism'. *Continental Philosophy Review* 38 (2006): 89–123.

Smith, Daniel W. 'The Conditions of the New'. *Deleuze Studies*, 2007: 1–21.

Smith, Daniel W. 'The Doctrine of Univocity', in *Deleuze and Religion*, edited by Mary Bryden, 167–83. London: Routledge, 2001.

Smith, Daniel W. 'G. W. F. Leibniz', in *Deleuze's Philosophical Lineage*, edited by Graham Jones and Jon Roffe, 44–66. Edinburgh: Edinburgh University Press, 2009.

Smith, Daniel W. 'Genesis and Difference', in *Deleuze and The Fold: A Critical Reader*, edited by Sjoerd van Tuinen and Niamh McDonnell, 132–55. London: Palgrave Macmillan, 2010.

Smith, Daniel W. 'Klossowski's Reading of Nietzsche: Impulses, Phantasms, Simulacra, Stereotypes'. *Diacritics* 35, no. 1 (Spring 2005): 8–22.

Stagoll, Cliff. 'Becoming', in *The Deleuze Dictionary*, edited by Adrian Parr, 21–2. New York: Columbia University Press, 2005.

Stagoll, Cliff. 'Event', in *The Deleuze Dictionary*, edited by Adrian Parr, 87–8. New York: Columbia University Press, 2005.

Stambaugh, Joan. *Nietzsche's Thought of Eternal Return*. Baltimore: The John Hopkins University Press, 1972.

Thiele, Kathrin. 'Of Immanence and Becoming: Deleuze and Guattari's Philosophy and/as Relational Ontology', *Deleuze Studies* 10, no. 1 (2016): 117–34.

Whitehead, Alfred North. *Modes of Thought*. New York: Simon and Schuster, 1968.

Widder, Nathaniel. 'Time is Out of Joint-and So Are We: Deleuzean Immanence and the Fractured Self'. *Philosophy Today* 50, no. 4 (Winter 2006): 405–17.

Williams, James. *Gilles Deleuze's Philosophy of Time* Edinburgh: Edinburgh University Press, 2011.

Worringer, Wilhelm. *Form in Gothic*. Translated by Herbert Read. New York: Schocken Books, 1957.

Zepke, Stephen. *Art as Abstract Machine: Ontology and Aesthetics in Deleuze and Guattari*. New York: Routledge, 2005.

Žižek, Slavoj. *Less than Nothing: Hegel and the Shadow of Dialectical Materialism*. London: Verso, 2013.

Žižek, Slavoj. *Organs without Bodies*. New York: Routledge, 2004.

Žižek, Slavoj. *The Parallax View*. Boston : The MIT Press, 2009.

Zourabichvili, François. *Le Vocabulaire de Deleuze*. Edited by Jean-Pierre Zarader. Paris: Ellipses, 2003.

Zourabichvili, François. 'Une philosophie de l'événement', in *La philosophie de Deleuze*, by François Zourabichvili, Anne Sauvagnargues and Paola Marrati, 4–116. Paris: Presses Universitaires de France, 2004.

Index